THE
DALMATIAN

ANNA KATHERINE NICHOLAS

With a special chapter
by Janis Butler

Title page: This magnificent photo, done by Martin Booth, Farmington, Michigan, is a classic in Dalmatian circles. The dog is Champion Green Starr's Colonel Joe, the Top Winning Dalmatian of All Time, owned by Mrs. Alan R. Robson, Glenmoore, Pa.

Dedication

To all the many handsome Dalmatians I have judged over the years, and to the thousands of "family Dalmatians" bringing constant pleasure to their owners.

© 1986 by T.F.H. Publications, Inc., Ltd.

Distributed in the UNITED STATES by T.F.H. Publications, Inc., 211 West Sylvania Avenue, Neptune City, NJ 07753; in CANADA by H & L Pet Supplies Inc., 27 Kingston Crescent, Kitchener, Ontario N2B 2T6; Rolf C. Hagen Ltd., 3225 Sartelon Street, Montreal 382 Quebec; in ENGLAND by T.F.H. Publications Limited, 4 Kier Park, Ascot, Berkshire SL5 7DS; in AUSTRALIA AND THE SOUTH PACIFIC by T.F.H. (Australia) Pty. Ltd., Box 149, Brookvale 2100 N.S.W., Australia; in NEW ZEALAND by Ross Haines & Son, Ltd., 18 Monmouth Street, Grey Lynn, Auckland 2 New Zealand; in SINGAPORE AND MALAYSIA by MPH Distributors (S) Pte., Ltd., 601 Sims Drive, #03/07/21, Singapore 1438; in the PHILIPPINES by Bio-Research, 5 Lippay Street, San Lorenzo Village, Makati Rizal; in SOUTH AFRICA by Multipet Pty. Ltd., 30 Turners Avenue, Durban 4001. Published by T.F.H. Publications, Inc. Manufactured in the United States of America by T.F.H. Publications, Inc.

Contents

About the Author

Since early childhood, Anna Katherine Nicholas has been involved with dogs. Her first pets were a Boston Terrier, an Airedale, and a German Shepherd Dog. Then, in 1925, came the first of the Pekingese, a gift from a friend who raised them. Now her home is shared with two Miniature Poodles and numerous Beagles.

Miss Nicholas is best known throughout the Dog Fancy as a writer and as a judge. Her first magazine article, published in *Dog News* magazine around 1930, was about Pekingese, and this was followed by a widely acclaimed breed column, "Peeking at the Pekingese," which appeared for at least two decades, originally in *Dogdom* then, following the demise of that publication, in *Popular Dogs*. During the 1940's she was a Boxer columnist for *Pure-Bred Dogs/American Kennel Gazette* and for *Boxer Briefs*. More recently many of her articles, geared to interest fanciers of every breed, have appeared in *Popular Dogs, Pure-Bred Dogs/American Kennel Gazette, Show Dogs, Dog Fancy*, and *The World of the Working Dog*, and for both the Canadian publications, *The Dog Fancier* and *Dogs in Canada*. Her *Dog World* column, "Here, There and Everywhere" was the Dog Writers' Association of America winner of the Best Series in a Dog Magazine Award for 1979. Also a feature article of hers, "Faster Is Not Better," published in *Canine Chronicle*, received Honorable Mention on another occasion.

In 1970 Miss Nicholas won the Dog Writers' Association Award for the Best Technical Book of the Year with her *Nicholas Guide to Dog Judging*. In 1979 the revision of this book again won this award, the first time ever that a revision has been so honored by this organization. Other important dog writer awards which Miss Nicholas has gained over the years have been the Gaines "Fido" on two occasions and the *Kennel Review* "Winkies" also on two occasions, these both in the Dog Writer of the Year category.

It was during the 1930's that Miss Nicholas's first book, *The Pekingese*, appeared in print, published by the Judy Publishing Company. This book, and its second edition, sold out quickly and is now a collector's item, as is her *The Skye Terrier Book* which was published during the 1960's by the Skye Terrier Club of America.

During recent years, Miss Nicholas has been writing books consistently for T.F.H. These include *Successful Dog Show Exhibiting, The Book of the Rottweiler, The Book of the Poodle, The Book of the Labrador Retriever, The Book of the English Springer Spaniel, The Book of the Golden Retriever, The Book of the German Shepherd Dog, The Book of the Shetland Sheepdog, The Book of the Miniature Schnauzer, The World of the Doberman Pinscher* and *The World of the Rottweiler.* Plus, in the newest T.F.H. series, *The Maltese, The Keeshond, The Chow Chow, The Poodle, The Boxer, The Beagle, The Basset Hound, The Dachshund* (the latter three co-authored with Marcia A. Foy), *The German Pointer, The Collie, The Weimaraner,* and numerous other titles. In the KW series she has done *Rottweilers, Weimaraners* and *Norwegian Elkhounds.* And she has written American chapters for two popular English books purchased and published in the United States by T.F.H., *The Staffordshire Bull Terrier,* and *The Jack Russell Terrier.*

Miss Nicholas's association with T.F.H. began in the early 1970's when she co-authored for them five books with Joan Brearley. These are *The Wonderful World of Beagles and Beagling* (also honored by the Dog Writers Association), *This is the Bichon Frise, The Book of the Pekingese, The Book of the Boxer,* and *This is the Skye Terrier.*

Since 1934 Miss Nicholas has been a popular dog show judge, officiating at prestigious events throughout the United States and Canada. She is presently approved for all Hounds, all Terriers, all Toys and all Non-Sporting; plus all Pointers, English and Gordon Setters, Vizslas, Weimaraners, and Wirehaired Pointing Griffons in the Sporting Group and Boxers and Dobermans in Working. In 1970 she became only the third woman ever to have judged Best in Show at the famous Westminster Kennel Club event at Madison Square Garden in New York City, where she has officiated as well on some sixteen other occasions over the years. She has also officiated at such events as Santa Barbara, Chicago International, Morris and Essex, Trenton, Westchester, etc., in the United States; the Sportsman's and the Metropolitan among numerous others in Canada; and Specialty shows in several dozen breeds in both countries. She has judged in almost every one of the United States and in four of the Canadian Provinces. Her dislike of air travel has caused her to refrain from acceptance of the constant invitations to officiate in other parts of the world.

6

Chapter 1

Origin and Early History of the Dalmatian

Since the mid-18th century references have been found by historians to the breed of dog known as the Dalmatian. His first established home, for which the breed was named was Dalmatia, a Western Yugoslavian area which at one time was part of Austria, located on the Adriatic. That these dogs were well-known throughout many parts of the world long before that time is authenticated by many types of antique art including engravings, paintings, models, and early writings which have established a familiarity and the presence of spotted dogs of similar size and type in such widespread areas as early Africa, Asia, and Europe. That so vast a territory had been covered by the dogs is explained by the fact that they were popular with ancient gypsies (Romanies). Many bands of gypsies were accompanied by the dogs in their wanderings around the world.

The Dalmatian quickly became a favorite and established some of his best known claims to fame in Great Britain. They were brought there by members of the British upper classes who in those days frequently made tours of Europe and often returned accompanied by some of the striking spotted dogs. Immediately they were adopted by the English aristocracy who used them to accompany their horse-drawn carriages, the trotting dog soon became a feature of these processions. The dogs were taught to station themselves beneath the rear axle of the coach, or in some cases to trot underneath the pole separating the horses, or to lead the procession, trotting smartly along ahead of the first horse. It was all very decorative and impressive!

Another activity with which the Dalmatian is synonymous, which also started, it is said, in Great Britain, is his very famous role of "firehouse dog." This began, we understand, with the dogs being acquired as ratters, for the purpose of killing vermin in London's stables and firehouses, which they did with expertise. But they loved the horses and the fire engine, so it was almost inevitable that they soon were racing ahead of them through the streets whenever the alarm was sounded. Now in modern times, many a Dalmatian can be seen riding on the firetrucks with their masters, as Dalmatians are still the mascots to be found in firehouses, not only in Great Britain but in the United States and undoubtedly other countries too, so firm is the association.

Dalmatians have worked in war times; done sentinel duty; served as shepherd's dogs; and as draft dogs. They have been seen in many a circus and vaudeville show, especially enjoying popularity with the clowns as "assistants," their intelligence, aptitude, and showy appearance having fitted them particularly well for this activity.

Jean Fetner driving "Top Hat" in 1953. Accompanied by Ch. Fobette's Frishka, C.D. and Ch. Coachman's Cake Walk, both Group winners.

Dalmatian Coaching, a tradition in the breed. Ch. Dymondee's Toy Soldier, C.D. owned by Mr. and Mrs. C. F. Lester, Jr., Itasca, Ill. Dalmatians were developed to be coach dogs but seldom have the opportunity to do that work these days.

Although not generally thought of as such, Dalmatians are splendid dogs for the sportsman, serving as retriever, bird dog, trailing, and even have been hunted in packs on boar and stag. We have read little speculation as to his ancestors but from similarity in appearance, we would assume that there is some trace of Pointer along the way in his developing background.

The oldest single activity for which the Dalmatian is noted is as a coach dog. He has been depicted plying this trade over many centuries, and holds the distinction of being the world's only true coach dog, substantiated, again, by the early engravings and drawings depicting spotted dogs accompanying Egyptian chariots, on through the ages.

Chapter 2

Dalmatians in Great Britain

We have already mentioned the strong bond existent in the past century between British dog fanciers and the Dalmatian. It is said that these dogs have been known there for the past 200 years, and there has even been exploration of a theory that they are actually partially descended from the early English hunting hounds, the Talbot in particular, so similar are they to these dogs in type, character, and hunting ability. Quite possibly a century or two ago there was some Talbot blood infused into the European dogs who, by their striking appearance, caught the eyes of travelers from Great Britain, then gained their admiration by their intelligence, along with their strong guard dog tendencies, and thus were brought back to Britain with the tourists. There seems no disputing the fact that the Dalmatian has his roots in very ancient times, and that the evolutions in the breed have been numerous.

When, in 1860, Great Britain held its second dog show there were only five breeds represented. These included Dalmatians, and so far as history records, this was the breed's initial appearance in dog show competition.

Were it not for a gentleman named Fred Kemp, who was President of the British Dalmatian Club and a third generation owner of this breed with which he himself was involved for more than half a century, Dalmatians might not have survived World War I. Mr. Kemp is credited with having kept alive dogs in his kennel through the difficult and in many cases devastating period be-

Westella Venture, another beautiful Dalmatian belonging to Miss Barnes, showing a classic head of the 1930's in England.

tween 1914 and the Armistice in 1918, providing breeding stock at the end of this period.

It is exciting to contemplate what happened to Dalmatians in England at the close of World War I. They fairly leaped ahead in popularity, the two Dalmatians registered with the Kennel Club in 1918 having increased to 125 by 1925 and to 889 by 1932.

When Crufts resumed holding its world famous dog show following World War I, there were two Dalmatians entered. In 1934, no fewer than 199 Dalmatian entries filled the classes for the breed, of which 15 were provided. Best of Breed, and gaining championship there, was Manor Mischief owned by Mr. Sorby Straw.

One of the most successful English breeders of Dalmatians at this period was Miss E.V. Barnes, whose outstanding winners included Champion Lucky James and Champion Venus of the

A well-known English champion of the 1930's, Ch. Golden Dawn of Coelan, was owned by Miss Stephenson whom she represented well at the dog shows.

Wells. Miss Barnes was the breeder of American Champion Tweedle Dum of the Wells, by Silverden Grandeur ex Tuppence, who was born in 1934. He came to America under the ownership of Mrs. Paul Moore, Hollow Hill Kennels, Convent, New Jersey, where he sired, among others, Champion Hollow Hill Atlas, who in his turn became the sire of Mrs. Leonard W. Bonney's incomparable Champion Tally Ho Sirius, a tremendously important Dalmatian in the United States in the 1930's-1940's.

Returning to English Champion Lucky James: he became a champion at under 18 months' age. He and his kennel-mate Champion Venus of the Wells won first prize in the International Brace Class at Crufts in 1934. Several Dalmatians from "of the Wells" were instrumental in the establishment of the important Dalmatian strains in the United States, and this kennel was the home of an impressive collection of leading British winners of its day.

Champion Snow Leopard was another unforgettable Dalmatian in English history, having scored as the winner of the Challenge Certificate wherever one was available for Dalmatians during his career. We have heard him described as a beautifully made dog with remarkably outstanding movement. He was bred and owned by Mrs. Hackney. A daughter of his was among the excellent bitches here in the United States at Hollow Hill Kennels, Champion Avenues Betty, who was bred by Mrs. Cash from Peggy of the Avenue and born in June 1932.

We have already mentioned Mr. Kemp and his third generation association with Dalmatians which kept the breed going through World War I. His famous dogs included Champion Tess of Coldharbour, Champion Panworth and King of Coldharbour among others. And, making for a fourth generation Dalmatian owner in the family, his daughter, (we assume), Miss Kemp, was the

A very lovely English dog who won well at Crufts and other important shows of the early to mid-1930's, Goworth Victor was owned by Miss E.V. Barnes in England.

breeder of Champion Silverden King of Coldharbour who belonged to Miss Shirley Mallion. This dog was a legendary show dog, winning consistently in breed and Variety Classes, as well as being a superlative stud.

Mrs. Walker Smith owned Champion Bookham Swell. Another important dog of this period was Champion Best of Cards owned by Fred Wardell. Then there was Mr. Proctor's Champion Hannah of the Harbour, a well admired bitch.

The majority of the Dalmatians who were successful in the 1930's in Great Britain were of the black spotted variety. We have

Champion Lucky James and Champion Venus of the Wells, two of the numerous winning Dalmatians owned by Miss. E.V. Barnes during the 1920's-1930's in Great Britain. Miss Barnes "of the Wells" dogs were behind many importations to America during the 1930's and a strong influence on the breed here. This print from the author's collection. Note excellence of these heads and spots.

Ch. Midstone Ebony was imported by Mrs. Leonard W. Bonney for her Tally Ho Kennels in its early days from Mrs. M.E. Walford of England. This bitch was especially admired for her beautiful head, neck, and elegant carriage.

heard special tribute, however, paid to Miss Smithers' Champion Bruno of Brow; and of Miss Stephenson's Champion Golden Dawn of Coelan. The latter produced Mrs. Paul Moore's Champion Golden Dusk of Coelan, another to join Mrs. Moore's Hollow Hill Kennels in America. All of this adds to the picture of the quality of these British Dalmatians of the "between World Wars" period, and of the part they played in our own Dalmatians in America.

The British Dalmatian Club celebrated its Diamond Jubilee in 1985, where 1,051 Dal fanciers were on hand for the event. Need we say more about the continuing popularity of these grand dogs in England?

Chapter 3

Dalmatians in the United States

The Dalmatian Club of America held its first National Specialty Show at Garden City, Long Island, on June 26, 1926. Nineteen Dalmatians competed in 21 entries for the judgment of Mrs. Charles G. West, Jr., who later became Mrs. James M. Austin and who is the mother of popular hound and terrier breeder Mrs. Philip S.P. Fell. Mrs. West found her Best of Breed in the highly admired winner of that period, Champion Tally Ho Last of Sunstar, with the rest of the awards a "clean sweep" for Gladmore Dalmatians' Gladmore Gaylass (Best of Opposite Sex and Winners Bitch) and Gladmore Guardsman (Winners Dog).

Tally Ho Dalmatians won Best of Breed at the following two Specialties as well, 1927 a repeat for Last of Sunstar while in 1928 the winner was a bitch, Champion Tally Ho Fore Thought. The entry of these two years was 24 and 27 Dals respectively, Dr. Thomas D'Arcy Buck and Mrs. C. Robinson the judges.

The Club did not hold a 1929 Specialty. When activity resumed in 1930 the locale was Whitemarsh, Pennsylvania, the judge Mr. Theodore Crane, and the entry had climbed to 40. Champion Gladmore Guardsman, who had been Winners Dog the first year at the National, returned as a special to go Best in Show. In 1931, entries again showed an increase to 46, Mrs. S.E. Beal who was judging found her Best of Breed in Champion Tally Ho Last of Sunstar, this splendid dog's third Best in Show award at the National.

Tally Ho Kathleen made her way from Winners Bitch to Best of Breed at the sixth National in 1932, as did another bitch, Mid-

One of the Dalmatians from D.S. Barnum's Toad Harbor Kennels. Ch. Polly of Toad House handled by Parker Harris taking Winners Bitch en route to the title at National Capital in 1962.

The great Ch. Reigate Bold Venture, noted Dalmatian sire and winner of the 1940's, was a son of Ch. Tally Ho Sirius ex Ch. Lady Culpepper of Reigate. He was bred by his owners, the Lanes, of Reigate Kennels in Virginia. His wins included Best of Breed twice at the National, and he was the sire of numerous champions. A widely admired and important dog of his day.

stone Ebony in 1933 who returned there as a special to repeat for Best of Breed in 1935, (after another "skipped year" in 1934) this time under the judgment of Dr. Henry Jarrett.

Jere F. Collins, in 1936, drew 43 Dalmatians in 50 entries, another of the many splendid Tally Ho Dalmatians, Champion Cruiser of Tally Ho, winding up in the Best of Breed position— the sixth time in ten National Specialties that Tally Ho had been the top winner. But then, no one could possibly dispute the excellence of these magnificent Dals owned by Mrs. Leonard W. Bonney of Oyster Bay, New York, nor the sincerity of her dedication

This important historic picture is one of the few we have been able to find of that great lady in Dalmatians, Mrs. Leonard W. (Flora) Bonney with one of her winners. Here she is, *left*, as judge A.W. Barrett awards Best of Breed to her Tally Ho Hesper at the 1951 National Specialty of the Dalmatian Club of America, Donald Sutherland, kennel manager, is handling the dog. Hesper was by Ch. Dr. Shoofly of Tattoo ex Tally Ho Felicity.

Best of Breed at the National Specialty, 1958. Ch. Coachman's Classic, C.D., owned by Mr. and Mrs. William Fetner, St. Louis, Mo.

and devotion to the breed. Mrs. Bonney spent a lifetime in the dog show world as a breeder, an exhibitor, and as a highly esteemed multiple breed judge. She was one of the truly great dog ladies of this century, and her contribution to the breeds she loved (Dalmatians, Chow Chows and Poodles especially) inestimable. She owned some of the greatest American-bred dogs of all time, and was a breeder of intelligence and expertise.

In 1937, Mrs. James M. Austin, who had judged the first National as Mrs. West, made her second appearance as judge of the National. This time it was Hollow Hill Atlas who came through from the dog classes to take Winners and Best of Breed for his owner, Mrs. Paul Moore, of Convent, New Jersey, another highly respected member of the Dalmatian world whose contributions to it deserve special recognition. Mrs. Moore owned the imported

Ch. Tally-Ho Last of Sunstar, bred and owned by Mrs. Leonard W. Bonney, Oyster Bay, N.Y. Noted sire and stud dog of his day.

Note the excellent head profile of Champion Barney Oldfield in The Valley, a big winner in the 1960's and the sire of champions. Owned by Mrs. Harland W. Meistrell, then of Great Neck, N.Y. now living in Vermont.

From the 1950's, this lovely bitch is Ch. Reigate Souvenir, by Ch. Reigate Bold Venture ex Reigate Dusk. Owned by Mr. and Mrs. Myron Greene, Greenland Dalmatians, Rochester, N.Y.

Ch. Roadcoach Roadmaster, full brother to the famed Ch. Roadcoach Roadster, with co-owner A.W. Barrett, Dover, Mass.

Ch. Battered Bentley in the Valley

Three of the famous Dalmatians owned by Mrs. Harland W. Meistrell in the 1950's-1960's. Bentley and Lady Callisto were well-known winners. Oros II, C.D., an obedience "star" in his own right, was sired by the unforgettable Am. and Can. Ch. Whiteside Sioux Oros, U.D.

Oros II, C.D.   Ch. Lady Callisto of Pine

Champion Tweedle Dum of the Wells (the sire of Atlas) and was the breeder of Atlas, born in March 1936, his dam Champion Avenue's Betty.

The entry climbed to 57 in 1938 for Mr. Frank Eskrigge, and the winner again came through from the classes, Master Patrick, Winners Dog along the way. This dog was the first National Best in Show winner owned by Mrs. A.W. (Mary) Barrett, and must have been acquired right at the beginning of her days as a Dalmatian breeder which have been so filled with outstanding dogs and exciting wins. Her Roadcoach Kennels are probably the oldest still active in Dalmatians in the United States, her interest being shared with Poodles. She has bred some very notable winners through the years.

Master Patrick was by Champion Gladmore Harper ex Champion Mistress Margaret, born in 1933, bred by Mary Powers.

It was in 1939 that the great Champion Tally-Ho Sirius won his first Specialty, repeating in 1941. Thirty-one Dalmatians that year were judged by F.W. Simmons: 65 in 1941 judged by Mr. Barrett.

In 1940 the National was held for the first time in the Mid-West, at Chicago, where Mrs. J. Homiller judged 38 Dals in 52 entries. Best of Breed was Champion Goworth Grenadier, Tapestry of Tattoo coming from Winners Bitch to Best of Opposite Sex.

There was quite a significant increase in the number of entries in 1940's National Specialty six months after Chicago, at Far Hills, New Jersey. Mr. A.E. Bonner was greeted by 75 Dalmatians here, choosing as Best of Breed Champion Four In Hand Mischief and as Best of Opposite Sex his Winners Bitch, Four In Hand Fantasy. At this show a magnificent young dog took Winners Dog, Reigate Bold Venture, who was destined to attain greatness.

In 1941, at Tuxedo Park, New York, Mr. Barrett chose Champion Twill of Tattoo as Best of Opposite Sex to Sirius.

In 1943 Mrs. W. Kenneth Close made Champion Duke of Gervais her Best of Breed at the February Specialty of the National in New York, the class bitch, Four In Hand Spatterdash from the classes to Best of Opposite Sex.

In 1944 and 1945, judged by Mrs. Lloyd Reeves and Mrs. Leonard W. Bonney respectively, Champion Reigate Bold Venture became the Best of Breed winner at the National both years.

Ch. Quaker Acres Eventide, a winning Dalmatian from the 1960's.

Am. and Can. Ch. China Doll of Dalmatia, born April 17, 1947, by Ch. Roadcoach Racing Colors ex Roadcoach Frou Frou, C.D.X. was one of Wendell J. Sammet's early important winners at his Dalmatia Kennels.

Then in 1946, at Rye, New York, with Mrs. Austin judging for the third time, an entry of 90 was assembled to be led by another great dog of that period, Champion Four In Hand Blackberry, bred by Leo M. Meeker in California and owned by Evelyn S. Nelson's Tomalyn Hill Kennels in New Jersey. Blackberry was sired by Champion Dal Dale Driver ex Champion Meeker's Tarberry and born in September 1939.In 1947, of an entry of 112 dogs, Mary Barrett again won Best in Show, this time with Champion Roadcoach Phaeton, a bitch, while Best Opposite Sex was the dog, Champion Sawyer's Duke, who himself won Best of Breed at the 1948 Specialty.

Champion China Doll of Dalmatia gained the top award at the 1949 Specialty for Wendell J. Sammet, with the Winners Dog, Tomalyn's Rascality, taking Best of Opposite Sex to her. China Doll was Best of Opposite Sex the following year, in 1950, to Champion Tally Ho Samson, that year's Best of Breed.

The great Ch. Tally Ho Sirius, outstanding Eastern winner of the early 1940's, was bred and owned by Mrs. Leonard W. Bonney, Oyster Bay, N.Y. Best in Show at Reading, Pa. in 1940. The sire of Champion Reigate Bold Venture and many other important Dals.

The well-known Ch. Lord Jim, by Ch. Coachman's Chuck-a-Luck ex Coachman's Candy Cane, in 1970. Winner of 13 all breed Bests in Show. Best of Breed at the National Specialty in 1970, where his daughter, Ch. Coachman's Carte Blanche, was Best of Opposite Sex. Another splendid representative of the Coachman Dalmatians, Jean and Bill Fetner, St. Louis, Mo.

During the 1950's, the National was won by the following Dalmatians: 1951 Tally Ho Hesper; 1952 Williamsview Riptide; 1953 Champion Williamsdale Rocky; 1954 Champion Colonel Boots From Dalmatia; 1955 Champion Head of the River Orangeman; 1956 Champion Roadcoach Roadster; 1957 Champion The Lash; 1958 Champion Coachman's Classic; 1959 Champion Green Starr's Undergraduate.

Ch. Four-in-Hand Mischief winning one of his 20 Bests in Show, making him the Top Winning Best in Show Dalmatian of his day, at Pasadena in 1940. Harry Sangster handling for Mr. and Mrs. Leo M. Meeker, Four-in-Hand Dalmatians, El Monte, Cal.

In 1960 the Dalmatian Club of America National held forth in California, at Santa Barbara, where Miss Evelyn Nelson found her Best of Breed among the 92 Dals entered in the dog, Champion Crestview Diamond Jim, with Best of Opposite Sex, Champion Pepper of Velvet Pennies.

By now the National Specialty was moving about a great deal to various sections of the country on a rotating basis. In 1961, with Mrs. A.W. Barrett judging, there were 68 Dals entered at Parsippany, New Jersey. Champion Roadcoach Roadster was Best of Breed; the bitch, Champion Crestview's Lisa, Best of Opposite

Sex. This started a trio of Bests for the Dalmatian Club of America Specialty Shows for Roadcoach Kennels, as Champion Roadcoach Spice won at Ravenna, Ohio, in 1962 over an entry of 71 under Mrs. Bonney and Champion Roadcoach Love Apple did so in 1963 at Sudbury, Massachusetts, in 62 entries assembled for Miss Kathleen Staples. The Bests of Opposite Sex on those occasions were Champion Greenland's Iron Liege and Champion Road Star's Black Maria respectively.

Long Beach, California, in 1964 had Mrs. Lloyd Reeves judging an entry of 97. Champion Coachman's Callisto was Best of Breed, Champion Pix Adhore of Cammar Best of Opposite Sex. The fol-

Phil Marsh handling Ch. Fobette's Frishka, C.D., the foundation bitch from the world-famous Coachman Kennels. Mr. and Mrs. William Fetner, owners, St. Louis, Mo. Marie Meyer judging. A picture filled with nostalgia for those who were active in the Fancy in the 1950's.

lowing year, at Sudbury, Massachusetts, Callisto had to content himself with Best of Opposite Sex to the Best of Breed won by Champion Blackpool Crinkle Forest. The judge on the latter occasion was Alva Rosenberg; the entry 78.

At Oak Brook, Illinois, in September 1966, the entry climbed to 116 for judge Louis J. Murr. Crinkle Forest repeated her previous year's Best of Breed. Pepper Spattered Teddy Bear came through from Winners Dog to Best of Opposite Sex.

Champion Rockledge Rumble took the chief award in 1967 at Whitehouse, New Jersey, from Mrs. Virginia Prescott. Thorndown Rabaletta was Winners Bitch and Best of Opposite Sex.

Mrs. Isabel R. Robson judged 117 at the National in Pico Rivera, California, October 1968. Champion Pacifica Pride of Posiedom was her choice for Best of Breed; Champion Korcula Salona, the bitch that took Best of Opposite Sex.

Mrs. Barrett again judged in 1969, at Hempstead, New York. Champion Zodiac's Snoopy was Best of Breed and Dottidale Cedelia came through the classes for Winners Bitch and Best of Opposite Sex.

As the 1970's opened, the National Specialty Shows of the Dalmatian Club of America hit the 100 entry mark consistently for the first time (there had been isolated entries exceeding this number upon occasion, but never on a year-to-year basis), and they have not retreated from this number since. In fact by 1977 they had exceeded the 200 mark for the first time, another milestone which held; and in 1980 the 200 mark was passed—an eloquent comment on the interest and popularity the breed has attained and is enjoying.

Best of Breed in 1970, 127 entries, judge Alfred Treen, was Champion Lord Jim; Best of Opposite Sex, Champion Coachman's Carte Blanche.

1971, Miss Marjory Van Der Veer, Wellesley, Massachusetts, 109 entries. Best of Breed, Champion Zodiak's Snoopy; Best of Opposite Sex, Champion Valto's Lady of Honor.

1972, judge Dr. David Doane, 162 dogs. Best of Breed, Champion Panore of Watseka; Best of Opposite Sex, Champion Dame Julia of Pacifica.

1973, Mrs. Alfred E. Treen, 143 entries, Alexandria, Virginia. Best of Breed, Champion Coachman's Canicula; Best of Opposite Sex, the bitch Champion Twin Gates Blue Bonnet.

Ch. Rickway's Topper winning Best of Breed at the Dalmatian Club of Southern New England Specialty, June 3, 1962. An admired and consistently winning dog of that period and area.

1974, Delafield, Wisconsin, Mrs. Winifred Heckman judging 153 dogs. Champion Panore of Watseka, Best of Breed (for the second time); Champion Melody Up Up and Away, Best of Opposite Sex.

The innovation of having more than one judge was introduced in 1975 at Louisville, Kentucky, when Mr. Fetner judged the bitches and Mr. Joseph Faigel the dogs and intersex competition. 197 entries resulted, Best of Breed being awarded to Champion Melody Ring of Fire; Best of Opposite Sex to the bitch, Champion Coachman's First Class.

29

Ch. Coachman's Callisto winning the Non-Sporting Group judged by the author at Westminster Kennel Club in 1963, owner-handled by Arthur Higgins, Pennydale Kennels.

Evelyn Nelson, who had then become Mrs. White, judged dogs and intersex at Norwich, Connecticut, in 1976; Dr. Sidney Remmele, bitches. Champion Crestview Dan Patch was Best of Breed; the bitch, Champion Altamar's Adastar, Best of Opposite Sex.

1977 in Crete, Illinois, Mr. Treen judging bitches and intersex; Mrs. Robson the dogs. 257 Dalmatians in 287 entries (the numbers difference reflect non-regular classes and the Sweepstakes). Champion Panore of Watseka winning Best of Breed for the *third time*; Champion Hopi Kachina Melody Mocha Best of Opposite Sex.

Then, in 1978, back to California where 204 Dals competed for the Specialty honors at Ventura, the judges Edd Bivin for bitches and intersex; Peter Knoop for the dog classes. Here it was that Champion Green Starr's Colonel Joe gained his first National Best in Show, which he repeated in 1979 and 1980, tying Last of Sunstar's triple wins. On these occasions, Best of Opposite Sex to Colonel Joe were Champion Melody Penny Lane in 1978; Champion Coachman's Hot Coffee (Mrs. Treen judging intersex) in 1979; and Long Last No Frills in 1980 (intersex judge Forrest Johnson).

Mrs. Curtis Brown judged intersex in 1981 at Lafayette, Ohio, her Best of Breed being the bitch Champion Korcula Midnight Serenade with Opposite Sex to Champion Wedgewood Tarmac High Brow.

In 1982 Anna Katherine Nicholas was the judge of intersex, the Specialty taking place at Norwich, Connecticut. Here it was that another milestone in Dalmatian history was reached when Champion Green Starr's Colonel Joe came through from the Veterans Class to take Best in Show, his fourth top award at this most prestigious of all Dalmatian events, thus becoming the only Dalmatian ever to have gained this honor *four* times there.

Over the years, the National has added obedience classes to its Specialty Shows, Junior Showmanship, and, of course, the Sweepstakes, making it an exciting occasion for the Dalmatian fancy no matter what facet of showing Dalmatians interests them.

Through these awards, one is able to reach a fairly accurate conclusion regarding the Dalmatians and their owners of prominence as the breed has moved along here in the United States. The legendary breeders of the decades prior to the 1960's set the pattern for our present day Dalmatians; and would, I feel certain, be proud of the results. We have already made specific comment on Tally Ho and Hollow Hill, where Mrs. Bonney and Mrs. Moore produced such great dogs.

Mrs. Moore evidently started out by attaining representatives of all the leading English kennels of the 1930's, as already noted in the British chapter where her importation of Champion Tweedle Dum of the Wells is noted, along with other dogs from leading British bloodlines. She used these dogs well, and they were soon to be found behind the winning Dalmatians bred by many of her contemporaries.

Mrs. Bonney was already well established with Tally Ho Dal-

31

matians by the 1930's. Tattoo Kennels from Newton Square, Pennsylvania, was establishing its own breeding program, again on fine English stock including Sally Who of Stubbington, a daughter of Great Britain's fabulous Champion Snow Leopard, and had a splendid bitch in Champion Fancy Free of Tattoo, bred by Edward W. Engs. Jr., by Boot Black of Tattoo ex Dixie of Maacama.

One of the most admired of all of Mrs. Bonney's dogs was Champion Tally Ho Last of Sunstar, who was homebred and who became the first Dalmatian to win the Non-Sporting Group when the Group System was changed to its present format in the 1930's. Another of Mrs. Bonney's dogs, Champion Gladmore Guardsman, was the first Dalmatian to win Best in Show under the present Group system.

Sunstar created somewhat of a dynasty, being grandsire of Champion Tally Ho Sirius, also bred and owned by Mrs. Bonney, who won Best in Show at Berks County in Reading, Pennsylvania, 1940, the first Dalmatian to gain such an award east of the Mississippi since Champion Gladmore Guardsman in still earlier days. Sirius's son, Champion Reigate Bold Venture (ex Champion Lady Culpepper of Reigate) carried along the family tradition when he took Best in Show at the big, prestigious Kennel Club of Philadelphia event in November 1944, to the delight of his many admirers. Incidentally, Mrs. Bonney believed in her show champions being outstanding in obedience as well. Her Champion Byron's Pennie (Champion Tally Ho Decision ex Champion Tally Ho Star of Sonia) was the first Dalmatian bench show champion to earn a C.D. degree, while Champion Tally Ho Black Eyed Susan, also bred by Mrs. Bonney (Champion Cress Brook Bang-Champion Tally Ho Copper Penny) was the first Dalmatian bench show champion to earn C.D.X.

Speaking of these early Best in Show Dalmatians, the one who accomplished most in this regard was the world famous dog from California, American and Canadian Champion Four In Hand Mischief owned by Mr. and Mrs. Leo M. Meeker, with whom Harry Sangster won something in the area of 20 times Best in Show. "Chief," as he was known, was a fabulous dog, more than living up to all the glowing terms in which you have heard him described. His untimely death was a true loss to the breed.

Mrs. Lloyd Reeves, one of the Pennsylvania fanciers, made her

THE WORLD'S LARGEST SELECTION OF PET AND ANIMAL BOOKS

T.F.H. Publications publishes more than 900 books covering many hobby aspects (dogs,

. . . BIRDS . .

. . CATS . . .

. . . ANIMALS . . .

. . . DOGS . .

. . FISH . . .

cats, birds, fish, small animals, etc.), plus books dealing with more purely scientific aspects of the animal world (such as books about fossils, corals, sea shells, whales and octopuses). Whether you are a beginner or an advanced hobbyist you will find exactly what you're looking for among our complete listing of books. For a free catalog fill out the form on the other side of this page and mail it today. All T.F.H. books are recyclable.

Since 1952, *Tropical Fish Hobbyist* has been the source of accurate, up-to-the-minute, and fascinating information on every facet of the aquarium hobby. Join the more than 50,000 devoted readers world-wide who wouldn't miss a single issue.

mark in Dalmatian history through her Tattoo Kennels, one of her earliest important dogs having been Champion Pied Piper of Tattoo, a homebred. Mrs. Edward P. Alker, famous lady of the Twin Pond Welsh Terriers, was well "into" Dals during the late 1930's. Reigate Kennels in Virginia bred a series of outstanding dogs, many of whom figured in the background of other successful kennels, and really made it big with their marvelous Champion Reigate Bold Venture and numerous other successful Dals. Williamsdale Kennels were among the most respected in the Dalmatian world, their headquarters in Ohio especially influential in the background of the Mid-Western dogs. Williamsview Kennels in New Jersey was another notable one. Dalquest Kennels, Margery L. Van Der Veer, at North Windham, Connecticut, was home to many a handsome Dal.

Evelyn Nelson White owned the Tomalyn Hill Dalmatians, for many years in New Jersey, then later in the South. This kennel was noted for fine homebreds, as well as for the California-bred Champion Four In Hand Blackberry, brought East from Leo Meeker's very famous kennel on the Pacific coast. Evelyn Nelson for years was Dalmatian columnist for the *Pure-Bred Dogs/American Kennel Gazette*. She was a lady who worked long and hard on anything beneficial to her beloved breed. She was also a well liked judge.

Mrs. Maurice Firuski owned the Sarum Kennels in Connecticut, which became active during the 1930's. Champion Reigate Dress Parade was a dog of hers I recall with special admiration. Her early stock included a daughter of Champion Tweedle Dum of the Wells; and her Champion Sarum Country Bumpkin.

Head of the River Kennels, at Smithtown, Long Island, were owned by Mrs. Prentice Sanger who was active on a large scale over a long period of time with her lovely Dals, and who was sadly missed following her death some years back—a dedicated and devoted Dal enthusiast.

Mr. and Mrs. Hugh Chisholm had a great interest in Dalmatians, especially during the 1940's, and there is an impressive list of champions to their credit and carrying their Strathglass prefix into other breeding programs. I especially recall with admiration a splendid dog of theirs, Champion Strathglass Buckshot, who made his presence felt both as a sire and in show competition.

Mildred and Frank Landgraf (he was the very well loved multi-

A beautiful headstudy of the famous Ch. Colonel Boots From Dalmatia. Courtesy of Wendell J. Sammet, Dalmatia Kennels.

ple breed judge who passed away during the early 1980's) were Dalmatian people in their breeding-exhibiting days. Very successful ones! Jean B. Whiting was known for the Whitlees. The Charles Thiessens played an active role.

An extremely influential Dalmatian establishment on Long Island during the 1950's-1960's period was that known as Pennydale owned by Mr. and Mrs. Arthur Higgins. Pennydale Partner's Choice, a Head of the River Hurricane daughter from Franklin's Soldier Girl, bred by Dr. and Mrs. H.A. Cordes, was being shown by them in the puppy classes of the early 1950's, and they also owned Head of the River Storm, by Champion Williamsview Carbon Copy ex Head of the River Sunshine during that same period, as well as Williamsview Bon Bon, by Champion The Ace of Fyrthorne ex Williamsview Wren, bred by William Hibbler, born September 1950.

Following these early dogs, the Higgins made an exciting acquisition from Dr. and Mrs. David Doane in the gorgeous bitch Champion Green Starr's Undergraduate, who made it big for them in the show ring then added to her laurels when, bred to Champion Green Starr's King Pin, she produced the stunning dog who became Champion Pennydale Pal Joey. Undergraduate was a daughter of Champion Beloved Scotch of the Walls ex Green Starr's Lady Luck. She and Joey were both liver spotted and they both surely blazed a trail of glory through the dog shows. In addition, Joey also became a highly respected sire.

When in 1963 Champion Coachman's Callisto made history by becoming only the third Dalmatian to go Group First at Westminster, his achievement was not reached again by a Dalmatian until early in 1985 when Champion Fireman's Freckled Friend repeated the honor Callisto had gained in 1963 under the author of this book. Those who had preceded him to the honor of Group First at Westminster were Champion Swabbie of Oz Dal and Champion

Ch. Princess Sarah, liver bitch owned by Pat Reed, handled by Barbara Partridge back in the 1960's.

Ch. Roadcoach Roadster, bred by Mary Barrett, owned by Sue Allman, and handled by Charley Meyer. An exciting and highly successful dog of the late 1950's. Handled here by Charley Meyer to one of his numerous Group 1sts.

Roadcoach Roadster. And he did so under the handling of his owner, Arthur Higgins. Callisto was a magnificent dog and did much to bring pride to the Higgins. A son of his, Champion Pennydale Mr. Roberts, was later owned by the Higgins with Dr. and Mrs. Doane of Green Starr.

Arthur Higgins passed away some years back, after which Muriel Higgins's interest as a breeder-exhibitor waned considerably, although she did remain active as a judge for a period thereafter. Now she has quite recently re-married, has moved to a different part of the country, and is seldom heard from by her friends who are interested in Dalmatians. The Pennydale contribution to Dalmatian quality is highly respected by all who recall these lovely dogs.

A very influential early kennel, to which we have been making reference, is "of the Walls" owned by Evelyn Wall at Plymouth, Massachusetts, which is *not* to be confused with the similarly named early English kennel, "of the Wells" owned by Miss E.V. Barnes in Great Britain. Dogs from both these kennels are found in lots of pedigrees from "way back there" of famous Dals. They are *not* the same kennel, nor is there any relationship between them.

Evelyn Wall bred many an outstanding Dalmatian and Dachshund at her kennel all of which carried the "of the Walls" identification. The noted Dalmatians included Champion Double Charge of the Walls, his daughter Teatotlar of the Walls, Champion Hi Balls of the Walls, Champion Tailgate of the Walls, Champion On A Binge from the Walls, Champion Beloved Scotch of the Walls (dam of the Doanes's great bitch Champion Green Starr's Darling Dotter); Champion Bitter Sweet of the Walls of Sarum (owned by Mrs. Firuski and the dam of Champion Symphony); Loaded Soda of the Walls; Creme de Cacoa of the Walls (dam of Champion Val-Kin's Chocolate Chips) and numerous others. From this list alone, it is easy to see the active part this kennel played in the development of the American Dalmatian a few decades back!

Chapter 4

Dalmatian Kennels in the United States

There is no better way to describe the progress of a breed than by telling you of the individual breeders and kennels that have contributed along the way. On the following pages we are proud to present summary descriptions of these breeders and their kennels and of many important Dalmatians and the background from which their success was attained. We tell you not only about the long-time breeders, many of whom are still active; but we also pay tribute to the comparative newcomers as well. Each has contributed to the well-being and development of these splendid dogs; and on the shoulders of the newcomers in particular, squarely rests the task of carrying on and preserving what has already been accomplished, and the responsibility for the future well-being of the breed. Study these pages well and you will come away with an increased knowledge of where the best Dalmatians have been bred, the care and forethought expended toward their progress and improvement generation after generation, and the exciting results of the efforts of these breeders.

ALBELARM

Albelarm Dalmatians are owned, along with highly successful show horses and a number of other breeds of dog, by Mrs. Alan R. Robson of Glenmoore, Pennsylvania. Breeds owned by Mrs. Robson over the past several decades have included Shetland Sheepdogs, Doberman Pinschers, Basset Hounds, Pekingese, Pugs, Boston Terriers, and Chow Chows. But it is with the Dal-

The great Ch. Green Starr's Colonel Joe winning Best of Breed at the Dalmatian Club of America National Specialty in 1982 judged by the author. Bobby Barlow handling for owner Mrs. Alan Robson.

matians that she has stayed most consistently, for which her kennel has gained world-wide fame and esteem.

Mrs. Robson's very first Best in Show award was won by one of her Dalmatians, Champion Coachman's Blizzard of Quaker Acres, handled for her by Bobby Barlow, at Susque-Nango Kennel Club on June 28, 1974.

Her most famous Dalmatian winner is the incomparable Champion Green Starr's Colonel Joe, who became the Top Winning Dalmatian of all time in the history of the breed.

Colonel Joe retired from show competition in the early 1980's having been awarded Best in Show all breeds on 35 occasions. His total record included 331 times Best of Breed, 136 times first in the Non-Sporting Group, 281 Group placements, and the Best in

39

Specialty Show at five independent Specialties. He was the Top Ranking Dal in 1977, '78, '79, and '80, and twice has ranked in the Top Twenty Non-Sporting Dogs of all time. He won the Dalmatian Club of America Parent Specialty four times, on the last occasion doing so from the Veterans Class.

Colonel Joe was born on May 6, 1974, bred by Mrs. Beverly Peters. He is a son of Champion Green Starr's Brass Tacks (Champion Green Starr's Corporal-Champion Dapplewhite Maid Marion) from Green Starr's Maggie Peters (Green Starr's Camelot-Champion Tandem Acres Victorious).

In between her first Best in Show win and Colonel Joe's success, Mrs. Robson had met success with a truly lovely bitch, Champion Coachkeep's Wingsong, who was the Top Winning Dalmatian Bitch for several years. Also with a dog from the same breeding but of a different litter, Champion Coachkeep's Blizzard.

Another estimable Dalmatian from this outstanding kennel is Champion Albelarm Bittersweet, a bitch whom Mrs. Robson considers to be one of the best of the breed she has owned or bred.

The Colonel Joe progeny and descendents are taking their own places in Dalmatian history as we write this book. Many of them are making their presence strongly felt both as producers themselves and in the show ring.

CANAL-SIDE

Canal-Side Dalmatians, owned by Pauline and Helene Masaschi, are located at Sandwich, Massachusetts, on beautiful Cape Cod.

The Masaschis acquired their first Dalmatian in 1971 from the Garretts' Ice Cream Dalmatians in California, whom they promptly started to campaign. He was American, Bermudian and Canadian Champion Pacific's Boston Bandit, and he had the distinction of becoming the first Dalmatian to win a Specialty Show in Canada, which he did under Langdon Skarda at Canada's very first Specialty for the breed. Bandit won many breeds and groups for his owners who had originally purchased him principally as a pet for their stable of show horses; they wanted a good looking Dal of whom they could be proud at the horse shows!

It was while showing their horses at the Devon, Pennsylvania, Horse Show back in the early 1970's that the Masaschis showed their Dal puppy, and another they had with them, to Bill Ken-

Am. and Can. Ch. Erin's Canal Side Drummer Boy, bred by John and Sharon Lyons, Erin Dalmatians, Bloomingburg, N.Y. Owned by Pauline and Helene Masaschi. Pictured going Winners Dog at the Dalmatian Club of Greater St. Louis Specialty Show, March 1984, completing title with this 5-point major. Judge, William W. Fetner. Owner-handler, Pauline Masaschi. Also was Best of Winners at Dalmatian Club of Greater N.Y. Specialty Show under judge Mrs. Alan Robson.

drick and Mrs. Alan Robson (she is famous for her American Saddlebreds as well as for her Dals) to evaluate Bandit for them. Encouraged by their comment that he "had the attitude and quality for a show dog," they entered Bandit in the Puppy Class at Cape Cod Kennel Club's Summer Show. When he won Best of Breed over top specials in competition at that time, the Masaschis were fired with enthusiasm and sought to purchase for their kennel more show quality Dalmatians.

The good liver male, American and Canadian Champion Coachman's Chocolate Soldier, was then obtained from Mr. and Mrs. William W. Fetner of St. Louis, Missouri. In this litter there were four champions, the dam being Coachman's Coffee Break who recently won the Veteran Bitch Class at the 1985 St. Louis Specialty at age thirteen.

Chocolate Soldier won many breeds and groups for the Masaschis, always owner-handled, and he is the sire of their famous American and Canadian Champion Coachman's Hot Coffee, a four-time Specialty winner (three times she won from the Veterans Class). This lovely bitch started her career owned by the Fetners with Jane Forsyth as her handler, and she is Chocolate Soldier's best known daughter.

Other famous champions sired by Chocolate Soldier include Champion Canal-Side's Soldier On Parade, Champion Dymondee's Toy Soldier, American and Canadian Champion Erin's Canal-Side Drummer Boy, and Champion Erin's Irish Coffee.

Chocolate Soldier is the foundation sire behind all of the Dalmatians at Canal-Side today. He is over 12 years old now and is enjoying the successes of his children and grandchildren in the show ring.

Hot Coffee produced one litter bred to the Masaschis' young male, American and Canadian Champion Erin's Canal-Side Drum-

Am., Bda., and Can. Ch. Pacific's Boston Bandit, liver and white, by Ch. Merithew Grand Slam (English import) ex Heidi of Edmonton, pictured winning the first Dalmatian Specialty ever held in Canada, the Dalmatian Club of Quebec, at Montreal. Judge, Langdon Skarda. Handler, Barbara Partridge. Owners, Pauline and Helene Masaschi.

mer Boy, the offspring from which the Masaschis are currently showing. One of these is Canal-Side's Strutt'n High, and he had the honor of taking Best of Winners for a 4-point major at the Dalmatian Club of Greater New York's Specialty Show in September 1984 under judge Joyce Haddon, following in his sire's pawprints, as Drummer Boy had been Best of Winners there the previous year under judge Isabel Robson.

Hot Coffee holds the distinction of being the first bitch ever to win Best Dalmatian at Westminster on *two* occasions, which she did in 1982 under Robert Sturm and in 1984 under breeder-judge Alfred Treen.

American and Canadian Champion Coachmaster's Ringmaster was acquired by the Masaschis from Robert and Shirley Hayes's famous Coachmaster Kennels in California. He was sired by Champion Coachmaster's Impressario ex Champion Coachmaster's Bernadette, and he was always owner-handled. At the Dalmatian Club of Southern New England Specialty under judge Nancy Riley, when he started out at a youthful age, he went Reserve Winners Dog from the Novice Class. A 4-point major at the Pittsburgh Specialty under judge Dr. Sidney Remmele gave him the final points for his championship at the Pittsburgh Dalmatian Club Specialty. Ringmaster is still hale and hearty at 12 years of age.

The Masaschis actively show their Dalmatians at all shows in New England and attend National and Regional Specialties. In 1985 Hot Coffee, from the Veterans Class, has taken Best of Breed at the Dalmatian Club of Greater Atlanta; Best of Breed from the Veterans Class at the Dalmatian Club of Southern New England (and on to Group 3rd that day); and Best of Breed from the Veterans Class at the Dalmatian Club of Detroit (Dalmatian Club of America National Specialty week). Her "credits" add up to an imposing list, including the following facts. She was the first Dalmatian Bitch ever to win *two* Bests of Breeds at Westminster Kennel Club (in 1982 owned by Coachman Kennels and Helene Masaschi, handled by Mrs. William Fetner and in 1984 owned and handled by Helene Masaschi), plus two Bests of Opposite Sex at Dalmatian Club of America National Specialties (1979 owned by Coachman Kennels and handled by Jane Forsyth and in 1984 owned and handled by Helene Masaschi). Coffee is a multiple Breed, multiple Group and multiple Specialty Show winner.

Ch. Cavalier Spring Sunshine taking the points at St. Hubert K. C. in 1980. Owned by Michael Manning, M.D., Cavalier Dalmatians.

CAVALIER

Cavalier Dalmatians are by way of being a dream come true for their owner, Michael T. Manning of Staten Island, New York, who from boyhood had thought longingly of one day breeding and showing dogs and having a kennel of that name.

Dr. Manning's first Dalmatian was his family's pet whom he trained to a C.D. The obedience lessons were to keep peace between Dr. Manning's father and the dog, but during them Michael Manning was bitten by the "show bug."

While attending medical school, Michael Manning purchased and trained Salimar's Napoleon through an Am. C.D. and a Can. C.D.X. The first brood bitch was acquired from Melody Kennels as a puppy and showed to become Champion Melody Ramblin' Rose, C.D. and Canadian C.D.

A linebreeding of Ramblin' Rose to Champion Melody Dynamic provided the first homebred champion for this kennel, Champion Cavalier Pretty Princess. Pretty was outcrossed twice to MGR Kennels' Champion Karastella Cadillac of M.G.R. The first of these litters produced Champion Cavalier Spring Sunshine and Champion Cavalier Lady Abigail Aubrey; from the second came Champion Cavalier Cover Girl.

Current efforts at Cavalier are to line and inbreed these daughters back to Cadillac with occasional outcrosses.

Although he has less time now for obedience work with his Dals than formerly, Dr. Manning lately has been working one of his champion males in Novice.

Dr. Manning is a practicing gastroenterologist living in Staten Island.

CENTURION

Centurion Dalmatians are owned by Paul K. and Elaine Ann Lindhorst at St. Charles, Missouri. This kennel has produced 12 Dalmatian bench champions and 14 who have earned obedience degrees. Four of the latter are multi-titled in obedience, and four of the breed champions have group placements. Six carry both champion and obedience titles.

Champion Centurion Star of Hope, C.D., by Champion Panore of Watseka ex Crown Jewels Crystal Crystaline Jade, C.D.X. has been an outstanding producer for this kennel. Of her 22 offspring, seven are champions and nine hold obedience degrees; in addition, three of the champions have Group placements.

Star herself was Winners Bitch at the Chicagoland Specialty in 1976 and Best of Opposite Sex at the Western Reserve Specialty.

She is the dam of a litter which produced four champions, sired by Champion Tosland's Tarr Baby. They are Champion Centurion Seraphim, C.D., a Group placer from the classes; Champion Centurion Bacchus, a Group 1st Winner, Champion Centurion Dealer Deacon, Group 1st Winner and No. 24 Dalmatian in 1980; and Champion Centurion Pride.

By Champion Raintrees Rooster Cogburn, Star produced Champion Centurion Special Edition, U.D., TT, who was the breed's Top Obedience Brood Bitch in 1983, and is one of very few Champion-UD Dalmatians. Star of Hope is the dam of two champions and 12 Dalmatians with obedience degrees. She herself was High in Trial at the Detroit Specialty. Also from this litter came Champion Centurion Flaming Fantasy.

Then by Champion Long Last Link to Paisley, Star of Hope became the dam of Champion Centurion Galactic General,

Ch. Centurion Roman Caesar, C.D., by Ch. Von Cross Gatabout Gatsby, C.D. ex Centurion Sea Gypsy, C.D., owned by Allen and Susan Bierman, St. Louis, Mo.

Ch. Centurion Cloudburst (*left*) and Centurion Texas Traveler are owned by Centurion Dalmatians, Paul K. and Elaine Ann Lindhorst.

C.D.X., High in Trial at the Davenport Specialty, owner-handled to the title.

Champion Centurion Pippin, by Champion Annles N. Belrine Dylan Flyer ex Champion Centurion Special Edition, U.D., TT, finished his championship in ten shows by going Group 1st for his final points. He had started out being a Group winner, owner-handled, from specials. The loss of so lovely a Dalmatian at only two years of age was certainly regrettable.

Current young winners include Champion Centurion Cloudburst and Champion Centurion Rainbow, littermates by Champion Indalane Bryans Knockout ex Showcase Centurion Sanpiper. Cloudburst, handled by 15-year-old Suzy Lindhorst, finished championship with three majors. Rainbow also finished with three majors and was owner-handled to the title.

Champion Centurion Roman Caesar, C.D. is by Champion Von Cross Gatabout Gatsby, C.D. from Centurion Sea Gypsy, C.D. He is doing well under the ownership of Allen and Susan Bierman.

An informal pose of Cheshire's Break Dancer at four months. Photo by owner, Cheryl Fales Steinmetz, Cheshire Dalmatians, Excelsior, Minn.

CHESHIRE

Cheshire Dalmatians are owned by Cheryl Fales Steinmetz at Excelsior, Minnesota, who started in purebred dogs in 1964 with a Miniature Poodle in obedience who earned a C.D. in 1965 and a C.D.X. in 1966. Cheryl purchased her first Dalmatian in 1970 from Mary Blair—a dog named Round Tower's Hickory Smoke, C.D. This dog was pointed in breed and also earned his American and Canadian C.D. in 1972.

After many false starts with other pups for the breed ring, Cheryl's first Dalmatian to finish was purchased in 1976. She was to become Champion Paisley's Star of Kirkland, C.D. This handsome liver bitch is a daughter of Champion Paisley's Five Card Stud, C.D.X., Canadian C.D. from American and Canadian Champion Melody Bobby McGee, American and Canadian C.D. She was bred by Marie Kirk.

Star completed her championship in 1979 and her C.D. the following year. In limited showing, she had multi-Bests of Breed and two Group placements, owner-handled. "Stripe's" third litter, whelped May 9, 1983, is by Champion Woodbury's Stonewall Jackson. In it she produced Champion Cheshire's Yankee Honor and Champion Cheshire's Earthquake (both black and white), both breeder-owner-handled in the ring. Yankee finished his championship with five majors and took a major Reserve at the 1984 Davenport Dalmatian Club Specialty, all before he had reached age 15 months. Earthquake finished at the age of two years. Yankee is now owned by Peggy Strupp in Utah; Quaker is co-owned with Thomas and Joelle Chatfield.

Ch. Cheshire's Earthquaker, by Ch. Woodbury's Stonewall Jackson ex Ch. Paisley's Star of Kirkland, C.D., owners, Thomas and Joelle Chatfield and Cheryl Steinmetz, the latter breeder and handler. Finishing title taking Winners Bitch St. Croix Valley, May 1985.

Ch. Cheshire's English Ivy, by Ch. Paisley's Five Card Stud ex Ch. Harmony Calais of Cheshire, was bred by Judy Box and Cheryl Steinmetz, owned and handled by the latter. Pictured winning Best of Breed at Chicagoland Specialty Show in 1984.

In 1979, Cheryl Steinmetz purchased Champion Harmony Calais of Cheshire, black and white, as an eight-week-old-puppy. She was bred by Janet and Douglas Nelson. "Cally" was Best in Sweepstakes at the 1980 Davenport Dalmatian Club Specialty, and completed her championship in 1981, following which she was sold to Judy Box in Texas with the agreement that a breeding be arranged and co-bred from her by Champion Paisley's Five Card Stud, C.D.X., Canadian C.D.

From that litter, whelped in 1982, came Champion Cheshire's

English Ivy (liver and white) and Champion Dobro's Perfect Harmony (black and white). When this litter was six weeks old, Cheryl flew to Texas to select her puppy, bringing Ivy home with her. Ivy was Reserve Winners Bitch at the Northern California Specialty the day following the 1983 National, later gaining her title with three majors, one of which included a Best of Breed over specials and a Group 4th placement. Always breeder-owner-handled, Ivy gave Cheryl her thrill as an exhibitor when she took Best of Breed in an entry of 120 at the Chicagoland Dalmatian Club Specialty in March, 1985.

Ivy has produced one excellent litter sired by Champion Fireman's Freckled Friend. Born in 1984, a black and white dog from this litter, Cheshire's Break Dancer, was Best in Sweepstakes at the Dalmatian Club of Greater Indianapolis Specialty on March, 1985.

Plans for the future include breeding Ivy to Champion Handsome Hugger of Croatia, owned by Andrea Prull and Forrest Johnson, and breeding Quaker to London's Cadbury Fudge, with major points to date, owned by Len and Sharron Podleski.

Current items of interest from Cheshire include the fact that Champion Cheshire's Yankee Honor now has a C.D. title, having been trained and handled by his new owner, Peggy Strupp.

Probably the most exciting of all the recent good wins for Cheshire is that Cheshire Break Dancer finished out May in a blaze of glory by taking Reserve Winners Dog at the Dalmatian Club of America National Specialty; Best Senior in Sweepstakes at the Canadian Specialty, and a 5-point major the final day of DCA weekend, at Monroe Kennel Club, where he was Winners Dog and Best of Opposite Sex over male specials. Then, several weeks later, at the Davenport Dalmatian Specialty, he was Best in Sweepstakes and Reserve Winners Dog.

COACHMAN

Coachman Kennels well live up to their motto of "Yesterday, To-day and Tomorrow" as their activity in this breed has been constant since the 1950's, something not too frequently found in these days of many changes. From the very beginning, Mr. and Mrs. William Fetner have been dedicated, conscientious, intelligent breeders, with results that have contributed tremendously to the quality of this breed.

51

To make it especially noteworthy, their daughter-in-law, Phyllis Fetner at Dallas, Texas, has been a staunch supporter and breeder who has helped immeasurably in keeping Coachman "alive and kicking" for the past ten years. Coachman is truly a family project in every sense of the word.

Looking back to yesterday, one notes the quality of the great foundation bitch, Frishka, who certainly put the breeding program off on the right foot with the outstanding offspring she produced. The results of this fact are noticeable today and almost certainly will continue to be so tomorrow, judging by the quality of young descendants of the original forebears who are just starting

The foundation bitch of Coachman Dalmatians. Ch. Fobette's Frishka, C.D. in 1955, by Ch. Chan-Dal-Sad-Snafu ex Ch. Prancing Lady of Fobette, was purchased from handler Nicky Finn. Owned by Mr. and Mrs. William Fetner.

Foundation stock at Coachman Kennels in 1958. Ch. Fobette's Frishka, C.D., by Chan-Dal-Sad-Snafu; and Ch. Fobette's Fanfare, C.D.X., by Ch Williamsdale Sunstar. The dams of these two are littermates from Fobette Kennels. Owned by Mr. and Mrs. William Fetner.

to make their presence felt. Here has been created a dynasty in Dalmatians, and we sincerely admire the Fetners who have accomplished so much so consistently for their breed.

Coachman Kennels and Stables are at St. Louis, Missouri, where more than 50 Dalmatian Champions have been bred and reared.

The wins of these various dogs have added up to impressive totals, and it is notable that numerous owners outside of the Fetner family themselves have shared in the glory of being in "the winners circle" due to them. The success of others with Coachman dogs is a source of special pleasure to the Fetners, who are proud of being able to say that more than a few big winning kennels are linebreeding to the Coachman dogs.

To the majority of dog show exhibitors, the symbols of success are wins at their breed's National Specialty and at Westminster. It is noteworthy that since 1958 no less than eight Coachman dogs have gone Best of Breed or Best of Opposite Sex at the Dalmatian Club of America National and that out of four Dalmatians in the history of Westminster to have won the Non-Sporting Group there, Coachman has been behind the winner twice. In 1963, it was Champion Coachman's Callisto who did it; in 1985, 22 years later, Champion Fireman's Freckled Friend, a linebred Coachman dog. The future? We shall have to just wait and see.

DAL ACRES

Dal Acres Dalmatians are at San Antonio, Texas, where they are owned by Dottie LaGassie and Marilyn Dusek who are the owners of Dal Acres Manufacturing Company in that city, which makes Western belts, weight lifting belts, and dog and cat collars and leads.

These two ladies are the breeders-owners of a most outstanding Dalmatian, Champion Dal Acres Banners Blazing, who was born November 1, 1979 and is a son of Champion Long Last Looksharp and Champion Dal Acres Ms. Kizzy, thus a combination of Long Last and Never Complain bloodlines.

Owner-handled, Blaze became No. 4 among Dalmatians in 1982, No. 6 in 1983, and No. 7 in 1984, all systems, plus being the No. 1 Owner-Handled Dalmatian in the country over that entire period. His Best of Breed wins add up to 84 with 11 Group 1sts, 15 Group 2nds, 11 Group 3rds, and 13 times Group 4th bringing his total Group placements to 50. Additionally he was Best in Specialty Show at the Chicagoland Dalmatian Club on September 25, 1982 under judge Frank Oberstar.

Blaze retired from the show ring to thoroughly enjoy a "dog's life" at home with his owners—a very outstanding Dalmatian who made friends everywhere for himself and his breed during his show career.

DALMATIA

Dalmatia identifies the Dalmatians bred, owned, and/or shown by noted professional handler Wendell J. Sammet, who back in the 1940's at Hingham, Massachusetts, laid the foundation for a highly successful breeding program which produced, and to this day, stands behind some of this country's most notable Dals. Now located at Bryantville, Massachusetts and most widely associated with the other breed he loves, Poodles, Wendell has never lost his interest in Dals. In fact it would be difficult to say which breed has brought him most enjoyment over the years as he has a host of truly notable successes in both.

The early names in the history of Dalmatia Kennels include, from the late 1940's, Champion Dalquest Rhythm from Dalmatia, born in 1947, by Champion Williamsdale Sunstar ex Champion Hamilton Belle. Wendell bred this splendid bitch to the well-known Champion Colonel Bones, son of Champion Williamsdale

Ch. Kareless Kiss From Dalmatia, daughter of the great Ch. Roadcoach Roadster, owned by Wendell J. Sammet.

Sunstar, and in February 1951 she produced a litter which included the bitches Bellehop From Dalmatia and Blue Bolero From Dalmatia, and the dog who was to become Champion Boot Black From Dalmatia.

This black spotted dog, breeder-owner handled by Mr. Sammet, had nine Group 1sts to his credit (in the days when dog shows were far and away less numerous than in modern times), and won Best of Breed at Westminster, Morris and Essex, and the Southern New England Dalmatian Specialty in 1954 and 1955 as well as the Chicagoland Specialty in 1955 and 1956. But it was not only as a show dog that Boot Black was outstanding, for among his ten champion offspring was the litter that included Champion Roadcoach Roadster and Champion Roadcoach Roadmaster, bred by Mrs. Mary P. Barrett.

Ch. Maestro From Dalmatia, owned by Wendell J. Sammet, Dalmatia, Bryantville, Mass.

Ch. Laced-Boots From Dalmatia in April 1959. One of the outstanding Dalmatians from this famous kennel owned by Wendell J. Sammet.

Boot Black's son, Roadster, was, like his sire, black spotted. He completed his championship at age 13 months and was sold to Mrs. S.K. Allman, Jr., of In The Valley Dalmatians at Doylestown, Pennsylvania. Handled by Charley Meyer, he climaxed his show career by winning Best in Show at the legendary Morris and Essex Kennel Club classic, which was one of a total of 17 Best in Show honors for this memorable dog. His 64 Group 1sts included such shows as Westminster, Eastern Dog Club and Chicago International in 1957. He was Best of Breed at the Dalmatian Club of America National Specialty in 1956, and at the Chicago Specialty in '57. His champion progeny included Champions Tioga Sportscar, Roadcoach Random, and Kiss and Tell From Dalmatia.

Another of Wendell's earliest bitches, Roadcoach Frou Frou, C.D.X., was bred by him to Champion Roadcoach Racing Colors, producing, in April 1947, the lovely bitch Champion China Doll From Dalmatia, with whom he won the Dalmatian Club of Amer-

Ch. She's So Lovely From Dalmatia, litter sister to Ch. He's So Handsome From Dalmatia, winning points towards her title in 1974. Wendell J. Sammet, owner-handler.

Ch. Dalquest Rhythm of Dalmatia, born in April 1947, was by Ch. Williamsdale Sunstar ex Ch. Hamilton Belle, and was the dam of Ch. Boot Black From Dalmatia. One of Wendell Sammet's earliest Dalmatians who figured strongly in the Dalmatia breeding program.

ica National Specialty in 1949 and Best of Opposite Sex to Best of Breed there in 1950. Among other offspring, China Doll gave Barbara Partridge her Gala Jubilee of Dalmatia who helped start this highly successful Dalmatian breeder and handler on her way.

Champion Kareless Kiss From Dalmatia and Shiney Boots From Dalmatia were of the 1950's era. Shiney Boots sired Champion Music Man from Dalmatia (a son, as well, of Champion Sparkling Rhythm). Champion Fine and Dandy of Dalmatia was another noted winner from this kennel. Then there was the bitch, Champion Lily White From Dalmatia, both an estimable representative and a notable producer.

Champion Colonel Boots From Dalmatia also brought home the National Best of Breed rosette, this in 1954. At the same event, Dress Boots From Dalmatia was Winners Bitch.

DALMATIANS OF CROATIA

Dalmatians of Croatia were established in 1962 by Forrest Johnson at Davenport, Iowa, who previous to that time had bred Chihuahuas and Miniature Poodles since 1954.

Over the years, this kennel has owned or bred 30 Dalmatian champions, despite the fact that the breeding and showing has been on a modest scale due to the Johnsons' preoccupation with the rearing of their five children and all of their activities.

The Johnsons' first homebred champion, Champion Mr. Diamond Chips of Croatia, was sired by their very first Dal, Champion Crown Jewel's Jubilee Diamond and out of Champion Crown Jewel's Pearl of Asia. Chips was judged Best Puppy at the 1970 Dalmatian Club of America National Specialty Show. Bred to Champion Crown Jewel's Nadana Topaz, Chips became the sire of four champions.

Paisley Jenny Lind of Croatia was acquired in the 1970's. She was an extremely elegant bitch out of the famous bitch Champion Melody Up Up and Away, and was sired by the multi-Best in Show dog Champion Panore of Watseka. She was bred to her half brother, Champion Bob Dylan Thomas of Watseka, the resultant litter producing Champion Jimmy Crack Corn of Croatia, Champion Mr. Paul Revere of Croatia, and Champion J.K. Jason of Croatia. Jimmy was Reserve Winners Dog at the Davenport Dalmatian Club Specialty. Paul Revere became a Specialty, multiple Best of Breed, and Group winner.

It was the Johnsons' good fortune to purchase a Champion Sugarfrost daughter out of the great producing Champion Melody Crimson and Clover, the latter a littermate to Champion Melody Up Up and Away. They were sired by the two-time Best in Show winning liver dog, Champion Melody Dynamic. When this puppy arrived, the Johnsons were both happy and disappointed, as she was rather heavily marked and substantial in build, actually quite homely and quite adorable, to quote Forrest Johnson. She was dubbed Daffy Duck, later shortened to Daffy. Always a consistent winner in the classes, she finished her title by going Winners Bitch and Best of Opposite Sex at the Detroit Dalmatian Club Specialty. Now she is formally known as Champion Melody Joleen of Croatia, and as a mature bitch she went Best of Opposite Sex to the great Champion Green Starr's Colonel Joe at the 1979 Davenport Dalmatian Club Specialty the day following the National.

Ch. Melody Joleen of Croatia taking Best of Opposite Sex at the Davenport Dalmatian Club Specialty in 1979. Owned by Forrest Johnson.

Obviously she had turned out well! Forrest Johnson notes that "ironically, she defeated 101 Dals that day" according to his records. Daffy was bred to Champion Jimmy Crack Corn of Croatia thus providing Champion Levi Zendt of Croatia and Champion Firewagins's Lucinda. Levi completed his title in 13 short days from start to finish, becoming a champion one day past his first birthday. Levi is a compact, brilliantly marked dog of excellent quality. Lucinda, a lovely liver bitch, is a breed and Group winner, and was in a tie for Top Producing Dalmatian Bitch for 1984.

Bred to Champion Paisley's Oh Henry, C.D., son of Champion Coachman's Red Carpet ex Champion Melody Up Up and Away, Daffy produced the magnificent Champion Sir Ike of Croatia. Ike finished easily and was Best in Sweepstakes at the Chicagoland Dalmatian Club Specialty. He is siring top quality puppies.

Champion Nicolette of Croatia was the result of a breeding between Daffy and Champion Mr. Paul Revere of Croatia. Nicolette went on a co-ownership basis when eight weeks old to Debbie Banfield, who is the trainer in the driving division for Friendship Farms Arabian Stables owned by Mr. and Mrs. William Hewitt (John Deere heritage). Interestingly, the puppy took to coaching like a duck to water, obviously her heritage of generations back coming to the fore! Four in Hand, Unicorn, and teams are hitched and trained there. Mrs. Hewitt's Arabians are sent all over the United States to compete and participate in driving exhibitions, and very often Nicolette is invited to "coach" under the carriages like the Dalmatians of long ago. No one goes near the expensive tack as Nicolette considers guarding it to be her principal job, which she performs well.

Encouraged by the breeder to do so, Debbie Banfield when Nicolette was two years old enrolled her in conformation classes to see how she might fare as a show dog. All went well until the judge tried to examine her. Nicolette did not want to be touched! Persistence paid off, however, and three months later Nicolette was entered in her first show, a Dalmatian Specialty judged by Tom Stevenson. This was the first time for both Nicolette and Debbie, in the actual show ring at a dog show so it was quite impressive that they went Winners Bitch and Best of Opposite Sex over a bitch special. It took all of seven shows to make Nicolette a champion. In the summer of 1985, she had her first litter, having been bred to Champion Count Miguel of Tuckaway, the sire of the 15-time Best in Show winner Champion Fireman's Freckled Friend. Forrest Johnson comments, "We reinforce superior shoulder and pigment by this blending."

Champion Miss Camielle of Croatia is the only liver resident at the kennel. She was Winners Bitch and Best of Winners at the Chicagoland Dalmatian Club Specialty when only nine-and-a-half months old, and finished a month later! Camielle is a daughter of Champion Levi Zendt of Croatia, and the dam of another Croatia Specialty winner, Champion Handsome Hugger of Croatia who is co-owned with Angie Prull of Fond du Lac, Wisconsin. Hugger's sire is also a Specialty winner, Champion Indalane Handsome of Croatia, the latter purchased for "new blood" and who has well proven his worth. "Handy" was Winners Dog and Best of Winners at the Detroit Dalmatian Club Specialty. In the breeding program, he has darkened eyes and given more depth of pigment and snow-white coats.

One more stud owned by the Johnsons is a son of Champion Green Starr's Colonel Joe. This is Champion Green Starr's Radar, who was purchased as a six-month puppy and finished quickly.

The latest addition to the Dalmatian family is the Canadian-born American and Canadian Champion Canusa's Kandi Kisses. She was Best of Breed at the Pittsburgh, Detroit, and Davenport Dalmatian Club Specialties, and she is a daughter of Champion Korcula King of Harts ex Champion Rolenet's Rhapsody.

DAUNTLESS

Dauntless Dalmatians are at Deland, Florida and owned by E. Anne Hutchins. This is the home of Champion Enchanted Tequila Sunrise, who when only nine weeks old was acquired by Anne Hutchins from Al and Midge Brown of Enchanted Dalmatians.

Sunrise finished under two years of age, going Best of Winners and Best of Opposite Sex under judge Richard Guevara on the January Florida Circuit. She won her first Non-Sporting Group under judge Jane Kay.

In October 1984, this lovely bitch was Best in Specialty Show at the Dalmatian Club of Greater Atlanta under judge Dr. Samuel Draper. She was No. 2 Bitch for 1983, and No. 1 Bitch and No. 7 Dalmatian for 1984.

"Sunny" is by Champion Tucwinn's Drumhille King Olaf ex

An informal photograph of Ch. Enchanted Tequila Sunrise owned by E. Anne Hutchins.

Enchanted's Majestic Miss. She was bred by D. Anne Wilson, and trained and shown by Charlie O'Hara.

Anne Hutchins purchased her first Dalmatian upon moving to Deland where she joined the West Volusia Kennel Club. This was King Oak's Mister Cocoa, by King Oak's Prince Mischief ex King Oak's Glory, bred by Olga Merwick Fenton. He was shown to Reserve a few times. At nine years old, he is now retired to being "big brother" to all the other Dalmatians who share his home.

Dauntless Annabel Lee and Dauntless Daisy Mae are littermates by Champion Rolenet's Ragtime Dandy ex Champion Enchanted Tequila Sunrise. Annabel was pointed prior to leaving for her new home, Cute As A Speckled Pup Kennels in Tennessee. Daisy Mae is pointed too, and still living in Florida.

Then there is Dauntless Chico of Enchanted, by Enchanted Sport Model ex Stormhawk's Rhapsody in Blue, a promising youngster who has taken his first point from the 6-9 months class.

DELTALYN

Deltalyn Dalmatians are owned by Judie and Bob Rivard and are located at Foster, Rhode Island.

The first champion owned by them was a lovely bitch, American and Canadian Champion Crown Jewels Delta Diamond, who was a daughter of Champion Crown Jewels Regent Diamond ex Crown Jewels Pendant Diamond. Holly, as she was called, was purchased from Norma and Vern Price of Crown Jewel Kennels at the age of eight weeks. She finished quickly for her new owners when she reached show age, her first two wins being four-point majors. She also gained title in Canada in short order, doing so during just one trip there.

Holly was bred twice, on each occasion to the same dog, Champion Coachman's Canicula, producing three champions in these two litters. Among these puppies was the Rivards' noted winner "Cooper," or, more formally, Champion Deltalyn's Decoupage.

The other two winners produced by Holly are Champion Deltalyn Mystic Brandy and Champion Deltalyn Daymon. Holly lived to the nice old age of fourteen-and-a-half years.

American and Canadian Champion Deltalyn Decoupage was the Rivards' first homebred champion, and the sort of dog that people sometimes work for years hoping and trying to produce! He won most of his points from the puppy class, and finished at 13 months of age. He returned to the ring at 18 months following a "growing up period," and within a couple of months' time he became one of the Top Dalmatians in the country. He was No. 1 Owner-Handled Dalmatian in 1975, 1976 and 1977. He was a multi-breed, Group, and Specialty Best of Breed winner; among his successes were five Regional Specialty Shows and Best of Breed at Westminster in 1976. He became a *Kennel Review* Top Producer in 1979, and to date is the sire of 20 champions with several more still to finish. He has sired ten Specialty winners and has over 30 champion grandchildren.

Cooper retired from the show ring with 126 Bests of Breed to his credit and more than 60 Group placements including 12 times Group 1st.

One of Cooper's daughters, Cale Dal Diamond Liver Lovely, finished her championship by going Winners Bitch at the Dalmatian Club of America National Specialty held in conjunction with the American Kennel Club Centennial Specialties in 1984.

Am. and Can. Ch. Deltalyn Decoupage winning at the Westchester Kennel Club in 1978. An important Group-winning Dalmatian, this splendid dog has won wide acclaim in hottest Eastern competition. Owned and bred by Bob and Judie Rivard.

Champion Deltalyn Dr. Pepper and American and Canadian Champion Deltalyn Dappled Lady Maby, American and Canadian C.D.X. are littermates by Champion Deltalyn Bold Lancer ex Deltalyn Prima Donna. Dr. Pepper finished his championship at 13 months old, almost completely from the puppy classes, with several Best of Breed wins over specials. Like her brother, Lady, too, finished quickly in a total of seven shows in which she won three majors and twice was Best of Breed over specials. Lady has the distinction of being a Group winner (under Bill Fetner from the Open Bitch Class), and is the Dalmatian seen representing the Non-Sporting Group on the Centennial cover of the *Pure-Bred Dogs/American Kennel Gazette*.

DOTTIDALE

Dottidale Kennels, for many years at Millbrook, New York, moved early in 1985 to a new home at Liberty, Kentucky, since owners Amy S. and Elli Lipschutz felt that a milder climate would be a pleasant change from their many years as residents of New York State. They are just about "settled in" as we are writing, and their many friends throughout the Dalmatian world I know are wishing them good fortune there.

Grand matriarch of the kennel was the lovely bitch Champion Windgap's Honey Bee, whom Amy was showing the very first time she brought a Dalmatian into the ring for my judicial opinion a couple of decades back. If memory serves me correctly, Honey Bee was the first of the Lipschutz's Dals, and what a marvelous foundation bitch she became for them!

Bred to a popular and well-admired dog of that period, Champion Pennydale Pal Joey, owned by Pennydale Kennels on Long Island, Honey Bee became the dam of Champion Dottidale Jo Jo, who proceeded to make history both in the show ring and as a sire. This handsome young homebred during 1967 became the Top Winning Liver Dalmatian in the United States; the Top Winning Owner-Handled Dal in the United States that same year; and the No. 4 Dalmatian in the Country under the Phillips System. Very nice going indeed.

Among Jo Jo's offspring have been an impressive number of champions. He sired the Winners Dog at the Dalmatian Club of America National Specialty for 1969; Winners Bitch and Best of Opposite Sex at this same show in the same year; Winners Dog at the Dalmatian Club of Southern New England Specialty in 1970; Best in the Sweepstakes, Dalmatian Club of Southern New England Specialty 1971; Reserve Winners Bitch at the Dalmatian Club of America Specialty 1972; and Best of Breed at the Westminster Kennel Club in 1972.

Champion Dottidale's Buster Brown was the result of Honey Bee being bred to her son, Jo Jo, a handsome liver dog who won well and produced another winning generation. Champion Dottidale Marco Polo was sired by Jo Jo from Dottidale Little Lu Lu. He was Best in Sweepstakes at the Dalmatian Club of Southern New England on the same weekend as his sire won the Veteran Dog Class at the Dalmatian Club of America Specialty. He, too, is the sire of champions.

Three generations of liver males, their linebreeding very apparent. *Left to right:* Ch. Dottidale Jo Jo, breeder-owner handled by Elli Lipschutz; Dottidale Mr. Chips, Jo Jo's grandson, bred by Elizabeth Baechtold and owned by Robert Kiernan, handling; and the link between the generations, Ch. Dottidale Buster Brown, breeder-owner-handled by Amy S. Lipschutz.

Ch. Dottidale Marco Polo, by Ch. Dottidale Jo Jo ex Dottidale Little Lu Lu, a homebred owned by Dottidale Kennels of Amy and Elli Lipschutz.

Ch. Dottidale Cedelia, black, by Ch. Dottidale Jo Jo taking Best of Winners at Longshore-Southport K.C. in 1969. Finished title in five shows including Dalmatian Club of America Specialty 1969 on her first ring appearance. R. Stephen Shaw handled for owners Pennydale and Green Starr Kennels.

The descendants of the early Dottidale dogs are continuing to uphold the family tradition. Champion Dottidale Captain Nemo is a current winner in the kennel, bred by George Enny, sired by Dottidale Golden Aslan. He was winner of the Stud Dog Class at the Dalmatian Club of Greater New York Specialty in 1979, and was doing well as a special when shown during 1983. Among his progeny was the Best of Winners at Westminster in 1982.

Now that they are moved and settled, there will be more time for Amy and Elli to concentrate on the dogs; we hope that there will be numerous future winners produced at Dottidale!

DYMONDEE

Dymondee Dalmatians (formerly known as Diamond D Kennels) are owned by Mr. and Mrs. C.F. Lester, Jr., at Itasca, Illinois.

The breeding at Dymondee is primarily a combination of Pryor Creek, Coachman, and Colonial Coach lines. One of their foundation bitches is Champion Poco Chimney Sweep, dam of American and Canadian Champion Range Trail Maple Creek Flagg, Champion Range Trail Maple Creek Maham, Champion Maple Creeks Someone Lovely, and Shady Lady from Maple Creek, all sired by

Ch. Colonial Coach Chess King, C.D., great-grandsire of Ch. Fireman's Freckled Friend. Dymondee Dalmatians, Mr. and Mrs. C.F. Lester, Jr.

A handsone head-study of Ch. Coachman's Lucky Coins. Dymondee Kennels, Mr. and Mrs. C.F. Lester, Jr.

The incomparable Ch. Coachman's Chuck-A-Luck, a most handsome and influential member of the Dalmatian breed. Owned by Coachman Kennels, Mr. and Mrs. William Fetner, St. Louis, Mo. Pictured winning the Non-Sporting Group at Lexington K.C. in 1965.

American and Canadian Champion Coachman's Chuck-A-Luck. Chimney Sweep was sired by Champion Colonial Coach Cheshire from Poco Nit Not Cinders. She is a Group placing Dal, and is great-granddam of the 1985 Westminster Non-Sporting Group winner, Champion Fireman's Freckled Friend.

Champion Snowcap's Never On Sundae, co-owned with Michael and Louisa Weinstein, also resides at Dymondee. Sundae is the multi-Group winning daughter of Champion Coachman's Chuck-A-Luck, and herself a champion producer.

Several Dymondee bitches have become foundations for other kennels, such as Diamond D's Dot to Dot, owned by the Robert Peths and the dam of the top winning Champion Fireman's Freckled Friend.

Other winning Dals at Dymondee include American and Canadian Champion Kale's Required Coachman, by Champion Roadking's Rome (Best in Show winning Chuck-A-Luck son) ex Domino Dolly. He is a champion producer and the grandsire of Freckled Friend. Champion Coachman's Lucky Coins is by Champion Coachman's Lucky Cuss ex Champion Coachman's Cup O'Tea. Champion Firesprite's Mist of Diamond D is by Champion He's So Handsome from Dalmatia ex Lady Sleeper, and is Dymondee's newest champion with multi-Best of Breed wins and Group placements.

Champion Robbsdale's Lady of The Knight, co-owned with Tim Robbins, Robbsdale Dalmatians, is a champion producer, a daughter of Champion Robbsdale's Baron Von Cross.

The Lesters are active exhibitors in conformation as well as obedience in the United States and in Canada. Their American and Canadian Champion Range Trail Maple Creek Flagg was Winners Dog and Best of Winners at the first Dalmatian Specialty held in Canada, that of the Quebec Dalmatian Club. He is the grandsire of multi-Best in Show winner, Canadian Champion Beachcomber's Mint Mark.

Both of the Lesters have officiated as judges in the obedience and conformation rings at A.K.C. sanctioned matches. Their daughter, Margaret, shares her parents' love of Dals, and is active in conformation, obedience, and junior showmanship.

Dalmatians bred by the Lesters or sired by their stud dogs can be found throughout the world, including England, Japan, and Canada.

ERIN

Erin Dalmatians are owned by John and Sharon Lyons at Bloomingsburg in Orange County, New York. The kennel was started in 1974.

Sharon grew up around horses and horse shows, her father having been highly respected horse trainer Walter Siefert. Through her horse show associates she became acquainted with Isabelle Robson and Jean Fetner, both of these ladies sharing an interest in horses.

Ch. Erin's Natasha of Overbrook, by Ch. Erin's Irish Rogue ex Ch. Coachman's Can Such Things Be, pictured going Best of Winners at Mid-Hudson K.C. in 1984. Bred and owned by John and Sharon Lyons.

Thus it was that a foundation bitch was purchased from Bill and Jean Fetner, leading John and Sharon into very exciting participation in our dog show world.

The foundation bitch was Champion Coachman's Paisley Candybar, acquired in 1976 at the age of nine months, who was later to become the Top Dalmatian Brood Bitch and No. 2 among all Non-Sporting Bitches in 1982.

To date the Lyons have bred 20 champions, including multiple Group and Specialty. Among the most notable are Champion Coachman's Hot Coffee, multiple Group and Specialty winner along with twice Best of Breed at Westminster; Champion Erin's Irish Whiskey, Best in Sweepstakes and Best Senior in Futurity at the Dalmatian Club of America National Specialty in 1982; and Erin's Nutmeg Candy, C.D., T.D., one of the few Dalmatians to have earned a tracking degree.

The Lyons are active in numerous dog clubs, including the Dalmatian Club of America, the Dalmatian Club of Greater New York, the Monticello Kennel Club, Stewards Club of America, and Senior Conformation Judges Association.

John is an American Kennel Club approved judge of Dalmatians and Junior Showmanship. He has served as President and Show Chairman of the Dalmatian Club of Greater New York, as well as President of the Monticello Kennel Club. Presently he is show chairman for the Monticello Dog Show.

Sharon has served for many years on the Board of the Dalmatian Club of Greater New York and Monticello Kennel Club. She is presently Specialty Chairman for the DCGNY.

FANFAYRE

Fanfayre Dalmatians came about due to their owner, Ronnie Ellen Fischler, having purchased her first horse from Dianne Reimer of Snowcap Dalmatians. Being around these athletic, intelligent, clean-cut dogs, Ronnie Ellen knew that it was only a matter of time before she must have one. This she did, acquiring a lovely bitch who became Champion Snowcaps Sparkle Plenty II after a good career in the show ring (following nine months off for recovery from a broken leg). When things had settled down, Ronnie Ellen bred Sparky to Champion Snowcap's Iago of Annle, a multiple breed and group winning dog. From this breeding came

Champion Snowcap's Special Edition. At her second dog show ever, when only seven months of age, "Noddy" (Special Edition) won Best in Sweepstakes at the Dalmatian Club of Southern New York first Specialty Show under breeder-judge P.J. Fetner, over 42 other puppies in competition. She completed her title in 13 shows, and went on to be successfully campaigned by Joy Brewster. In 1981 she was No. 3 Dalmatian Bitch in the country and No. 20 Dalmatian overall. A repeated breeding resulted in the birth of the puppy who became Champion Fanfayre's Ace In The Hole, C.D., Ronnie Ellen's first obedience champion who finished his title in his first three obedience trials.

The next litter from Sparky produced the dogs who really made a difference in Ronnie Ellen's breeding program and show career. Sparky was bred to Champion Snowcap's Sunscion, a beautiful liver dog who was the result of careful Snowcap breeding. This litter produced the dogs who swept the boards at the 1982 Dalmatian Club of America National Specialty. They are Champion Fanfayre's Beau of Short Acre, Champion Fanfayre's Best Foot Forward, and Champion Fanfayre's Belle Dame, who at that Specialty accounted for a Sweepstakes Class, Winners Dog and Best of Winners (Beau); Reserve Winners Bitch (Belle Dame); and then their dam, Sparkle Plenty, won the Brood Bitch Class with these two of her offspring, after which Beau and Best Foot Forward won the Brace Class—and a standing ovation!

As of May 1985, Champion Fanfayre's Beau of Short Acre, being campaigned by Joy S. Brewster for Robert Koeppel, is the No. 2 Dalmatian in the country, winning numerous Groups plus an all-breed Best in Show. Ronnie Ellen, as breeder, could not possibly be happier or more gratified. Beau's brother, Best Foot Forward, has also done well, going on to become a top breed and Group contender.

After barely taking time to recover from the excitement of that Specialty, Ronnie Ellen acquired Champion Williamsview Fame of Fanfare from Bill Hibbler, Williamsview Dalmatians. Fame was also sired by Champion Snowcap's Sunscion. As a puppy he won Best in Sweepstakes at the Southern New England Specialty under breeder-judge John Lyons. His first time in the Open Class, Fame won a four-point major. A few short months later he was Reserve Winners Dog at the 1984 National Specialty under Tom Stevenson. The next day at the Houston Specialty Fame again took Reserve Winners Dog. He finished his title shortly thereafter at 18 months, then took a short Bermuda vacation where he was undefeated in the breed.

Ronnie Ellen has five homebred champions out of three litters at her Spring Valley, New York kennel; eight champions in all, plus one C.D. dog. She comments, "They have been my close friends and companions and they have afforded me the opportunity to travel and to meet other people all over the country. With one litter due shortly and others planned for the near future, I hope to stay active in this breed for quite awhile. To me their intelligence and loyalty make the Dalmatian a cut above the rest!"

FIREMAN

The story of Fireman's Dalmatians is an exciting one, bound to make the heart beat faster of any fancier who has ever felt that only the big, established kennels can produce winners. Robert and Mary S. Peth found out in a big way that such is not the case, and we bring you here a thrilling success story in relating how the outstanding sensation of the current Dalmatian world, Champion Fireman's Freckled Friend, came to be and gained fame.

When Rob Peth, of St. Louis, Missouri, started working in the fire service, the Peths purchased their first "fireman's dog." Following the loss of this puppy in an unfortunate accident, it was decided that a Dalmatian should be purchased for this purpose, the traditional "fireman's dog," and so their first of the breed selected from Paula Moore was a bitch called Seagrave, who came originally from the Diamond D Kennels in Chicago.

Seagrave was the first pet who completely won the hearts of the entire Peth family. Naturally they wanted to breed her, and so the search began for a dog who conformed to Rob Peth's mental picture of a Dalmatian which had been pretty much implanted in his mind by discussions of the breed with Paula Moore. At a St. Louis Dalmatian Club Obedience Drill exactly the dog the Peths had been seeking appeared. His name was Mickey, and after contacting several knowledgeable Dalmatian breeders and discussing pedigree, it was discovered that Mickey would, indeed, be the ideal mate for Seagrave.

The breeding took place, and in due time the puppies arrived. One in particular took everyone's eye, as this puppy seemed to be saying, "Hey, look me over---and see how neat I am."

Here is where it all began! These puppies are by Ch. Count Miguel of Ruckaway ex Diamond D's Dot to Dot. Probably one of the most important litters ever produced, as the puppy second from *right* is the now so very famous Ch. Fireman's Freckled Friend, bred and owned by Robert A. Peth.

Right at this point, Rob Peth learned of a fellow-fireman's Dalmatian having just been stolen, and the family decided that this puppy, whom they had named "Spotty," would make a perfect replacement for the lost dog. But the owner of that dog was still too grieved to be ready for a replacement, and so the Peths held back Spotty hoping their friend would change his mind. But he did not and so, as the Peths put it, it looked as though they were "stuck" with him since they would not allow him to go to just any ordinary home.

About a year later, the Peths received a premium list for a dog show, the St. Louis Dalmatian Specialty, soon to be held in their area. They had always wondered what it would have been like to show Spotty's dam, Seagrave, so they decided that this time they would find out. After calling a good friend to learn a bit about what showing a dog entails, they were advised not to try to train and socialize their dogs themselves, and so a phone call was made to Bill Busch, noted Beagle breeder and professional handler from the St. Louis area. The rest is history!

At the Specialty itself, which was Spotty's first show, he took third in his class. The following day he was Best of Winners in an entry of more than 90, and he won Best of Winners at the Sunday show, too. Spotty became Champion Fireman's Freckled Friend with four consecutive majors, three five-point and one three.

In his first year of showing, entered at 35 events, Spotty, in addition to his championship, gained 24 Bests of Breed, won Group 1st twice, and 11 additional Group placements.

During his second year in the ring, eight Bests in Show were added to his victories, two Dalmatian Club of America Specialties, first in Group 23 times, plus 27 additional Group placements. At the Dalmatian Club of America National in Houston, Spotty swept the breed at all four shows. This was the first "clean sweep" of a DCA weekend since Champion Panore of Watseka did it in 1972.

Spotty finished up the year by winning the Dalmatian Club of America Centennial Specialty in Philadelphia becoming the only Dal in history to win two National Specialties the same year, and stopped on the way home to add a Best in Show at Danville under judge Florise Hogan.

Champion Fireman's Freckled Friend started 1985 with a bang, taking a Best in Show at Muncie K.C. under Gerhardt Plaga. From there the next stop was Westminster, and by the time the curtain had fallen on this prestigious event, Spotty had become only the fourth Dalmatian in history ever to have won the Non-Sporting Group there in its entire 109-year history, and the first in 22 years!

As of mid-1985, Spotty's record stands at 15 Bests in Show, 41 times Group 1st, 45 other Group placements, two National Specialties, three Regional Specialties, and 108 times Best of Breed.

Now Spotty's children are starting to appear at the dog shows, and his first litter, from Champion Robbsdales Lady Roslyn, produced four out of seven show prospects. Already started are Fireman's Strikeout the First, owned by the Peths, with points; Triggerhills Ragamuffin (Scattini) also pointed and with a Best of Breed; and Robbsdale's St. Louis Blues (Trevino and Robbins) is close to the title. Cheryl Steinmetz's Cheshire's Breakdancer, by Freckled Friend from Champion Cheshire's English Ivy, won Best in Sweepstakes at the first Dalmatian Club of Greater Indianapolis Specialty and Reserve Winners Dog at the 1985 Dalmatian Club of America. So we should be hearing lots from Spotty offspring in the future.

Ch. Fireman's Freckled Friend relaxing in the motor home at Philadelphia with his handler's daughter, Stacy Busch. "Spotty" seems to be saying, "How about a sip of that for me?" as he eyes Stacy's soft drink can! Owned by Robert A. and Mary S. Peth.

The Peths comment, "At this time we could not consider ourselves a kennel as we breed very limitedly. However, we are using the prefix of Fireman's on our puppies. We are carefully searching for that certain bitch that strikes our eye to perhaps start a serious breeding program. We certainly enjoy every aspect of our breed and the sport and hope to be around for some time to come."

To the author, this story is very special, for here we have a genuine fireman's dog owned by a genuine fireman making a name for himself in breed history for his excellence in the show ring. Who says such things cannot be done?

C.E. FLOCK, JR.

A very famous Dalmatian, Champion Melody Dynamatic, to whom you will find frequent reference in the pages of this book was bred, owned, and handled throughout his show career by C.E. Flock, Jr., of Palmer Lake, Colorado. This liver and white dog, by Champion Long Last Kelso ex Champion Melody Blue Velvet, was born on January 15, 1970.

With relatively little showing, Dynamatic amassed a record that made him the top winning dog of his color variety in the history of the breed at that time. He was ranked well in the national rating systems Top Ten Show Dalmatians for the years 1973, 1974, and 1975 and was a consistent Group winner as well as a Best in Show dog. Additionally he proved to be a premier sire, with 27 champion offspring to his credit having been used selectively in only about 20 breedings.

Dynamatic was the leading Dalmatian sire and the No. 7 Non-Sporting sire for the year 1980 and appears in the pedigree of many of the breed's current winning show dogs.

Ch. Melody Dynamatic was bred, owned and shown exclusively by C.E. Flock, Jr. Born January 15, 1970, this liver and white dog became one of the breed's most important and influential show dogs and sires of his color. The sire of Ch. Melody Up Up and Away (foundation bitch at Paisley) and of Ch. Melody Crimson and Clover.

Among Dynamatic's progeny are Champion Melody Up Up and Away, the foundation bitch for the MacMillans' Paisley Kennels; and Champion Melody Crimson and Clover, an important producer for Dr. and Mrs. White and the sire of Champion Hopi Kachina Melody Mocha and Champion Hopi Kachina Full Circle, foundation bitches for the current breeding program of Mr. and Mrs. Raymond Nogar of New Mexico.

Dynamatic's breeding is a combination of the most influential of English bloodlines, primarily Colonsay, with his sire's breeding from the *old* Long Last Kennels of Lorraine Donahue at Owings Mills, Maryland.

GREEN STARR

Green Starr Dalmatians at Jonesboro, Tennessee, are by way of being a dream come true for Dr. David G. Doane, co-founder and co-owner. He first grew to admire these handsome dogs while in the U.S. Naval Academy, where he used to see a lovely one being walked every evening at the base. The more he saw of this dog, the more determined he became that one day he would breed and show Dalmatians. So it was that in 1947 he purchased his first of the breed, as he puts it, "from a backyard breeder in Rhode Island," selecting two puppies for the sum of $300.00—at that time almost a full month's pay for a young Navy lieutenant. There were lots of ribbons hanging on the seller's wall which were impressive to a novice, and David's optimism was high as he entered his dogs in their first dog shows. Two years later it had become obvious that this was by way of being a lost cause, and the Doanes, David and his first wife Joan , (who is now Mrs. John J. Elliott, Jr.) found good pet homes for these two as they set out to find something more in keeping with their ambitions in the breed.

Then it was that Dr. Doane acquired Champion Beloved Scotch of the Walls from Mrs. Evelyn Walls whose kennel in Massachusetts was highly respected. "Scotcher" was the beginning of Green Starr. Dr. Doane comments that he feels that his two years of showing just ordinary dogs in competition was probably a most helpful learning experience for a future breeder-exhibitor and judge. His feeling is that the proud owners of an instant winner are somewhat at a disadvantage later on if their success does not continue at the same fast pace as it started.

What does a retired famous Best in Show "star" do to keep fit? He jogs with his master, as shown here by Ch. Green Starr's Colonel Joe and Dr. David G. Doane, Jonesboro, Tenn.

The great Ch. Green Starr's Masterpiece, liver and white owned by Dr. and Mrs. David G. Doane, the first liver spotted Dalmatian to win Best in Show all-breeds, back in the 1950's, is an outstanding representative of Dals of that period. Pictured winning Best in Show under judge Mrs. Leonard W. Bonney, *right.* On the *left,* Evelyn Nelson White, owner of the noted Tomalyn Hill Dalmatians.

Beloved Scotch proved to be a truly great sire. Although used only a few times, his impact on the breed was, and continues to be, profound. Bred to a granddaughter of the magnificent Champion Reigate Bold Venture, ("Scotcher" was a grandson of this same fabulous dog) the linebred combination produced six champions, among whom were the very important Champion Green Starr's Darling Dotter, considered by the Doanes to be the most outstanding of the many noted Dalmatians they have bred; Champion Green Starr's Dazzler, a noted Group winner who back in the early 1950's earned a Group placement at Westminster; Champion Green Starr's Kingpin, who was a strong part of the stud force at William Hibbler's prominent Williamsville Kennels; Champion Green Starr's Masterpiece, the first liver spotted Dalmatian to win Best in Show in this country and the first to do so on more than one occasion; and Champion Green Starr's Dynamite who was the grandsire of Champion Green Starr's Undergraduate, National Specialty winner, Westminster winner, and a top Group contender, owned and shown by Mr. and Mrs. Arthur W. Higgins of the Pennydale Kennels on Long Island.

During the early 1960's, activity in the kennel subsided for awhile as Dr. Doane was busily occupied with his full time obstetrical practice as well as trying to raise five children. In 1962 he met Margie, the present Mrs. Doane, and as the saying goes, they have "lived happily ever after." Their initial meeting took place at a dog show, indicating that Margie was already "into" dogs, an interest which they share with tremendous enjoyment.

Champion Green Starr's Corporal, a grandson of the outstanding Champion Green Starr's Masterpiece, produced Champion Green Starr's Brass Tacks who became an outstanding sire of Group winners, carried on in the Green Starr family tradition by winning the Stud Dog Class at the National Specialty, true to the tradition of his sire and grandsire. Brass Tacks will forever hold a special spot in this breed's history as the sire of the greatest winning Dalmatian of all time, Champion Green Starr's Colonel Joe who upon his retirement had won Best in Show on 35 occasions; 138 Group 1sts; close to 150 additional Group placements, and who is the only Dalmatian to have won the Dalmatian Club of America *on four occasions*, the last time from the Veterans Class. During his show career, Colonel Joe was campaigned under the banner of Mrs. Alan Robson and handled by Bobby Barlow. Since

Ch. Green Starr's Darling Dotter, the daughter of Ch. Beloved Scotch of the Walls, foundation of Green Starr Kennels, who Dr. and Mrs. David G. Doane consider to be the most outstanding of all Green Starr homebreds.

retirement he is living at home with the Doanes.

In the early days, Green Starr dogs were shown by Bob Kendrick and later by the late Parker Harris. Then Steve Shaw took over their handling until his retirement to become a judge. Colonel Joe began his fabulous career handled by Bobby Fisher, who piloted him through his championship and first two Groups. Nowadays the Green Starr Dals are handled by Mrs. Jean Lade.

Colonel Joe has proven himself the outstanding stud dog he was bred to be, with 30 champions already to his credit and more on the way although he has been used sparingly at stud. He is No. 9 on the All Time List of Dalmatian sires as of mid-1985, and there will undoubtedly be numerous additions to his champions as many are pointed and close to their titles at this time.

Within the past few years, Dr. Doane has retired from the Army (receiving the highest peacetime military award, the Distinguished Service Medal), and now is pursuing a new endeavor as Professor and Chairman, Department of Family Medicine, East Tennessee State University College of Medicine.

The Doanes now have time to continue their judging, breeding, and some limited showing. As judges, both place extreme emphasis on temperament, breed type, quality, balance and soundness—in that order.

The Doane children have been deeply involved with animals since they were youngsters. The late Stephen Doane, Medal of

Honor winner, actively competed with Dalmatians up until his departure for Vietnam; Eric, the youngest son, is showing Dals in the mid-West, and Leslie, the youngest and the only Doane daughter, has finished Champion Green Starr's Gentle Annie. She and Eric plan to "carry on" the Green Starr breeding program.

HAPI-DAL

Hapi-Dal Dalmatians are located at Santa Ana, California, where they are owned by Susie Wilson. There one finds the current young winner, Champion Hapi-Dal Knight Strider, who completed his title at the Dalmatian Club of Southern California Specialty Show during April 1985 where he took Best of Winners.

Strider was co-bred with Margaret Schools and is co-owned by Susie Wilson and 13-year-old Diana Wilson. It is Diana who has handled him all the way, having started him out at match shows (he was Best in Match at an all-breed event when only four-and-a-half months' age) prior to his reaching six months old.

He gained his championship in an impressive manner, finishing as described above. Along the way he was Best of Breed from the classes over six specials in an entry of 41 but most exciting of all to his owners was his having been selected Best in Futurity at the National Specialty in Houston, Texas, an entry of 89, in August 1984, judged by Jean Meader.

Sired by International Champion Dalwood's Knight Edition, Strider's dam is a very tightly linebred Hapi-Dal bitch, Champion Kipperdale's Eboni On Ice.

HARMONY

Harmony Dalmatians began in 1975, owned by Jan and Doug Nelson, Evergreen, Colorado. Their foundation bitch was purchased from Paisley Dalmatians in Minnesota, and is of Long Last and Melody breeding.

This is a small kennel that keeps its breeding program on a limited basis, averaging only one litter each year. Over the years they have added Watseka, Colonial Coach and Coachman bloodlines to their original stock to produce their own blending of the Dalmatian.

All potential breedings here are researched with utmost care, and the Nelsons take pride in the fact that dogs bred by them compete successfully in many areas of the United States and Canada, and their champion producers do well at reproducing their own high quality.

Harmony Dals have won top awards at Regional and National Specialty Shows as well as at all-breed shows, and part of the fun is that these wins have always been breeder- or owner-handled.

All of the Harmony Dalmatians are house dogs and companions, and they are shown in both conformation and obedience, the Nelsons believing that a complete Dal has a title on both ends of its name.

Litters are home-raised, carefully socialized, and, of course, are fully guaranteed.

The Dalmatians at Harmony include the handsome and successful Champion Harmony Real People who when only 13 months of age, went Best of Winners at the Dalmatian Club of America National Specialty in Kentucky. A full sister to Real People, Champion Harmony Calais of Cheshire, is a Group winner and multiple champion producer for her owner-handler Judy Box in Texas.

HEEGEE

He-Ge Kennels (name later changed to Heegee) was founded in 1970 by Geri and Helen Rosen of Danbury, Connecticut, with the purchase of Zodiac's Midernoch Shady Lady, a tightly linebred bitch and granddaughter of American, Canadian and Bermudian Champion Roadcoach Roadster, a top winning and producing dog of his time.

Shady Lady was shown for a very brief time, picking up her first major, but due to circumstances beyond her control never completed her championship. She was later bred to Champion Thaddans Beau Brummel, C.D.X. (by Champion Blackpool Bullshott ex Champion Crown Jewels Flawless Emerald, C.D.). A handsome male was kept from this union, He-Ge's Stitch in Time, who was later bred to High Jinks Kismet of He-Ge (Champion Pill Pedler's Boatswain ex Imperial Star of Blackpool), became the second foundation bitch for this kennel, thus combining the lines of Roadcoach, Blackpool, Crown Jewels and Pill Peddler.

The breeding program at Heegee Kennels has concentrated on the Blackpool and Roadcoach lines, lines that had produced such famous dogs as Champion Roadcoach Roadster and the top winning bitch Champion Blackpool Crinkle Forest.

Among the dogs bred by the Rosens are Canadian Champion He-Ge's Hellion and his litter brother Champion He-Ge's Thaddeus Cooper, sired by Champion Deltalyn Decoupage ex High Jinks Kismet. Hellion gained his Canadian title with ease, taking three placements in Groups along the way, and has ten points towards his title in the United States. A proven stud, Hellion is producing some very exciting young stock. Thaddeus Cooper was sold to fanciers in California and is now himself the sire of champions.

Champion He-Ge's Devilish Darling, by He-Ge's Stitch in Time ex High Jinks Kismet of He-Ge, completed her title in limited showing when only 18 months of age, almost always taking home either the purple ribbon or reserve, and was Best of Winners ten times en route to her championship. Her daughter, Heegee's Touch of Class, is just starting her show career as we are writing, and it is hoped to carry on in her dam's pawprints.

Champion He-Ge's April Promise, by Champion Rolenet's Buckshott ex High Jinks Kismet of He-Ge, is a Best of Breed winner from the classes with numerous other important wins on the way to her title. She finished with a 4-point major.

The Rosens are proud of the *Dog World Magazine* Award of Canine Distinction that has been awarded to High Jinks Kismet of He-Ge for having produced the above four champions.

All of the dogs at Heegee Kennels are homebred and loved. A constant improvement in quality and consistency in loving temperament is the Rosens' long term goal.

HIGHLANDER

Highlander Dalmatians were started in 1977 by Peter Kingan and Rick Weyrich at Houston, Texas. The Highlander prefix was chosen due to the 1946 Chrysler Highlander sedan that Peter owned at that time.

The first litter born at Highlander Kennels produced three champions. One of these was Champion Morgan's Highlander Harper, who was Best of Breed at two Specialty Shows of the Dalmatian Organization of Houston. Harper was a consistent breed winner and Group placer for several years in the Houston area.

The foundation bitch of Highlander Kennels is Champion Rob-bsdale's Highlander Lady L, who was the Best in Sweepstakes at two Houston Specialties. Her daughter, Champion Robbsdale's Highlander Chanel, won the Best in "Sweeps" at the 1984 St. Louis Specialty, and is currently winning Best of Breed honors at various shows in and around Texas.

LONG LAST

In 1947 the Long Last kennel prefix was registered by Mrs. Lorraine Donahue, the result of this lady having spent the war years with show horses and noticing the purebred Dals around the stable. When a litter of puppies arrived, she received a bitch from

Ch. Long Last Living Legend, by Long Last Coppersmith ex Ch. Long Last Limoge, bred at Long Last Kennels of Lorraine Donahue. An Important sire of multiple champions, Group and Specialty winners. Photo courtesy of Mike and Chris Jackson.

Ch. Long Last Looksharp, liver, a Regional Specialty winner. Sire of Group, Specialty, and Sweepstakes winners. Bred by Kitty Brown, owned by Mike and Chris Jackson.

among them as a gift. To quote the words of her late owner, "She was overmarked, patched, and unregistered." Nonetheless this unattractive little girl had brains, and became one of the top obedience dogs in the United States. her name was Spur of Victory, U.D.T. She was the first Dalmatian bitch and the third Dalmatian to achieve the U.D.T. title.

Mrs. Donahue became increasingly interested in show dog stock, and in breeding Dalmatians. Early purchases were from Reigate, Tattoo, Lorbryndale, and Dal Duchy Kennels.

Mrs. Donahue bred, imported, and owned more than 30 champions including Champion Long Last Kelso, Champion Long Last Ripcord, Champion Long Last Let's Pretend, and Champion

Ch. Long Last Talent Scout, liver, by Ch. Long Last Link to Paisley ex Ch. Long Last No Frills, finished with four majors, three times Best of Breed over specials, and winner of a Group 4th. Bred and owned by Mike and Chris Jackson.

Long Last Limoge, all of whom were multiple breed winners and producers of Group and Best in Show winners. Lorraine showed many of these dogs herself as she was an early member of the Professional Handler's Association.

In the mid-1950's, English bloodlines were introduced to Long Last. Three of the quality Washakie line bitches were imported and appear often in the pedigrees of Long Last dogs. The greatest import brought over by Mrs. Donahue was English and American Champion Colonsay Blacksmith, who was Best in Show at the 1957 British Dalmatian Club Specialty and won many breeds after completion of his U.S. championship. He was a dog of definite influence on the Dalmatians in this country.

Ch. Long Last Black Chrome, Best of Winners Dalmatian Club of America National Specialty in Texas 1984 and at the A.K.C. Centennial Dog Show. Bred by Chris Jackson and Kitty Burke. Owned by Mike and Chris Jackson.

Extended pedigrees show that Long Last has provided a solid foundation with the combination of American and English bloodlines, and this can be found behind many modern-day kennels throughout the United States and Canada.

Lorraine Donahue died in 1980. The line which she founded is still going strong. Long Last dogs share different kennel names now, but the breeding programs represent a unified effort to maintain and improve upon the virtues and accomplishments of the line.

The breeders working within the Long Last line are Barbara Allison, *Rimrock;* Kitty Brown, *Showcase;* Vickie and Dennis Emmel, *Fireside;* Barbara Greenspan, *Esquire;* Marilyn Hughes, *Autumn;* Jeanne Puglisi, *Silverspun;* Lynn Roberts, *Sundald;* Elaine Thomas, *Talisman;* and, of course, Mike and Chris Jackson who are carrying on the *Long Last* name at Owings Mills, Maryland.

MELODY

Melody Dalmatians have been in existence since 1964, during which time their owners, Jack and Beth White, have produced several Best in Show dogs, five Top Ten Dogs, one Dalmatian Club of America National Specialty Best in Specialty Show winner, two National Specialty Best of Opposite Sex winners, and too many Specialty winners to count. They won Best in Futurity the first year it was held in Chicago, and also still hold the title of All-

Ch. Melody Sweet, C.D. is the all Time Top Producing Bitch in the breed with 16 champions, including two Group winners. This bitch was in the Top Ten nationally for three years, shown mostly in the Intermountain region. Sweet won 10 Groups and was a multi-Specialty winner. She lived to be age 15½ years. Owned by Jack and Beth White.

Melody Diamond In The Dust, at age five months, is the "young hopeful" for the future at Melody Kennels. By Ch. Melody Nashville Brass ex the Specialty winning bitch Ch. Melody Joleen of Croatia. Jack and Beth White feel that this may be the one who will eventually take over for their famous older bitches.

Time Top Producing Bitch of the breed, Champion Melody Sweet, C.D., who is responsible for 16 champions, including two multiple Group winners. The Whites have also bred two other Top Producing bitches, Champion Melody Up Up and Away, who is the dam of 15 champions; and her sister, Champion Melody Crimson and Clover, C.D. with eight, including two Group winners.

Melody Dalmatians are house-raised on the Whites' Rim Rock Ranch, just outside of Fort Collins, Colorado. The Whites raise the dogs on the ranch in the Foothills, where they grow up with Appaloosa race horses, cattle, and even a few coyotes. They show on a limited basis, mostly within Colorado, yet are usually well represented at the National Specialty. Among their Dalmatians are two International, Mexican, and American Champions, including Champion Melody Ring of Fire of BB, C.D., who won the Mexican National Specialty and also a Group 1st at the International Shows at the ripe old age of ten years. His daughter, Champion Melody Penny Lane, secured her foreign titles when seven-and-a-half years old.

The Whites like to get in some obedience work with the dogs, too, although the pressures of other interests have unfortunately kept their obedience titles to a minimum. They do hope to become more active in the obedience rings soon.

A fact in which the Whites take special pleasure is that their homebreds have won *both* the Dalmatian Club of America Specialty and the Canadian National Specialty. The latter win was gained by Melody Moonlight Gambler who won Best of Breed from the classes and was also High Scoring Dog in Trial at the same show. Needless to say, they were quite proud of him and of his owners. This was in 1984.

It is very impressive to look at pedigrees and note the consistency with which the Melody influence has been felt in the breed. This kennel has certainly made a major contribution to the Dalmatian world, and deserves tremendous credit for the success attained with their dogs and the descendants of these dogs.

PAISLEY

Paisley Dalmatians are owned by Dave and Sue MacMillan who are located at St. Paul, Minnesota. When Paisley Peterbilt completed his championship in March of 1985, he became the 50th conformation champion owned or bred at Paisley. And during that same month, Paisley's QindaBritt became the 30th obedience Dalmatian to have earned a C.D. degree—all of which makes one want to say, "these people surely are doing much that is right."

Although she was actually their fourth Dalmatian and third champion, Champion Melody Up Up and Away, more familiarly known as "Pooka," is credited with being the true foundation of the Paisley breeding program, probably because she is to be found in the background of all but one champion carrying the Paisley name. All of the younger dogs are linebred on this remarkable bitch, some of them having as many as five crossed to her in their pedigrees.

Pooka was a liver colored Dal and a multi-Group winner. Her show credits include having been a Top Ten Dalmatian, and she was Best of Opposite Sex at the Dalmatian Club of America Specialty in 1974. But despite these accomplishments, it was in the whelping box that her most notable successes were achieved, such as becoming the dam of 15 champions, second in this number only to her half sister, Champion Melody Sweet, C.D. who exceeded her number by only one, making a total of 16 champions.

Adding to her success as a producer is the fact that Pooka's offspring seem to be following in her pawmarks in this regard, and a number of them are providing foundation for other highly successful Dalmatian kennels. Pooka is a daughter of Champion Melody Dynamatic, a Best in Show winner and a fine stud dog. Her dam is a litter sister to the lovely Champion Melody Crimson and Clover who produced well for Melody Dalmatians.

Paisley is basically a combination of Melody and Watseka lines with the addition of some Long Last and Coachman. Each of these lines has its strong points, and Sue is finding that the combination is giving them the look that they prefer. At the time their breeding program was started, Sue and Dave felt that there was no line that really possessed the combination of characteristics that they wanted in their Dals, and they saw no point in linebreeding just for the sake of doing so. Thus they started out by doing judicious outcrosses attempting to pick up the features they felt they needed to add.

Although initially they received considerable criticism for pursuing this course rather than the more conservative linebreeding, these outcrosses laid the groundwork by bringing in those qualities they had felt they wanted to improve upon, and thus incorporating them into the developing Paisley lines. Since the late 1970's they have turned mainly to linebreeding, with most of the young stock tightly pedigreed. They generally have studs within the line who are suitable for their bitches, so there is less chance of bringing a lot of variables into a given breeding. They still do an occasional outcross, but now only to special dogs with a specific goal in mind, and only to dogs they know personally and backgrounds with which they are entirely familiar.

Pooka's first litter was sired by Champion Panore of Watseka, who became one of the breed's leading sires. This litter of six produced five champions, and all six dogs were the producers of champions. Champion Paisley's A Touch of Class, or "Cary," remained at home with the MacMillans, where she became their Top Producing homebred bitch with ten champion offspring.

For her second litter, Pooka was bred to Panore's son, Champion Bob Dylan Thomas of Watseka, C.D., from which she produced three champions out of five puppies, including Champion Paisley's Five Card Stud, C.D.X., Canadian C.D. "Toby" sired many champions including the MacMillans' well-known Gr. Ch. Am., Br., Int., NAC Paisley Torch of Kirkland. Another from the Dylan-Pooka litter was Champion Paisley's Pandora, C.D., who was Winners Bitch at D.C.A. and C.D.C. in 1975.

The decision was made to add some Coachman to the MacMillans' breeding program, and so Pooka was taken to Champion Coachman's Red Carpet, a handsome young liver who was actually half Blackpool breeding. This combination produced four liver champions including Champion Paisley's Oh Henry, C.D., who himself produced a number of fine liver champions including the well-known Champion Paisley's First Things First, a multi-Group winning and 1982 Dalmatian Club of America Best of Opposite Sex. "Snickers," as we write is currently working with the MacMillans' daughter Jessica as her Junior Showmanship Dog and in obedience.

Pooka's daughter Cary, by Panore, was the next one bred, to Champion Coachman's Caliber, a breeding which produced three champions including American and Canadian Champion Paisley's Pride of Willowood, who eventually sired "Jocko."

Next it was decided to add a bit of Long Last to the strain, breeding both Pooka and Cary to Champion Long Last Living Legend. Pooka's litter produced Champion Paisley's Harmony Bouquet, C.D. who had a superb Specialty record and produced a Dalmatian Club of America winner and a Group winner in her first litter. Cary's litter produced three champions including the well-known stud dogs Champion Paisley's A Change of Pace, C.D. (Murphy) and Champion Long Last Link To Paisley (Pirate). Murphy stayed with the MacMillans; Pirate went to Long Last and was also the 1979 Dalmatian Club of America Best in Futurity. Both dogs have proven themselves useful sires.

Another productive outcross with Pooka was to Champion Karastella Cadillac of MGR. Of the three pups, the male finished and one of the bitches, Paisley's Betsy Ross, had a wonderful litter bred back to a Paisley dog. From the latter came two exceptional liver bitches and Champion Paisley's Special Export.

There is much more one could write about the Paisley dogs, but space limitations are upon us. So we will finish up with a note of congratulations to the seven Paisley Dals who completed their obedience titles during 1984, of which three additionally were show champions. Also, note should be made of the fact that as of May 1985, 21 liver-colored Dalmatians from Paisley completed championship, with several others "knocking on the door"—a point of pleasure to the MacMillans who do have a very special weakness for this color. Additionally it should be noted that 21 Paisley champions are Group placers, 26 have major awards at Specialties, and 18 of the 30 obedience titles at Paisley are held by champions.

PROCTOR

Proctor Dalmatians are owned by Kenneth and Eva Berg at Moraga, California, who have been breeding, showing and loving the breed since 1967. The Bergs have bred more than 20 champions, and have also been quite active in obedience. Their primary goal is to provide outstanding pets with sweet dispositions and stable temperament. As Eva remarks, "most of our dogs are smilers," and with the full recognition that most dogs, their own included, are loving family pets, their breeding program seeks to accomplish that end. They also breed carefully to the Standard. Their success in the show ring, owner-handled, on the very competitive California circuit further endorses their program.

The foundation bitch at Proctor is Champion Paisley of Proctor, C.D., a daughter of Champion Panore of Watseka ex Champion Melody Up Up and Away. She is the dam of six champions and numerous obedience titled dogs, and was among the Top Producing Dams in the United States for two years. At the 1978 Dalmatian Club of America Club Specialty, Paisley was winner of the Brood Bitch Class.

The foundation dog here was Champion Merry Polka of Tallara, now deceased. Sired by Gemini of Tallara ex Bri-Dal's Victoria, he himself became the sire of seven champions and numerous Dals with obedience degrees. A Specialty winner, he was nationally ranked in the Top Ten Dals (all systems) in 1969 and 1970.

96

Ch. Legendary Cottondot of Proctor, by Ch. Cottondot Toleak of MGR ex Ch. Proctor's Creole of Cottondot. "Callie," the swimmer at Proctor Kennels, is displaying her fine diving style.

Champion Joe Forrester of Proctor, C.D., by Champion Merry Polka of Tallara ex Champion Paisley of Proctor, C.D., an outstanding liver male, is the sire of six champion progeny and several more Dals who are close to finishing. Bosco was nationally ranked for two years in the Top Twenty, always owner-handled.

Champion Beauregard O'Hara of Proctor, by Champion Joe Forrester of Proctor ex Maggie O'Hara of Proctor, is a Specialty Best of Breed winner over an entry of 265 Dals.

Ch. Joe Forrester of Proctor, C.D., by Ch. Merry Polka of Tallara ex Ch. Paisley of Proctor, C.D., owned by Kenneth and Eva Berg.

Champion Forrest Fire, by Champion Forrest Ranger of Proctor, C.D.X. ex Champion Forrest Greensleaves, finished championship at the age of 12 months and was nationally ranked in the Top Ten (all systems) in 1983 and 1984, always owner-handled. He has many youngsters ready to finish. His elegance and style made him a natural to achieve his 41 breed wins at the age of two years and ten months.

Champion Proctor's Hi-Ho Cheerio is the Bergs' newest champion, adding a strong English pedigree to the breeding program at Proctor. He is by Champion Count Miguel of Tuckaway ex Champion Washakie Belleamie. His owners feel that his outstanding structure and good movement will be an asset to their kennel for years to come.

RAMBLER

Rambler Dalmatians are owned by James and Joanne Nash at Los Altos, California, and were named after the "little Nash Rambler" cars. The cars are no longer being made, but the Rambler line of Dalmatians is definitely still in production, working on their owners' goal of breeding sound, stable, healthy Dals which can (and do) succeed in both conformation and obedience. It is a source of satisfaction to these fanciers that Rambler dogs have won championships and have earned obedience and temperament test degrees as well. The Nashes have bred or co-bred National Specialty Futurity and Best Opposite winners, regional Specialty Best of Breed and High in Trial winners, and nationally ranked obedience Dals. They like to see their dogs compete in both rings; most of their champions also are C.D.'s; most of their obedience dogs are successful in conformation, too.

The Nashes also have worked with other breeders and they have bred to or leased Dalmatians from such bloodlines as Royal Oak, Melody, Paisley, Long Last, etc. They point with pride to the fact that their Rambler dogs are to be found in the foundation breeding stock for Sunspot, Rally, St. Florian, Driftwood, and Pisces, all of which are young kennels doing well.

Rambler Dalmatians began in 1971 with the linebred Tallara bitch, Sweet Abigail, C.D., TT. Her daughter, Pacifica Tiffany Belle, C.D., is the dam of the Nashes' first homebred champion, Champion Rally's Candy Dapple Rambler, C.D. (co-owned with Marsha Knight, Rally Dals) who is also a champion producer herself. The first champion and first male owned by the Nashes was Champion Rambler's Seaspot Bogart, C.D., a dog they bought from Mark Sachau.

Champion Royal Oaks Liberty Belle was leased by the Nashes from Eric and Ardith Dahlstrom, Royal Oaks Dalmatians, for three litters. Belle is the dam of eight champions, five of them Rambler-born, with more pointed and showing. She also has produced six C.D. degree holders (including a High in Trial dog) and five who have earned TTs for passing the temperament tests.

Champion Rambler Quintessence, C.D., TT, is owned by the Nashes, a Belle daughter by Champion Paisley's A Change of Pace, C.D. This bitch started her show career with a Specialty reserve and points at six months, won the 1983 Dalmatian Club of America Futurity at nine months, and is now a multi-Best of Breed winner.

Champion Rambler's Raisin Cane, TT, is co-owned by the Nashes with Jim Schreiber, and is an older sister of Quintessence. She finished with four majors and two Bests of Breed from the

Left to right, Ch. Royal Oaks Sunspot Rambler, CD., TT, owned by J. Otto; Ch. Rambler's Quintessence, C.D., TT, owned by J. Nash; and Ch. Sunspot's Rambler Ottomatic, owned by L. Oesau. Ch. Royal Oaks Liberty Belle is the dam of these three Champion C.D. and TT Dals.

classes. Her three-month-old son by Count Miguel of Tuckaway just won Best Puppy at the Dalmatian Club of Northern California Spring Match.

Another Belle son, Champion Sunspot's Rambler Ottomatic, C.D., TT, recently finished and is now working with owner Loyal Oesau in Open A and tracking. This dog was High in Trial at the 1983 Dalmatian Club of Southern California Specialty.

Champion Royal Oaks Sunspot Rambler, C.D., TT, was co-owned by the Nashes with Jill Otto (Sunspot Dals). She is herself a multi-Best of Breed winner and is the dam of two nationally ranked C.D.X. bitches and two champions, including a Group winner. Her younger puppies started their show careers in July 1985.

Champion Saint Florian Sunspot Ad-Lib is a Group winning daughter of Holly (Sunset Rambler), co-owned by Dawn Mauel and Jill Otto. The Mauels (St. Florian Dals) also own Champion Rowdy J. Rambler, C.D., a son of Raisin Cane and Champion Melody Dynamatic, who was Best of Breed at the 1984 Dalmatian Club of Northern California Specialty.

100

Driftwood's Sunspot Rambler, C.D.X. (owned by Kathy Blink, Driftwood Farm), and Pisces Rambler Sunspot Dawn, C.D.X. (co-owned by Linda Fish, Pisces Dals and Joanne Nash, Rambler) are litter sisters out of Champion Royal Oaks Rambler, C.D., TT, by Champion Paisley's A Change of Pace, C.D. Bonnie was High in Trial at the Dalmatian Club of Northern California's Specialty and Dawn won a Dog World Award for her Novice title. Both have been nationally ranked obedience Dals for two years, and are now entering the Utility ring.

Ch. Rambler's Seaspot Bogart, C.D., by Ch. Panore of Watseka ex Ch. Majestic K'ls Dapple McDor. Bred by Mark Sachan. Owned by James and Joanne Nash. This is Rambler Kennel's first Champion C.D.

RAVENWOOD

Ravenwood Dalmatians, owned by Kathy and Lee McCoubrey, Chuluota, Florida, had their beginning purely by accident, the result of a series of events.

The McCoubreys' German Shepherd Dog had disappeared, leading them to make a wide search for this animal, including all the pounds. One day while they were checking out a dog pound they came upon a gentle and beautiful liver spotted Dalmatian bitch who had been abandoned. They immediately agreed that they could not permit so lovely a dog to be put to sleep, and so Tammy was adopted to join this family. They had her spayed, then entered her in obedience classes. She took to these with ease, her aptitude amazing the instructors, and the McCoubreys were encouraged to apply for an Indefinite Listing Privilege and show her.

The refugee from the pound became Ravenwood Tammi, U.D., and for several years she was one of the top competitors, surely well rewarding her owners who had saved her in her time of need!

While showing Tammi in obedience, Kathy McCoubrey decided that she would like to have a good dog for breed competition as well, to use as the foundation for a breeding program, one in which intelligence and trainability would be as important as conformation. She purchased a young male from Emily Hoover of Atlantis Dalmatians, and he became Champion Atlantis Conquestador, C.D.X., AD, and with two legs toward Utility. From then on, the McCoubreys were hooked, and became highly active and enthusiastic members of the fancy.

The Ravenwood breeding program has accounted for American and foreign champions and title holders at the various obedience levels. They take pride in the fact that all but their very latest champions are obedience trained, and feel sure that the latter will be following this lead shortly.

Champion Atlantis Conquestador, C.D.X., AD (Int., Am. and Mex. Ch. Melody Ring of Fire, C.D. ex Ch. Atlantis Love of Pacifica), black spotted, is the sire of Champion Ravenwood Knight Games, C.D.; Champion Ravenwood Polished Pebbles, U.D.; and American and Bahamian Champion Ravenwood China Clipper, American and Bahamian C.D. To the best of his owner's knowledge, Conquestador is the only Dalmatian Champion to have earned a Schutzhund endurance title (AD). He was bred by E.

and T. Hoover. He is making his presence felt now as a sire, and is already a Specialty Stud Dog Class winner.

American and Bahamian Champion Ravenwood China Clipper, American and Bahamian C.D., is a Conquestador son ex Ravenwood Fabled Attraction. He is a multiple Best of Breed winner in both countries, bred and owned by Ravenwood Dalmatians.

American and Bahamian Champion Ravenwood State of the Art is by American and Brazilian Champion Vicor of the Ebony Spots, C.D. ex Champion Ravenwood Polished Pebbles, U.D. "Stacey" was exclusively owner-handled to both her championships.

Champion Ravenwood Polished Pebbles, U.D., by Champion Atlantis Conquestador, C.D.X., AD ex Champion Surrey Rhodes Kady of Santana, C.D., was bred by Kathy McCoubrey and Sharon Boyd. "Candy" is described by her owner as "the resident over-achiever." She earned her C.D. at age ten months and finished both C.D.X. and U.D. with placements in very large classes. She had some lovely wins en route to her championship, including a Best of Breed from the classes over Best in Show competition, and she is the dam of American and Bahamian Champion Ravenwood State of the Art and Bahamian Champion Ravenwood Sign of the Times, American and Bahamian C.D.

Then there is Champion Ravenwood Playing With Fire (Dub'l D's Rip Van Winkle ex Ravenwood Tessellation). She is living proof that a good dog will finish in spite of size, being only 20″ tall. Nonetheless, breeder-owner-handled, she took three majors including several wins from the Bred-by Exhibitor Class and has been well admired for her quality despite lack of size.

ROADCOACH

Roadcoach Kennels were started by Mr. and Mrs. Alfred W. Barrett somewhere around 1930 as closely as we can pinpoint it, in Massachusetts; and as Mary Barrett has been active right up until a very short time ago, still showing dogs and as a judge, we feel that she certainly qualifies as the longest-time Dalmatian breeder currently in the United States.

The number of famed Dalmatians bred, owned, and exhibited by Mr. and Mrs. Barrett over the years could fill a book in themselves. From the 1930's, Champion Gambler's Luck (son of Champion Tally Ho Ian) and Champion Master Patrick,

Ch. Roadcoach Winston, by Ch. Roadcoach Roadmaster ex Penelope Tioga, was born on August 3, 1962. One of the many splendid Dalmatians owned by Mary Barrett's Roadcoach Kennels.

both of these from the same dam, Champion Mistress Margaret. Mary Powers was the owner of Margaret. By the 1940's (and even a bit earlier) Alfred and Mary Barrett were going "full steam ahead" under the Roadcoach banner and at the same time both were becoming extremely busy and respected judges.

Among the famed Roadcoach Dalmatians have been Sue Allman's 17 times Best in Show winner Champion Roadcoach Roadster and his litter brother Champion Roadcoach Roadmaster; Champion Duke of Roadcoach, Champion Roadcoach Victorious, Champion Roadcoach Revelry, Champion Roadcoach Brian Boru, Champion Roadcoach Racing Colors, Champion Roadcoach Chocolate Royale, C.D.; Champion Roadcoach Bandit; Champion Roadcoach Phaeton, Champion Roadcoach Sportsman, Champion Roadcoach Timber Topper, the exquisite bitch Champion Roadcoach Spice, Champion Roadcoach Love Apollo, and a great many more.

Since Mrs. Barrett is ill as we are working on this book, it is to Wendell Sammet, who gathered photos and information together for us, that our readers owe thanks for the pleasure of sharing photos of a goodly number of her most important dogs. This is truly a legendary kennel in the Dalmatian world which will live on through its descendants for years to come.

Ch. Roadcoach Sportsman with his breeder-owner-handler Mrs. A.W. Barrett, Roadcoach Kennels.

Ch. Robbsdale's Baron Von Cross, liver and white, born November 1976, is the No. 1 Liver Sire alive today in the United States. This sire of 17 champions is owned by Timothy S. Robbins.

ROBBSDALE

Robbsdale Dals, at La Porte, Texas, were started in 1967 by Tim Robbins when he received a Dalmatian puppy as a high school graduation gift. A pet quality bitch, Tim bred her and as a result whelped his first litter of the breed in November 1968. Keeping one of these puppies from this first litter, Tim started showing his dogs throughout Texas and the South. This first show dog completed championship in March 1970.

About this same time, Tim purchased a puppy bitch from the Crown Jewels Kennels in Chicago. She was named Crown Jewels Texas Topaz, to which she added the title "champion" in due time. She became the kennel's foundation bitch throughout the early 1970's, as Tim continued to breed on the Crown Jewels line.

Then, in 1976, Tim purchased through Crown Jewels Kennels a liver and white male who was 3⁄4 Crown Jewels and 1⁄4 Coachman breeding. This dog has become the foundation of the present day Robbsdale Dals. He is Champion Robbsdale's Baron Von Cross, and he is the sire of an impressive 17 champions to date.

Beginning in the late 1970's, Robbsdale has continued to breed to several Coachman line studs, combining the Crown Jewel and Coachman strains. During the past few years, Robbsdale has produced many top winning Dals at Specialty Shows and all-breed events.

Tim Robbins has been an active member of the Dalmatian Club of America since 1968. He has served as the President of the Dalmatian Organization of Houston for six years, and has helped in Houston area kennel clubs and dog shows. He is currently serving as editor of *The Spotter*, the official publication of the Dalmatian Club of America.

ROUGHRIDER

Roughrider Dalmatians are owned by Cyril and Kathryn Braund, at Great Falls, Montana.

Kathryn Braund was introduced to the Dalmatian breed while a young girl growing up in San Francisco, when she met one owned by friends of hers. Right then she decided that this would be the breed she'd own when she was grown up, and forty years later her dream came true when her husband gifted her with a Dalmatian puppy as a Valentine. From that day onward she has owned and been in love with the breed.

Kathryn's first Dalmatian had an ILP number only from the American Kennel Club. He was purchased in Great Falls from friends who now own two Roughrider dogs, one of them a champion. This first Dal of Kathryn's made a name for himself, however, when he became the Braunds' first obedience-titled dog, Kamper of Big Sky Country, C.D.X.

Her love of Dalmatians got Kathryn Braund started writing about dogs, and she sold her first article to *Dogs* magazine, which was about housebreaking a puppy, with Kamper the model used for the photographs. Since then Kathryn has won many awards

Kathryn Braund's retrieving Dalmatian, Can. Ch. Roughrider Decotah, Am. and Can. C.D., gives a fine example of "success on the wing." Roughrider Kennels.

for her writing, and has four books on the market, in addition to having been Obedience Editor for *The Spotter* for ten years.

Because Cyril Braund was a technical co-ordinator and engineer for the field in the Minuteman Missile program, the Braunds moved almost every year. Thus they were not able to indulge in a breeding program of Dalmatians until 1982 when they retired to Great Falls. They did, however, own three or four Dalmatians during most of their working years. As Kathryn says, "We put up many acres of fences around the yards of houses in which we lived while traveling and working in the field."

Roughrider's foundation bitch is Champion Colonial Coach Klassic, C.D.X. She was born in 1983, and came to live with the Braunds when they were in Cheyenne, Wyoming. Her first son,

Canadian Champion Roughrider Dacotah, American and Canadian C.D.X. was the pup the Braunds could not sell. He was a lightly spotted and big boned Dal, with a beautiful conformation and superb temperament. So the Braunds kept him. Subsequently the late Jack Godsil, obedience and hunting dog trainer, trained him for upland bird hunting. Kathryn has written stories about him and this training, and about "Koda's" prowess in hunting.

Unfortunately, Dacotah was never used at stud until he was six years old. Kathryn says "unfortunately" because they discovered that this dog threw his own great pedigree in temperament, structure, and beautiful spotting patterns. From the three litters he sired, two bitches won their championships and several others earned obedience titles. Sad to say, "Koda" passed on in 1984, the victim of a jumping accident in which several cervical discs were ruptured.

The Braunds kept one bitch from the first litter Dacotah had sired. She is now American and Canadian Champion Roughrider Koda's Kid, U.D. K.D. won her Utility title at only four-and-one-half years of age. At three she had earned her C.D. and C.D.X. degrees while shown in the breed ring as well. When retired from being shown at less than three years of age, she had ten Bests of Breed, two Group 2nds and a Group 3rd plus several Group 4th placements. K.D. throws true to her great pedigree. Three of her children from her first litter, sired by Champion Tamarack's Tennyson v Watseka, born in July 1983 are already champions. K.D. whelped five show quality puppies in her first litter and five in her second litter, the latter born in September 1984. Roughrider believes that if all the owners exhibit these dogs in the breed ring, it can be anticipated that K.D. will earn a place on the Top Bitch Producing Dams polls in the Dalmatian breed. Her son, American and Canadian Champion Roughrider's Rogue, at 20 months has 17 Bests of Breed to his credit, a Group 1st award, and three Group 2nds. He won the Group 1st at the Bonneville Basin K.C., May 20, 1985. He won his American Championship when just 13 months old with three Bests of Breed along the way. Rogue also has sired two litters with his puppies looking of above average promise.

K.D. will be bred again to Tennyson because the two obviously nick well, pulling from their gene banks the best qualities of the great heritage behind them.

SHORT ACRE

Short Acre Dalmatians belong to Anne M. Nicholson and are located at Greenwood Lake, New York. They are founded on bloodlines from Snowcap Kennels owned by Diane Riemer. Some of the famous names to be found in Short Acre pedigrees include those of Champion Blackpool Crinkle Forrest, Champion Panore of Watseka, Champion Coachman's Chuck-A-Luck and Champion Snowcap's Contessa. At the present time, all of the Short Acre Dals are sired by Snowcap's Y.A. Tittle, and his son, Champion Snowcap's Sunscion, both of them Specialty winners and sires of many champions.

Showcase Gold Standard, liver and white, by Ch. Long Last Looksharp ex Ch. Greenway's Velvet Dancer, was Best of Winners at the Dalmatian Club of America National Specialty in Philadelphia 1984. Bred by Kitty A. Brown and Thomas M. Brown. Owned by Elaine Thomas and Kitty Brown.

Anne Nicholson's Best in Show dog, Champion Fanfayre's Beau of Short Acre, who is now being campaigned by Joy Brewster for Mr. Robert A. Koeppel, completed his championship in seven shows undefeated in the classes, finishing under the author at the 1982 Dalmatian Club of America Specialty. He began his career as a special by going Best of Breed at Westminster, and has gone on to become No. 1 in the U.S.A. with Best in Shows to his record. He has won or placed in the stud dog class at Specialty Shows, and his progeny are of a lovely type with many pointed from the puppy classes.

In her breeding program, Anne has used Snowcap bitches, such as Champion Snowcap's Special Edition, (No. 2 in 1982), or her dam, Champion Snowcap's Sparkle Plenty II, in combination with the above-mentioned Snowcap's Y.A. Tittle or his son Champion Snowcap's Sunscion. In other cases she has blended the Snowcap line with Williamsview bloodlines, also very outstanding. It is her plan to work with the lines from these two kennels in an effort to create her own "perfect dog."

One such blend resulted in Champion Short Acre's Calgary Stampede, with the breeding of Williamsview Bonnie Blue to Sunscion. "Cody," as Stampede is called, completed title in five shows, at age six months, with a Best of Breed from the classes, and two 4-point majors.

Anne has been breeding Dals for only about six years which is not very long but, in her case, has surely been successful.

SHOWCASE

Showcase Dalmatians are owned by Thomas M. Brown and Kitty A. Brown at Landover Mills, Maryland, where numerous fine Dalmatians are owned and have been bred.

A very excellent bitch from this kennel is Champion Greenway's Velvet Dancer. Shown exclusively in major competition, Velvet has among her honors Winners Bitch and Best of Winners at the Dalmatian Club of America National Specialty in Ohio in 1981 under Mr. Fetner, who awarded her Winners Bitch, and under Thelma Brown, awarding Best of Opposite Sex. She also has a 5-point major under Mr. Rivard in a Dalmatian Club of America Supported Entry.

Velvet is proving as exciting a producer as she is a show bitch, and in her first litter, by Champion Long Last Looksharp, there is a daughter who certainly seems to be following right along in her dam's pawprints! This is Showcase Gold Standard who, like her mother, was Best of Winners at a Dalmatian Club of America National Specialty, in this case at Philadelphia 1984.

SNOWOOD

Snowood Dalmatians, at Elgin, Illinois, are the result of Meg and Mike Hennessey's idea of replacing their fourteen-year-old pet Dalmatian bitch with a show dog. With this in mind, Meg attended a Chicagoland Dalmatian Club Specialty Show where she saw a dog who really appealed to her. Sensibly, she contacted the owner of this dog's sire, who was Sue MacMillan of Paisley Dalmatians. After waiting through several litters, the Hennesseys finally selected an affectionate liver puppy bitch called "Dixie," who has grown up to become Snowood Dancer of Paisley, C.D.

After showing Dixie in conformation and obedience, Meg decided to try her hand at breeding. After much research of pedigrees and discussions with the various breeders, Dixie was bred to Champion Sir Ike of Croatia. This linebreeding on Paisley and Melody resulted in a lovely liver and white show bitch, Snowood Ja Sam Jedan.

This bitch, whose name means "I am first" in Croatian, was the Hennesseys' first homebred and she is off to a very excellent start for them. At the 1985 Dalmatian Club of St. Louis Specialty, she was Best Junior Puppy and Best in Sweepstakes. Then was Best Senior in Sweepstakes at the 1985 Indianapolis Dalmatian Club Specialty. Jedan also has to her credit two Best of Breed wins from the classes over specials and a Group 4th placement —all accomplished with a novice owner-handler. Another recent win for her was Winners Bitch, Best of Winners and Best of Opposite Sex at Burlington Kennel Club in July 1985, judged by the author, and has since completed her championship and is bred to a Paisley dog.

The current plan for Snowood Dalmatians is to remain a small kennel, breeding only about one litter a year. Meg and Mike are becoming more enthusiastic every day over their breed and showing dogs, so it would seem likely they will remain active fanciers for a long time to come.

SPLASH O'EBONY

Splash O'Ebony Show Dogs are owned by Debbie Nierman at Dallas, Texas, where they are dedicated to producing a few litters of quality Dalmatians.

World International, Champion of the Americas, and American Champion Splash O'Ebony's Woodbury Jaki is a Group winning bitch with multiple placements.

Jaki was Best of Opposite Sex at the 1983 National Specialty as well as at the Dalmatian Organization of Houston.

Making her presence felt as a producer of quality along with winning in the show ring, Jaki's first litter has resulted in multiple champions, one of them a Group winner and multiple Group placer.

STARBORN

Starborn Kennels are owned by Jack and Karol Bush and located at Sweeney, Texas. The kennel was started in 1975 on foundation stock which was a combination of Watseka, Crown Jewel, and Blackpool bloodlines.

Recent champions at this kennel include Champion Starborn's Big Dipper, Champion Starborn's Summer Breeze, and Champion Starborn's Summer Sunshine.

Sunshine was the Best of Winners at the Dalmatian Organization of Houston's 1983 spring Specialty.

In addition to the Dalmatians, Starborn Kennels also breed and exhibit Beagles.

SUGARFROST

Sugarfrost Dalmatians are owned by Janet Ashbey of Stewartsville, New Jersey, who has been both an active and highly successful breeder-exhibitor over a good number of years.

The key bitch in Janet's breeding program, and the one who truly established the Sugarfrost winning line, is her beloved American and Canadian Champion Sugarfrost Top Choice, C.D.

As a puppy, this splendid young bitch was Best in Sweepstakes at the Dalmatian Club of America National Specialty in 1976. She finished her championship easily from the Bred-by Exhibitor class, and then went into the whelping box. Her first litter pro-

113

duced four champions: Champion Sugarfrost Flying Parson; Champion Sugarfrost Jenifer Valentine, C.D.; Champion Sugarfrost Foxy Lady; and Champion Karosel's Most Happy Fella. After her second litter, which produced Champion Sugarfrost Can't Stop Dancin', she started out in obedience for her C.D., which she gained with ease.

Next came her third litter, which included Champion Sugarfrost Bonnie Belle, Champion Scardal Sugarfrost Lancer, Champion Sugarfrost Buttons and Bows, and Z-Dalz Sugarfrost Xanadu (as yet needing a major to finish title). This was followed by a trip

Janet Ashbey with Ch. Sugarfrost High Fashion winning a Group placement at Glens Falls in 1984.

Ch. Sugarfrost Flying Parson with Ross Petruzzo. One of the many splendid winning Dalmatians from Janet Ashbey's noted kennel.

to Canada to attain her championship north of the border.

From Top Choice's fourth and final litter came Champion Sugarfrost Flying Dutchman (finished at age nine months) and Champion Sugarfrost High Fashion, winner of 17 points in six days, beginning the day she turned one year old.

SUMMERHILL

Summerhill Dalmatians belong to Edith and Nelson Gladstone of Kernersville, North Carolina, and this is the home of Champion Albelarm Starr of Summerhill, who is the kennel's foundation dog and a very impressive one! He is an all-breed Best in Show winner, the winner of 114 times Best of Breed, first in 30 Non-Sporting Groups, and the holder of 48 additional Group placements. "Chipper" is in the Top 25 All-Time Breed Winners among Dalmatians; was No. 1 Owner-Handled Dalmatian (all systems) in

Ch. Albelarm Starr of Summerhill, foundation of Summerhill Dalmatians, Best in Show winner, is in the All Time Top 25 Dalmatian winners and was the No. 1 Owner-Handled Dal for 1980, '81 and '82, plus ranked in the Top Ten four years consecutively, 1980-1983. Sired by the Famous Ch. Green Starr's Colonel Joe ex Ch. Coachman's Windsong of Q.A. Owned by Edith and Nelson Gladstone.

1980, 1981, and 1982; and ranked in the Top Ten for four consecutive years, 1980 through 1983.

A son of Champion Green Starr's Colonel Joe ex Champion Coachkeeper Windsong of Quaker Acres, Chipper is currently among the country's top Dalmatian sires. Among his progeny, the lovely daughter, Champion S. and P. Starlet of Summerhill was the No. 1 bitch for 1982 and 1983. Tragically she died at the height of her career only a few weeks past her fourth birthday. She was a daughter of Chipper and Champion Windstorm Weezie

116

of S. and P. who, in her short career, gained first in four Groups, 21 other Group placements, 38 times Best of Breed, and is the only bitch to have ranked in the Top Ten since the early 1970's. Another Chipper daughter, Champion Summerhill's Stardust Melody, finished at age 11 months with three Bests of Breed over specials. His son, Champion S. and P. Squire of Summerhill, finished in five consecutive shows with two Bests of Breed over specials. His grandson, Champion Red Coach's Dallas, in mid-1985 ranked No. 4 Dalmatian. In addition, numerous other young sons and daughters around the country are either finished or pointed.

The Gladstones have been breeding Dalmatians since 1973. Summerhill's breeding program represents a combination of Green Starr, Quaker's Acre, and Coachman lines from which its own strain is being developed through a carefully selective program of linebreeding.

Edith and Nelson Gladstone place particular emphasis on temperament in their dogs and their breeding program. It is their feeling that a Dalmatian is intended to be a loving, happy companion; thus their puppies are born and raised in their home where they enjoy a great deal of love and companionship.

ALFRED AND ESMERELDA TREEN

When Mrs. Alfred E. Treen of Brookfield, Wisconsin, states in her kennel notes that "there is very little to tell about us in Dalmatians or in any other breed for that matter," she is really being far too modest. For both Al and Esme have been active and devoted workers for the Dalmatian over a period of many years and have contributed as breeders of some outstanding dogs. Esme has done a super job as editor of the Dalmatian magazine, *The Spotter* until her resignation awhile back; and she and Al are authors of another fine, comprehensive and very worthwhile book on this breed which is a popular and widely read best seller in this field.

As a child Esmerelda had Boston Terriers, Pointers, and Setters. Then she and Al together owned some very nice Cockers and Boxers prior to acquiring their first Dalmatian. The latter breed took over with them from then on, and they have bred, owned, and won with them over a period of 34 years. Nor was the enthusiasm limited to just Esme and Al in the family. Their two children shared it as well, both as Junior Showmanship kids. Their

117

Ch. Saint Rocco's Polka Dot, C.D., an important early winner owned by Mr. and Mrs. Alfred E. Treen, Brookfield, Wis.

Ch. Pryor Creek's Tuxedo Satin was one of the handsome Dalmatians owned by Mr. and Mrs. Alfred E. Treen.

son, Joe, was invited to compete in Junior Showmanship at Westminster in 1959. Unfortunately the family was in the process of moving at the time, making it impossible for him to go East to compete.

Esme says, "our claim to fame is having bred American and Canadian Champion Champion Coachman's Chuck-A-Luck." He was intensely inbred following a dream pedigree which Esme had worked out herself on paper during the early 1950's. She had fully expected the great dog to appear in his dam's generation, but while "Rosie," his dam, was a delightful Dalmatian she was not especially interested in shows. Hunting, fishing, or anything of that sort were much to her liking; but the moment she walked into a show ring she folded.

When the Treens moved to the Milwaukee area it was necessary that they disperse most of their dogs. Rosie was placed in co-ownership with a Mr. Smith, who was to breed her to the stud of the Treens' choice from which litter they were to have a puppy. The one they chose grew up to become Coachman's Clotheshorse, a lovely animal who could not be shown as his dam had stepped on his foot in the whelping box, the result being that he walked with a peculiar gait. The bloodlines were, however, excellent for the Treens' breeding plans.

Littermate Chuck-A-Luck, call name "Brewster" after the famous carriage works in Philadelphia, was taken by the Fetners as a stud fee puppy and sold. The rest of the pups were also sold to become pets. But fate stepped in where Chuck-A-Luck was concerned, as Bill Kramer, who then was a handler, saw the dog and immediately wished to show him. The upshot was that Chuck-A-Luck swept through a show career which included three all-breed Bests in Show, 19 Group Firsts, and 127 times Best of Breed. Additionally he became the sire of 27 champions, two of whom, like their sire, becoming Best in Show dogs. The Treens were making arrangements to have semen collected from him to be frozen for future breeding when he died quite suddenly, a victim of bloat. During his show career Chuck-A-Luck was owned by Mr. and Mrs. Blair, who turned him over to the Treens when they were divorced.

The Treens had other delightful and important Dals in addition to this famous dog. Champion Saint Rocco's Polka Dot, C.D., their foundation bitch; Champion Pryor Creek's Firecracker;

Champion Pryor Creek's Tuxedo Satin; Champion Fobette's Fanfare, C.D.X., the dog Esme used for the inbreeding, to name a few.

The Treens surely contributed well with their inbred pedigree, which, again quoting Esme, "produced a great dog who has left his mark on the breed." The winning dogs in the show ring today include many who trace back to Chuck-A-Luck, including the current successful winner, Champion Fireman's Freckled Friend, who in 1985 became only the second Dalmatian to win a Non-Sporting Group at the Westminster Kennel Club Dog Show in New York.

Pryor's Creek Sweet Basil when only 15 months of age at a match show in Racine, Wis. Mr. and Mrs. Alfred E. Treen.

Brood Bitch Class at the National Specialty in 1977. *Left to right,* Ch. Labyrinth Sleighbelle, Ch. Tuckaway Jason James, and Ch. Tuckaway Bold and Brave. Sleighbelle, the dam, owned by Dr. Sidney Remmele, Tuckaway Kennels, Lexington, Ky. The judge is noted Dalmatian breeder, Mrs. Alan Robson.

TUCKAWAY

Tuckaway Kennel, Lexington, Kentucky, was established in 1963 by Dr. Sidney Remmele who had been "in" Dals actually more than ten years at that time. Few kennels have had such impact during the past two decades as this one! Over the years, Tuckaway has bred, raised, or shown some 36 champions. Much of this success can be attributed to the great stud dog, Champion Coachman's Canicula, who was purchased by Dr. Remmele from the Coachman Kennels of Bill and Jean Fetner.

Canicula, crossed on the outstanding bitch Champion Labyrinth Sleighbells (one of the top producing bitches in Dalmatian history), set the stage for notable success. Sleighbells, co-owned with Christine Dyker, produced the famous litter from which seven finished, the eighth produced champions, and there were four multiple Group winners as well as Specialty winners.

121

Ch. Tuckaway The Pill Peddler, handled by Tom Glassford, winning Best in Show for the Tuckaway Kennels.

Direct descendants of the Canicula-Sleighbells lines are ever present today, both in the show ring and in the backbone of numerous prominent kennels in various sections of the United States. To name a few: Champion Tuckaway Gallant Man, Champion Tuckaway Traveler Indalane, Champion Count Miguel of Tuckaway, Champion Fireman's Freckled Friend, Champion Deltalyn Decoupage, Champion Viking Bred D, Champion Indalane's Rhett Butler, Champion Indalane's Scarlett O'Hara, Champion Korcula Midnight Hannah, Champion Korcula Midnight Margi, Champion Korcula Midnight Serenade, Champion Indalane's Bryan Knockout, and Champion Pic-A-Dilly's Classic Peach.

To quote Dr. Remmele, "Of course all of the above is attributed to the tremendous influence in the breed of Champion Coachman's Chuck-A-Luck."

Tuckaway is still very active in both breeding and in showing.

Dr. Remmele served on the Dalmatian Club of America Board for nine years, and was President for two terms. He twice served as Specialty Show Chairman. As a judge, he has twice officiated at the National Specialty, has done many regional specialties, and has judged the breed at Westminster.

Spoken like a true breeder, Dr. Remmele's reply to the query regarding wins he considered especially notable was, "Winning the Dalmatian Club of America Specialty in 1973 with Canicula was a great thrill. But the greatest honor was to win both the Stud Dog and Brood Bitch Classes at the National in 1977 with Canicula and Sleighbells."

A family portrait of part of the famed Canicula-Sleighbelle litter. *From left to right:* Canicula, Ch. Tuckaway Bold and Brave, Ch. Tuckaway Gallant Man, Ch. Tuckaway Jason James, Ch. Labyrinth Tuckaway Julep, Ch. Tuckaway Dinah, and Ch. Labyrinth Sleighbelle. Dr. Sidney Remmele, Tuckaway Kennel.

WATSEKA

Watseka Dalmatians are owned by Carol Schubert at Park Forest, Illinois, where some of the most famous members of this breed in history have been housed over the years. Carol's husband, Don Schubert, who was also active as a breeder, owner and handler, died of a heart attack in the early 1980s.

Champion Panore of Watseka is one of the especially notable dogs from here whose name you will find in many a pedigree. By Champion Colonial Coach Carriage Way ex Champion Tamara of Watseka, he is the winner of ten all-breed Bests in Show, plus more than 50 Group 1sts and three National Specialty Bests of Breed. He is the No. 2 all-time Dalmatian sire.

Ch. Panore of Watseka, by Ch. Colonial Coach Carriage Way ex Ch. Tamara of Watseka. One of the most famous Dalmatians, this dog has 10 Bests in Show and many other important wins to his credit. Owned by Carol Schubert, bred by Carol and Sherry Schubert.

Ch. Tamarack's Tennyson v Watseka, bred by Robert and Sharon Freeman, handled by Carol Schubert, owned by Allen M. Sheimo, here is winning the 1983 Dalmatian Club of America National Specialty. Also an All-breed Best in Show dog with many honors to his credit.

Then there is Champion Bob Dylan Thomas of Watseka, Panore's son from Newsprint N U of Watseka, bred by James and Kathleen Cox, owned by Carol Schubert, who is the sire of more than 50 champions which, we understand, makes him the No. 1 Dalmatian Sire of all time. He, too, is a multiple Group winner with a long succession of high honors to his credit.

Champion Jack Daniels of Watseka, in the family tradition, is also proving to be an outstanding sire, stamping his kids with his style and beauty. He is by Champion Woodlyn's George of Watseka from Champion Willowmount Saucy Success, and was bred by Donald and Carol Schubert.

Ch. Bob Dylan Thomas of Watseka, C.D., the No. 1 all time Dalmatian sire, bred by James and Kathleen Cox, owned by Carol Schubert.

Ch. Jack Daniels of Watseka, an outstanding sire and show dog, bred by Carol and Donald Schubert, owned by Carol Schubert.

Currently Carol Schubert has been handling a very exciting dog for Allen Sheimo, doing so with tremendous success. This is Champion Tamarack's Tennyson v Watseka, bred by Robert and Sharon Freeman, a son of Bob Dylan Thomas ex Champion Tamarack's Taylor Maid. He was Best of Breed at the 1985 Dalmatian Club of America National Specialty and is also a Best in Show, all-breeds, winner with numerous Group victories as well to his credit.

WHISKEY CREEK

Whiskey Creek Dalmatians began in 1976 when their first of the breed joined Tony Castellano's and Michelle Sager's kennel. Growing up to become Champion Whiskey Creek's Budweiser, this promising pup became his owners' constant companion, ruler of the roost, and show dog at heart. He proved the latter recently by going Best of Breed at the Dalmatian Club of Greater New York's Specialty in 1984, then on to Group 3rd from the Veterans Class.

In 1981 Champion Erin's Irish Whiskey was acquired as a puppy from John and Sharon Lyons of Erin Kennels. "Riley" went Best in Sweepstakes and Best Senior in Futurity at the 1982 National Specialty, and has produced multiple champions, one of them a Specialty Best of Breed winner. His offspring include Champion Whiskey Creek's Texas, the kennel's first homebred champion. Michelle and Tony also are especially proud of the accomplishments of Whiskey Creek's Raisin Cain, C.D., owned by Sally and Dave Lakness of Massachusetts. Pointed in the breed ring, she earned her C.D. in three consecutive trials with scores in the 190s, earning her third leg by going High Dalmatian in Trial at the Dalmatian Club of Southern New England 1984 Specialty.

The current show stock includes Champion Erin's Whiskey Creek Cheers, a liver bitch who just completed her championship with four majors, a Specialty reserve, and Specialty Best in Sweepstakes at the Dalmatian Club of Greater New York 1984 Specialty. Her owners have big plans for "Jenna" after her first litter, sired by Champion Count Miguel of Tuckaway, is born and she will return to the show ring.

Whiskey Creek Kennels are situated at Franklin, New Jersey.

127

WINEMALL

Winemall Dalmatians are owned by Janis Butler at Kissimmee, Florida, who also owns Labrador Retrievers and Vizslas, and does a good deal of tracking with her dogs.

Champion Roadrunner's Skye of Winemall, co-owned by Janis with breeder C.G. Gamble of the Roadrunner Kennels, is, to her knowledge, the only show champion Dalmatian with a Tracking ·Degree in the state of Florida.

Another excellent Dalmatian from this kennel is Roadrunner Sassi of Winemall, also a show winner and also co-owned with Mrs. Gamble.

NOTE: The story of Janis Butler training and working Skye to the Tracking Degree appears in another chapter of this book.

AMERICA'S TOP DALMATIAN WINNERS THROUGH 1984

NAME	BOB	BIS	G1	G2	G3	G4
Ch. Green Starr's Colonel Joe	336	35	138	76	51	17
Ch. PGR Heiloh Samson	242	2	21	47	45	26
Ch. Spottsboro Rebel Streak	219	0	9	9	17	21
Ch. Fire Star's Sonny Boy	187	8	33	46	33	23
Ch. Ye Dal Dark Brilliance	177	7	46	51	33	15
Ch. Tally Ho's Sir Charles	167	0	27	31	30	18
Ch. Colonial Coach Son of York	150	0	5	14	16	29
Ch. Lord Jim	149	13	50	35	20	13
Ch. Rolenet's Ragtime Dandy	144	8	36	34	23	21
Ch. Panore of Watseka	141	10	51	26	13	16
Ch. Little Slam's Major Game	136	0	19	26	23	20
Ch. Roadcoach Roadster	127	17	75	33	7	3
Ch. Deltalyn Decoupage	126	1	12	14	20	15
Ch. Pacifica Pride of Poseidon	124	1	13	21	29	23
Ch. Coachman's Chuck-A-Luck	121	3	31	37	15	11

1▲ 2▼

◆ Overleaf:

1. Family portrait! On the *left* Am. and Can. Ch. Coachman's Hot Coffee takes Best of Breed, Helene Masaschi handling, as Coffee's sire, Am. and Can. Ch. Coachman's Chocolate Soldier, takes Best of Opposite Sex to his daughter. Pauline Masaschi handling. The judge is Melbourne Downing; the show Cape Cod K.C. Both Dals owned by Canal-Side Kennels, Sandwich, Massachusetts.

2. Ch. Sugarfrost, for whom the kennel is named, on the *left*, sire of Ch. Te Ja's Jack Frost, C.D., *second from left,* the sire of Am. and Can. Ch. Sugarfrost Top Choice, C.D., *second from right,* who is the dam of Ch. Sugarfrost Flying Parson, *right.* Family portrait of some of the Sugarfrost Dals. Janet Ashbey, Stewartsville, New Jersey.

1. Am. and Can. Ch. Coachman's Hot Coffee, owner-handled by Helene Masaschi, taking Best of Opposite Sex at the Dalmatian Club of America-American Kennel Club Centennial Specialty, November 16, 1984. Alfred Treen was judge.

2. Ch. Cheshire's Yankee Honor is by Ch. Woodbury's Stonewall Jackson ex Ch. Paisley's Star of Kirkland, C.D. Bred, owned, and handled by Cheryl Fales Steinmetz, Cheshire Dalmatians, Excelsior, Minnesota.

3. Snowood Ja Sam Jedan taking Best of Winners and Best of Opposite Sex at Burlington, Wisconsin, K.C. under A.K.N. in July 1985. Handled by co-breeder Meg Hennessey. Owned by Meg and Mike Hennessey, Snowood Farm, Elgin, Illinois.

4. Ch. Coachkeep's Windsong was Top Winning Bitch for several years consecutively during her show career. Here winning a Non-Sporting Group during the mid-1970's for owner Mrs. Alan R. Robson, Glenmoore, Pennsylvania, for whom Bobby Barlow handled.

5. Cheshire's Break Dancer, by Ch. Fireman's Freckled Friend ex Ch. Cheshire's English Ivy, at 11 months. Bred, owned, and handled by Cheryl Fales Steinmetz, Cheshire Dalmatians, Excelsior, Minnesota. Shown winning the Sweepstakes at the Dalmatian Club of Greater Indiana, March 1985.

6. Ch. Texas Ranger v Tucwin (liver and white), was Winners Dog and Best Junior in Sweepstakes at 1983 Dalmatian Club of America Specialty. Bred by Tucwinn Kennels, owned by Barden Dalmatians and handled by Tim Robbins. Currently being campaigned by Dr. Sidney Remmele, Tuckaway Kennels.

7. Canal-Side's Struttin' High, by Am. and Can. Ch. Erin's Canal-Side Drummer Boy ex Am. and Can. Ch. Coachman's Hot Coffee, bred by Coachman Kennels and Helene Masaschi, owned by Pauline and Helene Masaschi. Pictured taking Best of Winners at Ramapo K.C. in 1984.

8. Ch. Robbsdales Lady Roslyn (liver and white) by Ch. Robbsdales Baron Von Cross ex Sascha Underfoot, owned by Edward Trevino and Robbsdale Dals.

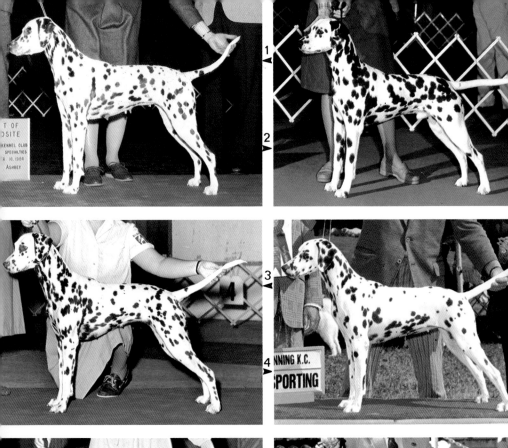

1 ◄

2 ◄

3 ◄

4 ◄

5 ◄

6 ◄

◀ Overleaf:

1. Ch. Harmony's Calais of Cheshire at three months old. Ch. Paisley's Star of Kirkland, C.D. at the age of three years. Owned and photographed by Cheryl Fales Steinmetz, Excelsior, Minnesota.

2. Australia's Top Winning liver spotted Dalmatian bitch, Aust. Ch. Kirindal Fancy Free with some of her trophies after winning Best Exhibit in Show, Dalmatian Club A.C.T. Specialty in 1984, under American judge Mrs. Esme Treen. Owned by Mrs. Jan Kirin, Kirindal Kennels, Canberra, Australia.

3. Ch. Paisley's Star of Kirkland, C.D. bred by Marie Kirk, owned by Cheryl and Thomas Steinmetz, Excelsior, Minnesota.

4. Ch. Royal Oaks Liberty Belle and her newborn litter, bred by Joanne Nash and Ardith Dahlstrom. Note the absence of spots on these brand-new puppies. Spots will come in as the puppies mature. Belle is the dam of eight champions, six C.D. holders, and 5 TTs. Owned by Eric and Ardith Dahlstrom, Hydesville, California.

5. Ch. Sugarfrost Bonnie Belle owned by Janet Ashbey, Sugarfrost Dalmatians, Stewartsville, New Jersey.

6. Am. and Bah. Ch. Ravenwood China Clipper, Am. and Bah. C.D., and a Best of Breed winner in both countries, is owned and bred by Ravenwood Dalmatians, Kathy and Lee McCoubrey, Chuluota, Florida.

1. Ch. Starborn Summer Breeze (liver and white), by Ch. Robbsdale's Baron Von Cross ex Ch. Cottondale's Candlelight, is owned by Starborn Kennels of Jack and Carol Bush, Sweeney, Texas.

2. Ch. Paisleys Twilight Fantasia, by Ch. Paisley's A Change of Pace, C.D. ex Ch. Paisley Spirit O Hopi Kachina, bred and owned by Dave and Sue Mac-Millan. This Dalmatian is a multiple Group placer and the dam of several champions.

3. Ch. Paisley Peterbilt is the 50th Paisley Champion, and won his first Group 1st award before the age of 18 months. He is by Am. and Can. Ch. Paisley's Pride of Willowood ex Ch.Paisley's Perfectly Preppie, C.D.

4. Am. Ch. He-Ge's Thaddeus Cooper, bred by Geri and Helen Rosen, owned by Jim and Sue Cahill, Santa Rosa, California. This dog is a litter brother to Hellion.

5. Gr. Ch., Am., Brz., and Int. NAC Paisley Torch of Kirkland (liver), by Ch. Paisley's Five Card Stud, C.D.X., Am. C.D. ex Am.and Can. Ch. Melody Bobby McGee, Am. and Can. C.D., pictured winning the Dalmatian Club of Greater New York Specialty in 1978. "Torchie" went on to become the Top Winning Dog for all breeds in Brazil for 1980. Breeder, Marie Kirk; owners, Sue MacMillan (U.S.) and Alberto Salim Saber Filho (Brazil).

6. Williamsview Gambler's Luck, Janet Ashbey handling, taking the points at Longshore-Southport in 1983.

1 ►
2 ►
3 ►
4 ►
5 ►
6 ►

1 ◄

2 ◄

3 ◄

4 ◄

5 ◄

6 ◄

-SPORTING
OUP THIRD
DEN VALLEY
ENNEL CLUB
NOV 1983

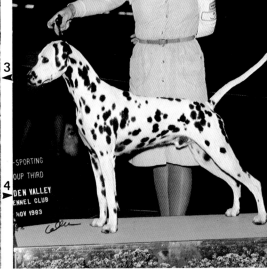

◀ Overleaf:

1. The handsome Am. and Can. Ch. Roughrider's Rogue winning the Non-Sporting Group at Bonneville Basin K.C., May 1985. Owned by Kathryn Braund, Roughrider Dalmatians, Great Falls, Montana.

2. Am. and Can. Ch. Countryroad Pippi Longstocking winning her class at the 1983 National Futurity. She is now one of the brood bitches at Countryroad Kennels, and producing well. Mr. and Mrs. Charles Cyopik, owners, Puslinch, Ontario, Canada.

3. Ch. Erin's Midas Touch going Reserve Winners Dog from the Puppy Class at the Western Reserve Dalmatian Club in 1981. Owner, Ann Thornhill. Breeders, John and Sharon Lyons. Midas is now a multi-Best of Breed winner.

4. Ch. Forrest Fire, by Ch. Forrest Ranger of Proctor, C.D.X. ex Ch. Forrest Greensleaves, C.D., is nationally ranked in the Top Ten, all systems, for 1983 and 1984. This handsome dog is owned by Proctor Dalmatians, Kenneth and Eva Berg, Moraga, California.

5. Ch. Morgan's Highlander Harper, twice Best of Breed at the Houston Dalmatian Specialty, is a son of Ch. Robbsdale's Baron Von Cross ex Dominoes Lady Morgan. Owned by Highlander Kennels, Peter Kingan and Rick Weyrich, Houston, Texas.

6. Ch. Williamsview Fame of Fanfayre owned by Ronnie Ellen Fischler, Fanfayre Kennels, Spring Valley, New York.

Overleaf: ▶

1. Ch. Rolenet's Ragtime Dandy winning Best in Show at Galveston County in 1979. Handled by Ann Schwartz for Irene Meister Mexic, Oakville, Ontario, Canada.

2. Am. and Can. Ch. Deltalyn Dappled Lady Maby, Am. and Can. C.D. is a Non-Sporting Group winner, by Ch. Deltalyn Bold Lancer ex Deltalyn Prima Donna, homebred by the Rivards.

3. Am. and Can. Ch. Delta Dals Mr. D, by Pill Pedler's Cinders ex Tammy's Lucky Lady, the first Dalmatian male owned by Bob and Judie Rivard. He came to them from Alberta Holden's Pill Peddler Kennel but was actually bred by David Gebow. Pictured taking Best of Winners at Framingham in 1973. Deltalyn Dalmatians, Foster, Rhode Island.

4. Ch. Deltalyn Dee Dee of Indalane, by Am. and Can. Ch. Deltalyn Decoupage ex Ch. Indalane Korcula Kristabel going Winners Bitch and Best of Opposite Sex from the Puppy Class at the Dalmatian Club of Southern New England Specialty Show in 1978. Owned by Bob and Judie Rivard, Foster, Rhode Island.

5. Am. and Can. Ch. Roughrider Koda's Kid, U.D., Can. C.D., by Can. Ch. Roughrider Dacotah, Am. and Can. C.D.X. from Flair's Black Berry, belongs to Cyril and Kathryn Braund, Great Falls, Montana.

6. Am. and Can. Ch. Sugarfrost Top Choice, C.D. Owner-handled by Janet Ashbey.

7. Ch. Rolenet's Ragtime Dandy winning the Spring 1982 Specialty Show of the Dalmatian Club of Houston. Handled by Ann Schwartz for Irene Meister Mexic, now of Oakville, Ontario, Canada.

8. Ch. Deltalyn Dr. Pepper, homebred by Ch. Deltalyn Bold Lancer ex Deltalyn Prima Donna, taking Best of Breed at Newtown Kennel Club in 1980. Dr. Pepper gained his title entirely as a puppy. Owned by Judie and Bob Rivard, Foster, Rhode Island.

◄ Overleaf:

1. Ch. Paisleys Oh Henry, C.D., by Ch. Coachman's Red Carpet ex Ch. Melody Up Up and Away, C.D., bred and owned by Dave and Sue MacMillan.

2. Ch. Centurion Roman Caesar, C.D. and Centurion Sea Gypsy, C.D., two splendid obedience performers, owned by Allen and Susan Bierman, St. Louis, Missouri.

3. Sitting *behind,* Ch. Rambler's Seaspot Bogart, C.D. and Ch. Rally's Candy Dapple Rambler, C.D. In *foreground,* Pacifica Tiffany Belle, C.D. and Sweet Abigail, C.D. TT. Owned by Rambler Dalmatians, James and Joanne Nash, Los Altos, California.

4. Two of the handsome Dalmatians owned by Forrest Johnson, Dalmatians of Croatia, Davenport, Iowa. The one sitting is Ch. Handsome Hugger of Croatia, co-owned with Angie Prull, Fond du Lac, Wisconsin.

5. Our favorite dog people are the ones who love and respect their older dogs. Thus we take special pleasure in bringing you this picture of two geriatrics at Dottidale Kennels. On the right, Ch. Windgap's Honey Bee, grand matriarch of the kennel, on her 16th birthday. *Left,* her son, Dottidale Black Buttons, at 13 years 8 months. Owned by Amy and Elli Lipschutz.

6. Dottidale puppies at 10 weeks depicting a good black and good liver color at this age.

7. Practicing to join the Rockettes?? A trio of Dal puppies owned by Mr. and Mrs. William Fetner, St. Louis, Missouri.

8. Ch. Rowdy J. Rambler, C.D., by Ch. Melody Dynamatic ex Ch. Royal Oaks Liberty Belle, was bred by Joanne Nash and Ardith Dahlstrom and is owned by Dawn and Clark Mauel. This lovely Dal is a Specialty Best of Breed winner.

Overleaf: ◗

1. Ch. He-Ge's Devilish Darling, bred and owned by Geri and Helen Rosen, taking Winners at Trap Falls K.C. in 1980. Joy S. Brewster, handler.

2. Ch. Robbsdale's Lady of the Knight, co-owned by Tim Robbins, Robbsdale Dalmatians and the C.D. Lesters, Dymondee Dalmatians, winning points on the way to the title.

3. Am. and Can. Ch. Roughrider's Rogue, whelped July 1983, by Ch. Tamarack's Tennyson v Watseka ex Am. and Can. Ch. Roughrider Koda's Kid, Am. and Can. C.D. Owned by Cyril and Kathryn Braund, Great Falls, Montana. Handled by Larry Sinclair.

4. Aust. Ch. Paceaway Nutcracker with owner-handler Dianne Besoff, Abermain, N.S.W., Australia.

143

1

2

3

4

1

2

3

4

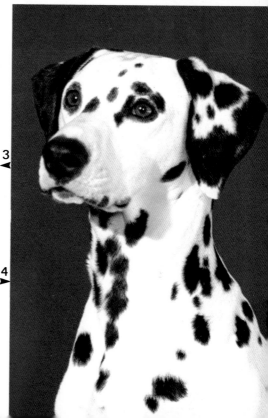

◆ Overleaf:

1. The great show mare Hot Fudge with her filly Hot Sundae and their Dalmatian friend Coachman's Coffee Break, the *first* Coachman liver and white Dal, from Ch. Coachman's Carte Blanche. Painting by Walter Brown courtesy of owners Mr. and Mrs. William Fetner, St. Louis, Missouri.

2. Ch. High Mountain Jim Jim, by Ch. Dottidale Jo Jo ex Bits of Ebony, bred and owned by Mr. and Mrs. Fred Vanderbeck, taking Best of Breed at Suffolk County K.C. in 1975 under famous Dalmatian breeder Mrs. Muriel Higgins who judged. Jim Jim was handled by Elli Lipschutz, Dottidale Kennels.

3. Ch. Ravenwood Knight Games, C.D., by Ch. Atlantis Conquestador, C.D.X., AD ex Ch. Surrey Rhodes Kady of Santana, C.D., winning points towards the title in 1980. Breeders, Kathy McCoubrey and Sharon Boyd. Owners, Kathy and Lee McCoubrey, Chuluota, Florida.

4. Can. Ch. Countryroad Betty Boop owned by Mr. and Mrs. Charles Cyopik, Puslinch, Ontario, Canada.

1. Ch. Dottidale Captain Jinks, by Ch. Dottidale Captain Nemo ex Dottidale Busterita Brown, was bred by Dottidale Kennels. Owner Patricia McCormack entirely handled this splendid dog to the title with wins that included Best of Winners at Westminster in 1982.

2. Am. and Can. Ch. Kale's Chequered Coachman is a champion producer and the grandsire of Ch. Fireman's Freckled Friend. Dymondee Kennels, Mr. and Mrs. C. F. Lester, Jr., Itasca, Illinois. Here winning Best of Breed at Canada's prestigious National Sportsmen's Dog Show in 1978.

3. Ch. Albelarm Starr of Summerhill winning the Non-Sporting Group at Durham K.C. 1983. This noted winner is owned by Edith and Nelson Gladstone, Kernersville, North Carolina.

4. Ch. Dottidale Chipper, by Ch. Dottidale Jo Jo ex Countess of Charbet, going Best of Breed from the classes at Del-Otse-Nango 1970. Owned by Anne Rojas.

5. The very successful currently winning Ch. Fireman's Freckled Friend, owned by Rob and Sherry Peth, St. Louis, Missouri. Handled by Bill Busch to Best in Show under judge Mrs. Jane Forsyth, Waukesha K.C. 1984.

6. Ch. Firesprite's Mist of Diamond D owned by Dymondee Kennels, Mr. and Mrs. C.F. Lester, Jr., Itasca, Illinois, winning Best of Breed in June 1976.

7. Ch. Poco Chimney Sweep, Dymondee Dalmatians, Itasca, Illinois, is the dam and granddam of champions. Her grandchildren include Ch. Fireman's Freckled Friend. Owned by Mr. and Mrs. C. F. Lester, Jr.

8. Ch. Dottidale Captain Nemo, by Dottidale Golden Aslan ex Dalmor's Diamond Nicole, bred by George Enny and owned by Dottidale Kennels, here taking Best of Breed. Owner-handled by Amy S. Lipschutz, at Chenango Valley in 1983.

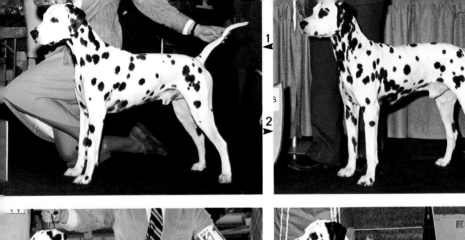

1

2

3

4

5

6

7

8

1

2

3

4

5

6

7

8

STER HATTIESBURG
KENNEL CLUB
TER PHOTO BY KATHY

ST OF
REED

◆ Overleaf:

1. Am. and Can. Ch. Canusa's Kandi Kisses taking Best of Breed at the Greater Pittsburgh Dalmatian Club Specialty in 1984. Forrest Johnson, owner, Dalmatians of Croatia, Davenport, Iowa.

2. The very important Aust. Ch. Brackleigh Aquarius, 1969-1982, whose bloodlines have contributed greatly to his breed. Sired by Aust. Ch. Kayell Bunting ex Lady Lollipop of Exhurst (U.K. import), Aquarius was bred by Mrs. R. Patterson and owned by R. and M. H. and P. H. J. Young, Dumbledeer Dalmatians. Elanora Heights, N.S.W. This outstanding stud dog was the sire of 37 champions, an Australian record that still stands!

3. Ch. Ragtime's Candy Kiss, black-spotted bitch born February 14, 1981, is the daughter of Ch. Rolenet's Ragtime Dandy ex Ch. Orleans' Candy of Atlantis. Shown winning a Group placement at Greater Hattiesburg, 1983. Handled by Ann Schwartz for Irene Mexic Meister, Oakville, Ontario, Canada.

4. Am. and Can. Ch. Range Trail Maple Creek Flagg, by Am. and Can. Ch. Coachman's Chuck-A-Luck ex Ch. Poco Chimney Sweep is a multi-Group winning Dalmatian and the sire of champions. Owned by Mr. and Mrs. C. F. Lester, Dymondee Kennels, Itasca, Illinois.

5. Australia's present day Top Winning Bitch (liver spotted), Champion Kirindal Fancy Free. A daughter of Eng., Aust., and N.Z. Ch. Clydevale Mastermind ex Sidlaw Happy Hogmanay of Leagarth (U.K. import). Handled here by owner-breeder Jan Kirin, Kirindal Kennels, Canberra, Australia.

6. Ch. Nicolette of Croatia owned by Debbie Banfield and Forrest Johnson here is taking Best of Winners on the way to her title.

7. Roughrider Montana's Cody winning 2nd Best Puppy in Sweepstakes and Best Puppy in Breed competition at six months and five days old. Judge, Mrs. Tom Stevenson. Owner, Kathryn Braund. Lethbridge K.C., Alberta, Canada.

8. Amigo's Rosita De Miguel, owned by Michael and Suzanne Willey, winning Best in Sweepstakes at the Dalmatian Club of America National in 1980. The judge was Wendell J. Sammet, famous professional handler and Dalmatian breeder whose Dalmatia Kennels is one of the oldest for Dals in the country and has produced scores of famous names.

1. Ch. Beauregard O'Hara of Proctor, by Ch. Joe Forrester of Proctor, C.D. ex Maggie O'Hara of Proctor, is a Specialty winner who exemplifies the type and style being achieved in the Proctor Dalmatians' breeding program. Kenneth and Eva Berg, owners, Moraga, California.

2. Ch. Green Starr's Colonel Joe winning an all-breed Best in Show at Charleston K.C. in 1979. Bobby Barlow handled, as usual, for Mrs. Alan R. Robson. The author was judge on this occasion.

3. Ch. Dymondee's Toy Soldier, C.D. is Dymondee Kennels' newest champion in the spring of 1985. A multi-breed winner with Group placements, he is by Am. and Can. Ch. Coachman's Chocolate Soldier ex Dymondee's Paper Rose. Pictured winning a Non-Sporting Group placement in September 1984.

4. Ch. Dymondee Toy Soldier at the start of his show career, winning his first points at Skokie Valley K.C. Owned by Mr. and Mrs. C. F. Lester, Jr., Itasca, Illinois.

5. Ch. Paisley of Proctor, C.D., by Ch. Panore of Watseka ex Ch. Melody Up Up and Away, C.D., is the foundation bitch at Proctor Kennels. Kenneth and Eva Berg, owners, Moraga, California.

6. Winning the Veteran's Class at the Dalmatian Club of America in 1974, Am. and Can. Ch. Coachman's Chuck-A-Luck at 10½ years of age. Handled by Carol Schubert for Mr. and Mrs. Alfred E. Treen, Brookfield, Wisconsin. The judge was the late Mrs. Winifred Heckman.

1 ▶

2 ▶

3 ◀

4 ◀

NON-SPORTING GROUP

5 ◀

6 ◀

1 ►

2 ►

3 ►

4 ►

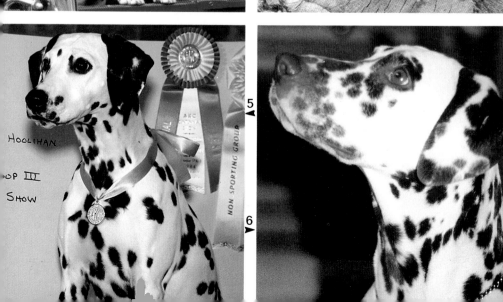

HOOLIHAN

op III

SHOW

NON SPORTING GROUP

5 ►

6 ►

1. Ch. Snowcap's Sparkle Plenty II, by Ch. Snowcap's Hannibal Hayes ex Snowcap's Priceless Gem, foundation bitch at Fanfayre Dalmatians, Ronnie Ellen Fischler, Spring Valley, New York.

2. Creme de la Creme is this liver spotted puppy by Ch. Coachman's Trump Card ex Ch. Coachman's Circus Wonder. From Coachman Kennels, St. Louis, Missouri.

3. Can. Ch. He-Ge's Hellion, a homebred owned by Geri and Helen Rosen, Danbury, Connecticut.

4. Driftwood's Sunspot Rambler, C.D.X., bred by Jill Otto and Joanne Nash, is owned by Kathryn L. Blink, Woodside, California. "Bonnie" was High in Trial at the 1984 Dalmatian Club of America National Specialty, and nationally ranked in obedience for two years.

5. Ch. Green Star's Major Hoolihan, by Ch. Green Starr's Colonel Joe ex Williamsview Majorette, had the distinction of being adjudged Best of Breed and third in the Non-Sporting Group at the A.K.C. Centennial Dog Show in November 1984 at Philadelphia. Bred by Mr. and Mrs. David G. Doane, owned by Linda Hazen Lewin, Rockville, Maryland.

6. Am. and Can. Ch. Coachman's Hot Coffee, noted Dalmatian bitch owned by Canal-Side Kennels, Sandwich, Massachusetts.

1. Ch. Coachman's Hot Coffee winning Group 1st at North Shore K.C. in 1979. Handled by Jane Forsyth for Mr. and Mrs. William Fetner, Coachman's Kennels, breeders and owners at that time.

2. Cavalier Chief of Staff taking first in class at the Dalmatian Club of America Centennial Specialty in 1984, owner-handled by Michael T. Manning, M.D., Staten Island, New York.

3. Ch. Erin's Whiskey Creek Cheers, by Ch. Erin's Canal-Side Drummer Boy ex Ch. Erin's Adorable Abby. Owned by Tony Castellano and Michelle Sager, Whiskey Creek Kennels, Franklin, N.J. Breeders, D. & L. Checki and Sharon Lyons. Handled by Tony Castellano.

4. Ch. Homestead Peppermint owned by Evelyn and Bob Stolting, handled by Bob Forsyth.

5. Ch. Paisleys Pandora, C.D., by Ch. Bob Dylan Thomas of Watseka, C.D. ex Ch. Melody Up Up and Away, C.D., was Winners bitch at the Dalmatian Club of America National Specialty in 1975 and Best of Winners and Best of Opposite Sex at the 1975 Chicagoland Specialty. Bred by Dave and Sue MacMillan. Owned by Cathy Vesley and Sue MacMillan.

6. Ch. Snowcap's Never On Sundae, multiple Group winner and champion producer, was No. 3 Dalmatian bitch in U.S. in 1976 and No. 2 in 1977. Owned by Dymondee Kennels, Mr. and Mrs. C. F. Lester, Jr., Itasca, Illinois.

1 ►

2 ►

3 ►

4 ►

5 ►

6 ►

1 ▶
2 ▶

3 ▶
4 ▶

5 ▶
6 ▶

◀ Overleaf:

1. Am. and Can. Ch. Countryroad Cool Classic taking a Group placement at Kennel Club of Northern New Jersey in 1983. Bred by Mr. and Mrs. Charles Cyopik, owned by Linda Bartley of Hawleyville, Connecticut, this dog was Winners at the 1981 Dalmatian Club of America National Specialty.

2. Ch. Coachman's Carte Blanche, multi-Group and Specialty winner, pictured taking Best of Opposite Sex at Dalmatian Club of America Specialty in 1970. Daughter of Ch. Lord Jim. Coachman Dalmatians, St. Louis, Missouri. Jay Fetner handled at this event.

3. Ch. Atlantis Conquestador, C.D.X., AD. This dog is a well-known winner, the sire of champions, and so far as is known, is the *only* Dalmatian Champion also to have earned a Schutzhund Endurance Title (AD). Bred by E. and T. Hoover. Owners, Ravenwood Kennels, Kathy and Lee McCoubrey, Chuluota, Florida.

4. Int., Mex., and Am. Ch. Melody Ring of Fire of BB, C.D. is owned by Melody Dalmatians, Jack and Beth White, Fort Collins, Colorado. Pictured at the age of 10 years winning his last Group 1st at the International Shows in Mexico City. This sire of about 18 champions is himself an all-breed and Specialty Best in Show winner.

5. Ch. Short Acre Calgary Stampede, homebred owned by Anne Nicholson, by Ch. Snowcap's Sunscion ex Williamsview Bonnie Blue, finished in five shows at six months of age. Here taking Best of Winners at Twin Brooks in 1982. Short Acre Kennel, Greenwood Lake, New York.

6. Ch.Fanfayre's Best Foot Forward *(left)* and Ch. Fanfayre's Beau of Short Acre, by Ch. Snowcap's Sunscion ex Ch. Snowcap's Sparkle Plenty II, owned by Anne Nicholson and bred by Ronnie Ellen Fischler. They were Best Brace under the author at the Dalmatian Club of America National Specialty in 1982.

1. Ch. Coachman's Loving Cup, C.D. winning the Novice Class at the Dalmatian Club of America, August 1980.

2. Ch. Melody Rambler's Rose, C.D. completing her degree, Top Ten Obedience Dal of 1978. This dam of the first homebred champion at Cavalier Kennels, Ch. Cavalier Pretty Princess, was handled to conformation and obedience titles by owner, Michael T. Manning, M.D., Staten Island, New York.

3. *Left* to *right:* High Jinks Kismet of He-Ge, Ch. He-Ge's Devilish Darling, and Can. Ch. He-Ge's Hellion, all owned by Geri and Helen Rosen, Danbury, Connecticut. Here winning the Brood Bitch Class at Westchester 1980.

1 ▶

2 ▶

3 ▶

◀ Overleaf:

1. This youngster is by Ch. Fireman's Freckled Friend ex Ch. Canusa's Kandi Kisses and is owned by Forrest Johnson, Dalmatians of Croatia, Davenport, Iowa.

2. Ravenwood Tammy, U.D. was the first Dal owned by Kathy and Lee McCoubrey, Chuluota, Florida. From a portrait by Elizabeth Baugh.

3. Ch. Proctor's Hi-Ho Cheerio, by Ch. Count Miguel of Tuckaway ex Ch. Washakie Belleamie, newest champion at Proctor Dalmatians, Kenneth and Eva Berg, Moraga, California.

162

1. Ch. Whiskey Creek's Budweiser is by Ch. Tuckaway Gallant Man ex Tuckaway Jewels Reward. Owned by Tony Castellano and Michelle Sager, Whiskey Creek Kennels, Franklin, New Jersey. Shown placing in the Group at Westchester K.C. 1984. Handled by Joy S. Brewster.

2. Ch. Centurion Star of Hope, C.D., by Ch. Panore of Watseka ex Crown Jewels Crystaline Jade, C.D.X., dam of seven champions and nine obedience degree holders. Owned by Centurion Dalmatians, Paul and Elaine Lindhorst, St. Charles, Missouri.

3. Ch. Rambler Quintessence, C.D., TT, by Ch. Paisley A Change of Pace ex Ch. Royal Oaks Liberty Belle, winning Best in Futurity at the Dalmatian Club of America National Specialty in 1983. Bred by Joanne Nash and Ardith Dahlstrom. Owned by James and Joanne Nash, Rambler Dalmatians, Los Altos, California.

4. Ch. Roadrunner's Skye of Winemall, C.D., T.D. owned by C.G. Gamble and Janis Butler, Winemall Kennels, Kissimmee, Florida. To the owners' knowledge, this is the only champion Dal with a Tracking title in Florida.

5. Roadrunner Sassi of Winemall, owned by C.G. Gamble and Janis Butler, Winemall Kennels, Kissimmee, Florida.

6. Int., Mex., and Am. Ch. Melody Penny Lane is a multiple Specialty Best of Breed and 1978 Dalmatian Club of America National Best of Opposite Sex winner. The dam of four champions, including two Specialty winners both here and in Canada. Melody Kennels, Jack and Beth White.

1 ◄
2 ◄
3 ◄
4 ◄
5 ◄
6 ◄

1

2

3

4

5

6

◆ Overleaf:

1. Ch. Hapi-Dal Knight Strider taking a Specialty Best of Winners to complete his title. Handled by Diana Wilson, co-owner with Susie Wilson, Santa Ana, California.

2. Am. and Can. Ch. Coachman's Chocolate Soldier winning the second Specialty Show held by the Dalmatian Club of Quebec at Montreal. Judge, Mrs. Mary Barrett of Roadcoach fame. Co-owner and handler, Pauline Maraschi, Sandwich, Massachusetts.

3. Mrs. Arthur W. (Mary) Barrett of Roadcoach Kennels with her Ch. Roadcoach Kittiwake, Best of Winners en route to the title at the 1973 Dalmatian Club of America National Specialty.

4. Best of Winners at the National Specialty, Ch. Fanfayre's Beau of Short Acre. Handled by Joy S. Brewster. The author was judge.

5. Ch. Coachman's Blizzard of Quaker Acres here is winning Mrs. Alan R. Robson's first Best in Show award in any breed, in June 1974 at Susque-Nango K.C. Handled by Bobby Barlow who, until his retirement from handling piloted Mrs. Robson's dogs to numerous top awards over the following years. Mrs. Robson's Albelarm Kennels are located at Glenmoore, Pennsylvania.

6. Ch. Coachman's Lucky Coins, by Ch. Coachman's Lucky Cuss ex Ch. Coachman's Cup O'Tea, was handled by Margaret Lester who won First Prize in Junior Showmanship at the Dalmatian Club of America National Specialty in 1982.

1. Ch. Centurion Special Edition, U.D., TT, was the Top Obedience Brood Bitch in 1983. One of very few Champion-UD Dalmatians, she has produced two champions and 12 obedience degree holders. Special Edition was High in Trial at the Detroit Specialty. Owner-handled by Jeannine Kerr, St. Ann, Missouri.

2. Can. Ch. Alfredrich Handsome, Tall 'n' Dark completing his championship in three straight shows at the age of nine months, and taking Best Puppy in Group. Owned and bred by Alfredrich Dalmatians, owner-handled by Mr. Jean-Richard Millaire, Alfredrich Kennels, Casselman, Ontario.

3. Ch. He-Ge's April Promise, bred and owned by Helen and Geri Rosen, taking Best of Breed at Chenango Valley, December 1983.

4. Ch. Harmony Real People, by Ch. Karastella Cadillac of MGR ex Ch. Paisley's Harmony Boquet, C.D. pictured at 13 months old going Winners Dog and Best of Winners at the 1980 Dalmatian Club of America National Specialty in Kentucky. Judge, Forrest Johnson. Breeder-owner-handler, Jan Nelson, Evergreen, Colorado. There were more than 240 Dalmatians entered in the classes at this event.

5. Can. Ch. Alfredrich Fantastica pictured going Winners Bitch at the Dalmatian Club of Canada National Specialty in 1984. Owned by Mr. Jean-Richard Millaire, Alfredrich Dalmatians, Casselman, Ontario, Canada.

6. Ch. Robbsdale's Highlander Lady L, (liver and white), Best in Sweepstakes on two occasions at the DOH Specialty in Houston, Texas was by Ch. Robbsdale's Baron Von Cross ex Crown Jewels Turkish Tera. This foundation bitch of Highlander Kennels is owned by Peter Kingan and Rick Weyrich.

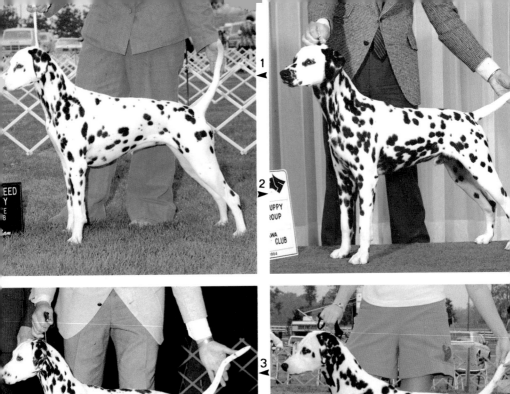

1

2

3

5

6

◀ Overleaf:

1. Ch. Whiskey Creek's Texas, by Ch. Erin's Irish Whiskey ex Coachman's Raisin Cereal, owned by Patti and Joe Sirriani. Breeders, Michelle Sager, Tony Castellano, and P.J. Fetner. Handled by Michelle Sager to Best of Winners at Somerset Hills, 1984.

2. Ch. Erin's Calculated Risk, by Ch. Coachman's Caliber ex Ch. Coachman's Paisley Candybar, first homebred champion for Erin Dalmatians, is now a multiple Best of Breed winner. Bred and owned by John and Sharon Lyons, Bloomingburg, New York.

3. Ch. Patz Magic Dancer of MGR taking Best of Breed at Twin Brooks K.C. in 1984. Bonnie Threllfal handled for Michael Manning, M.D., Staten Island, New York.

4. Ch. Fanfayre's Beau of Short Acre winning Best in Show, Albany K.C. Handled by Joy S. Brewster for Richard Koeppel, New York City. Photo courtesy of Anne M. Nicholson, Short Acres Dalmatians, Greenwood Lake, New York.

5. Ch. Harmony Bright Eyed Susan, C.D., by Int. Ch. Paisley Torch of Kirkland, NAC, ex Ch. Paisley's Smart Alice v Watseka, a multiple Best of Breed winner, group placer, and the dam of champions, here taking Best of Breed in a sizable entry at the age of seven years.

6. Ch. Robbsdales Highlander Chanel, (liver and white) by Ch. Robinwood's Union Jack ex Ch. Robbsdales Highlander Lady, was Best in Sweepstakes 1984 at St. Louis Specialty. This multi-Best of Breed winner is owned by Robbsdale Dals and Highlander Kennels.

170

1. Ch. Paisley's A Change of Pace, C.D., by Ch. Long Last Living Legend ex Ch. Paisley's A Touch of Class, C.D., bred and owned by Dave and Sue MacMillan, Paisley Dalmatians, St. Paul, Minnesota.

2. Ch. Paisley's Five Card Stud, C.D.X., Can. C.D. is by Ch. Bob Dylan Thomas of Watseka ex Ch. Melody Up Up and Away, C.D. This sire of 12 champions including the well-known Torch was bred by Dave and Sue MacMillan. Owned by Judy Box.

3. Ch. Long Last Living Doll, by Ch. Long Last Living Legend ex Ch. Long Last Larceny, bred by Mike and Chris Jackson is owned by Elaine Thomas and Chris Jackson. She was Best of Breed over Specials during her Open Class competition.

4. Ch. Melody Up Up and Away, C.D. (liver), by Ch. Melody Dynamatic ex Calculator Miss Sincerity, bred by Dr. Jack White. Owners, Dave and Sue McMillan, St. Paul, Minnesota. The dam of 15 champions, "Pooka" is the foundation bitch at Paisley Kennels.

5. Ch. Enchanted Tequila Sunrise taking Best of Breed at Atlanta K.C. in 1984. Owned by E. Anne Hutchins, Dauntless Dalmatians, Deland, Florida.

6. Am. and Braz. Ch. Vicor of the Ebony Spots, C.D. (liver) bred by Alberto Salim Saber Filho, co-owner with Sue MacMillan. This is a Brazilian-bred dog from Paisley stock. He came to the U.S. to earn his titles, and sired numerous champions during his stay.

7. Am. and Can. Ch. Evomack's Tsar of Carlsbad winning a Non-Sporting Group for Alfredrich Dalmatians, Jean-Richard Millaire, Casselman, Ontario, Canada.

8. Can. Ch. Alfredrich Happy Hour, by Ch. Count Miguel of Tuckaway ex Am. and Can. Ch. Sunkist Singalong, winning points on the title at Credit Valley. Mr. Jean-Richard Millaire, Casselman, Ontario, Canada.

1

2

3

4

5

6

7

8

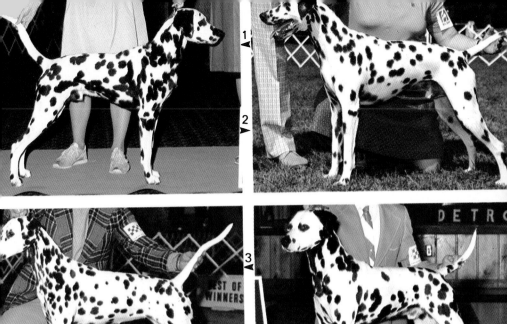

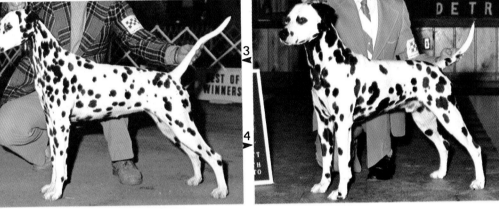

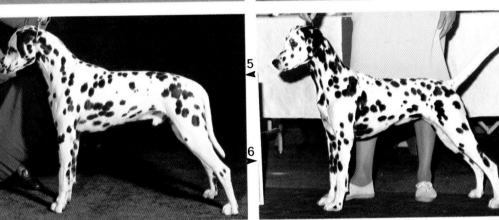

◀ **Overleaf:**

1. Cheshire's Break Dancer at 11 months, by Ch. Fireman's Freckled Friend ex Ch. Cheshire's English Ivy, winning Best in Sweepstakes at the Dalmatian Club of Greater Indianapolis in 1984. Bred, owned, and handled by Cheryl Fales Steinmetz, Cheshire Dalmatians, Excelsior, Minnesota.

2. Ch. Fanfayre's Best Foot Forward, by Ch. Snowcap's Sunscion ex Ch. Snowcap's Sparkle Plenty II, taking points on the way to the title in 1982. Joy S. Brewster handled for owner, Ronnie Ellen Fischler, Spring Valley, New York.

3. Ch. Tuckaway Second Hand Rose finished at seven months with four majors and is a multiple breed winner. Owned by Tuckaway Kennels, Dr. Sidney Remmele, Lexington, Kentucky.

4. Ch. Indalane Handsome of Croatia taking Best of Winners at the 1983 Dalmatian Club of Detroit Specialty. Owned and handled by Forrest Johnson, Dalmatians of Croatia, Davenport, Iowa.

5. Ch. Fanfayre's Beau of Short Acre, by Ch. Snowcap's Sunscion ex Ch. Snowcap's Sparkle Plenty II, at the age of one year. This handsome dog has piled up a notable number of important victories during his show career.

6. Ch. Melody Spotlight Angel winning Best in Sweepstakes at the Davenport Dalmatian Club Specialty at 10 months old. The current winning bitch from Melody Kennels, she is consistently taking Best of Breed at the shows. Melody Dalmatians, owners, Jack and Beth White, Fort Collins, Colorado.

7. Ch. Ravenwood Polished Pebbles, U.D. taking Best of Breed at Spartanburg K.C. 1981.

8. Ch. Splash O'Ebony Woodbury Jaki, owned by Debbie Nierman, Splash O'Ebony Dalmatians, Dallas, Texas. Pictured winning Best of Opposite Sex at the Dalmatian Club of America National Specialty in August 1982.

1. What an interesting and historic photo! *Left* is Int. Mex. and Am. Ch. Melody Ring of Fire of BB, C.D.; *center* is Ch. Melody Crimson and Clover just starting her career; and *right* is her sire, Ch. Melody Dynamatic. This was one of Beth White's first dog shows, and it was an exciting occasion for her as, additionally, Ch. Melody Ring of Fire BB, C.D. went on to win the Group.

2. Three generations of Janet Ashbey's Sugarfrost Dalmatians. The puppy on the *right* is Sugarfrost Flying Parson at four months, grandson. On the *left,* his sire, Ch. Sugarfrost Melody Commander; in *foreground,* Commander's sire, Ch. Sugarfrost, at 11 years, the dog for whom the kennel was named. Janet Ashbey, owner, Stewartsville, New Jersey.

1 ▲ 2 ▼

2 ◄

3 ◄

5 ◄

6 ◄

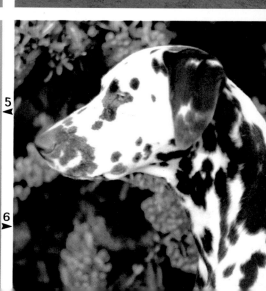

◆ Overleaf:

1. A headstudy of the excellent liver bitch Showcase Gold Standard, Best of Winners at the National Specialty in 1984. Owned by Elaine Thomas and Kathy Brown.

2. Paisleys Southern Pair O Dice, by Ch. Paisley's Oh Henry, C.D. ex Wiki-uppe Domino, bred by Bob and Anne Simpson. Owned by Jody Peterson.

3. This lovely photo of Ch. Green Starr's Major Hoolihan shows all the intelligence and beauty of the breed. A multiple Group winning and placing Dal, "Hot Lips" finished with three majors, one from the Puppy Class. Best of Breed at the Chicagoland Dalmatian Club 25th Anniversary Specialty in an entry of 140. Best of Breed and Group 3rd at the A.K.C. Centennial. Always owner-handled by Linda Hazen Lewin.

4. Ch. Fanfayre's Best Foot Forward *(left)* and Ch. Fanfayre's Beau of Short Acre *(right)* were bred by Ronnie Ellen Fischler and are owned by Anne Nicholson, Greenwood Lake, New York.

5. Pisces Rambler Sunspot Dawn, C.D.X. won the Dog World Award for completing her C.D. in her first three trials with scores of 195 or better. She is the No. 1 *Obedience Dalmatian* for 1984, her second year for being nationally ranked. Owned by Linda Fish and Joanne Nash, the latter co-breeder with Jill Otto.

6. Ch. Coachman's Cup O'Tea owned by Coachman Kennels, St. Louis, Missouri.

1. Aust. Ch. Swiftgait Mylord Duke is by Aust. Ch. Paceaway Nutcracker ex Swiftgait Sugar N'Spice. Owned by Miss M. Reid, Abermain, N.S.W., Australia. Photo by M. Bennett.

2. Ch. S. and P. Starlet of Summerhill, C.D. winning Best of Breed at Old Dominion K.C. 1983. Owned by Edith and Nelson Gladstone, Kernersville, North Carolina.

3. Ch. Miss Camielle of Croatia taking Best of Winners on the way to the title. Owned by Forrest Johnson, Dalmatians of Croatia, Davenport, Iowa. Judge was Wilma Hunter.

4. Ch. Handsome Hugger of Croatia winning First in the Sweepstakes at the A.K.C. Centennial Dog Show, Philadelphia 1984. Forrest Johnson handled for himself and co-owner Angie Prull, Fond du Lac, Wisconsin.

5. Aust. Ch. Swiftgait Lyndall, by N.Z. and Aust. Ch. Korrandulla Twist n'Time (N.Z. import) ex Swiftgait Gabriella, owned by R. and D. Besoff, Swiftgait Dalmatians, Abermain, N.S.W., Australia.

6. Ch. Ramblers Raisin Cane, TT, by Ch. Paisley's A Change of Pace, C.D. ex Ch. Royal Oaks Liberty Bell, finished with four majors and with multi Bests of Breed from the classes. Bred by Joanne Nash and Ardith Dahlstrom. Owned by Joanne Nash and James Schreiber.

7. Ch. Cavalier Lady Abigail Aubrey, owned by Michael T. Manning, M.D., Staten Island, New York, taking points towards title on the 1982 Florida Circuit. Joy S. Brewster handled.

8. Ch. Cavalier Pretty Princess taking Best of Winners at Danville K.C., March 1979.

1

2

3

4

5

6

7

8

1 ▶

2 ▶

3 ▶

4 ▶

BEST IN
SWEEPSTAKES
DALMATIAN CLUB
OF AMERICA
1982
Ashbey

5 ◀

EST OF
BREED
CAN KENNEL CLUB
NNIAL SPECIALTIES
EMBER 16,1984
ASHBEY

6 ◀

OF
ERS
MYERS
CLUB
R 1984
Graham

7 ◀

GROUP
FIRST
WESTMINSTER
KENNEL CLUB
1985

8 ◀

FIRST
IN GROUP
NON-SPORTING
GOLDEN GATE
KENNEL CLUB
17th ANNIVERSARY
FEBRUARY 1985
Callea

◆ Overleaf:

1. Ch. Erin's Adorable Abby finished with three majors including Best of Breed over Specials at K.C. of Philadelphia 1982. Owners, J. and S. Lyons and D. and L. Checki. Breeders, John and Sharon Lyons.

2. Ch. Erin's Irish Coffee, by Ch. Coachman's Chocolate Soldier ex Ch. Coachman's Paisley Candybar, taking Best in Sweepstakes at the Dalmatian Club of Greater New York Specialty, 1982, at seven months old. Breeders-owners, John and Sharon Lyons, Bloomingburg, New York.

3. Ch. Paisley's First Things First (liver) was sired by Ch. Paisley's Oh Henry, C.D. ex Ch. Paisley Spirit O Hopi Kachini. Bred and owned by Dave and Sue MacMillan. This multiple Group winner, Best of Opposite Sex at the 1982 National Specialty under the author is currently a Junior Handling and Obedience Dog for Jessica MacMillan.

4. Ch. Erin's Irish Whiskey, by Ch. Erin's Irish Rogue ex Ch. Coachman's Can Such Things Be, owned by Tony Castellano, Michelle Sager, John and Sharon Lyons, taking Best in Sweepstakes at the Dalmatian Club of America National Specialty in 1982. John Ashbey, judge. Sharon Lyons, handler.

5. Ch. Fireman's Freckled Friend, owned by Rob and Sharri Peth, winning the Dalmatian Club of America National Specialty in Philadelphia November 16, 1984. Bill Busch, handler, Alfred Treen, the judge.

6. Am. and Bah. Ch. Ravenwood State of the Art owner-handled by Kathy McCoubrey to Best of Winners at Ft. Myers Dog Club, November 1984. Ravenwood Dalmatians, Chuluota, Florida.

7. Ch. Fireman's Freckled Friend is only the fourth Dalmatian in the 109-year-history of the Westminster Kennel Club to have won the Non-Sporting Group there. Bill Busch handled for owner Robert A. Peth, St. Louis, Missouri, February 1985.

8. Ch. Saint Florian Sunspot Ad-Lib, by Am. and Braz. Ch. Vicor of the Ebony Spots, C.D., TT ex Ch. Royal Oaks Sunspot Rambler, C.D., TT, here winning Group 1st at Golden Gate in February 1985. Bred by Jill Otto and Joanne Nash. Owned by Jill Otto and Dawn Mauel, Palo Alto, California. This Dalmatian finished with five majors in five weeks.

1. Am. and Can. Ch. Snowcap's Special Edition, by Ch. Snowcap's Iago of Annie ex Ch. Snowcap's Sparkle Plenty II, belongs to Fanfayre Dalmatians, Ronnie Ellen Fischler, Spring Valley, New York. Handled by Joy S. Brewster.

2. Ch. Fanfayre's Belle Dame taking Reserve Winners bitch at the Dalmatian Club of America Specialty in 1982. Bred by Ronnie Ellen Fischler, owned by Anne Nicholson, and handled by Joy S. Brewster.

3. Can. Ch. Alfredrich Danski Dancer is here winning a U.S. major and going Best of Breed over specials at Onondaga Kennel Association in 1982.

4. Ch. Deltalyn Bold Lancer, Best of Breed at Greater Pittsburgh Dalmatian Club Specialty in 1980, is one of the outstanding winners owned by Judie and Bob Rivard, Foster, Rhode Island.

5. Am. and Can. Ch. Crown Jewels Delta Diamond, by Ch. Crown Jewels Regent Diamond ex Crown Jewels Pendant Diamond, is the first champion at Deltalyn Dalmatians owned by Bob and Judie Rivard, Foster, Rhode Island.

6. Ch. Centurion Dealer Deacon, C.D. is a Group winner who ranked No. 24 among Dalmatians in 1980. Owned by Centurion Kennels, Paul K. and Elaine Ann Lindhorst, St. Charles, Missouri.

1 ►

2 ►

3 ►

4 ►

5 ►

6 ►

1. Am. and Can. Ch. Countryroad Cool Million, noted show winner and Top Producer, at home with his owners, Charles and Linda Cyopik, Countryroad Dalmatians, Puslinch, Ontario, Canada.

2. Ch. Skardal Sugarfrost Lancer with Janet Ashbey taking Winners at Long-shore-Southport 1983.

3. Royce Jackson and his Dal, Smokey. Photo by Cheryl Fales Steinmetz, Excelsior, Minnesota.

4. Am. and Can. Ch. Canusa's Kandi Kisses, a lovely Canadian-born daughter of Ch. Korcula King of Harts ex Ch. Rolenet's Rhapsody. This is the latest addition to Dalmatians of Croatia owned by Forrest Johnson, Davenport, Iowa. For winning Best of Breed at the Davenport Dalmatian Club Specialty Show, June 1984, Kandi received a life-like Dalmatian model trophy.

1. Ch. Royal Oaks Liberty Belle, bred and owned by Eric and Ardith Dahlstrom, here at 10 years of age, is winning the Veteran Bitch Class at the Dalmatian Club of Northern California Specialty in June 1984. "Belle" is the dam of eight champions, six C.D. degree holders, and five TT (Temperament Test) degrees. Her grandchildren include Group and High in Trial winners.

2. Ch. Sugarfrost Jenifer Valentine, C.D.

3. Dymondee's Poetry in Motion and Dymondee's Sunday Best, a Group and Specialty winning Dalmatian Brace, owned by Dymondee Kennels, Mr. and Mrs. C.F. Lester, Jr., Itasca, Illinois.

4. Ch. Fanfayre's Beau of Short Acre and Ch. Fanfayre's Best Foot Forward taking Best Brace at the Dalmatian Club of America Specialty in 1982.

5. The noted Ch. Deltalyn Decoupage in 1976 winning a Best of Breed. Homebred by Bob and Judie Rivard, "Coop" has a long list of credits to his record including Groups. Deltalyn Kennels are at Foster, Rhode Island. Handled by Judy Rivard, judged by the author.

6. Ch. Cavalier Cover Girl, one of the handsome Dalmatians belonging to Michael T. Manning, M.D., Cavalier Dalmatians, Staten Island, New York.

◆ **Overleaf:**

1. Ch. Long Last No Frills (liver) was Best of Opposite Sex at the Dalmatian Club of America 1980. This Regional Specialty winner and Best in Sweepstakes was bred by Barbara Greenspan. Owned by Mike and Chris Jackson, Long Last Kennels.

2. Can. Ch. He-Ge's Hellion, by Ch. Deltalyn Decoupage ex High Jinks Kismet, completed his Canadian championship with two Group 2nds and one Group 4th and is also on his way in the U.S. Owned by Heegee Kennels, Geri and Helen Rosen, Danbury, Connecticut.

3. Am. and Can. Ch. Countryroad Cool Million, the sire of 22 American Champions and 20 Canadian Champions, is by Am. and Can. Ch. Colonial Coach Caballero ex Willowmount Go Go Dancer. Owned by Mr. and Mrs. Charles Cyopik, Puslinch, Ontario, Canada. Pictured winning Best of Breed in 1981 at the Dalmatian Club of Detroit Specialty.

4. Ch. Harmony Calais of Cheshire, by Ch. Karastella Cadillac of MGR ex Ch. Paisley's Harmony Bouquet, C.D., winning the Non-Sporting Group. Owner-handled by Judy Box, of San Antonio, Texas. "Callie" is a multiple champion producer from her first litter.

5. Ch. Centurion Pippin is a Group winner by Ch. Annles N. Belrins Dylan Flyer ex Ch. Centurian Special Edition, U.D., TT. Owner-handled by Paul K. and Elaine Ann Lindhorst, Centurion Kennels, St. Charles, Missouri.

6. Ch. He's So Handsome From Dalmatia winning Best of Breed his first time shown at Maryland K.C. This son of Ch. Pill Peddler's Boatswain from a Roadcoach bitch finished from the Bred-by Class at an early age. Bred, owned, and handled by Wendell J. Sammet.

7. Ch. Harmony Fantasy Fanfare, C.D., by Ch. Paisley's A Change of Pace, C.D. ex Ch. Harmony Bright Eyes Susan, C.D. finishing her championship with Best of Winners from the Bred-by Exhibitor's Class at the Dalmatian Club of Las Vegas Specialty in October 1984. This multiple Best of Breed winner and Group placer from the classes also finished her C.D. in straight shows with all scores over 190. Breeder-handler, Jan Nelson. Judge, Roy Ayers.

8. Ch. Dal Acres Banners Blazing winning the Non-Sporting Group at Danville K.C. in 1983. Owned by Dal Acres Kennels, Dotty LaGassie and Marilyn Dusek, San Antonio, Texas.

1. Ch. Coachkeep's Blizzard and Ch. Coachkeep's Windsong are full brother and sister but from different litters. Pictured taking Best of Breed (Blizzard on *left* handled by Bobby Barlow) and Windsong on the *right).* Owned by Mrs. Alan Robson, Albelarm Kennels, Glenmoore, Pennsylvania.

2. Am. and Can. Ch. Deltalyn Decoupage winning the Stud Dog Class at the Dalmatian Club of Greater New York Specialty. The progeny are *center,* Wedgewood Ship in a Bottle and, *right,* Indalane Scarlett O'Hara, who at this Specialty had taken five points each as Winners Dog (and Best of Winners) and Winners Bitch respectively. Judie Rivard, co-breeder-owner, handling "Coop" on the *left.*

BEST OF BREED OR VARIETY
BEST OF OPPOSITE SEX

1▲   2▼

FIRST
WESTCHESTER KENNEL CLUB
SEPTEMBER 1978

Chapter 5

The Dalmatian Club of America

The Dalmatian Club of America, existent since the 1920's, is a most efficient and progressive Specialty Club Organization, doing a truly super job for the benefit of its breed. Its projects are numerous, including the publication of an excellent quarterly magazine, *The Spotter*, for its members; a very active Judges Education Committee working hard to encourage and assist in holding educational seminars; periodic reviews of the American Kennel Club/Dalmatian Club of America slide shows, ever watchful for possible up-dating and improvement to become necessary; a Standard Committee studying for the possible need of revision there; a Membership Education Committee which makes every effort to be helpful, in addition to all the other Committees, each in capable hands, that help to keep a Parent Specialty Club running well. By no means is this the type of Parent Club that considers that holding an Annual Specialty Show fulfills its obligation to its breed and thus goes no further. The Dalmatian Club of America has a true sense of obligation to the breed, and works hard 12 months of the year towards that end.

1985 Officers of the Dalmatian Club of America are as follows:

President .... Charles Garvin, M.D.
Vice-President .... Forrest G. Johnson
Corresponding Secretary .... Mrs. David G. Doane,
325 Old Mill Spring Road
Route 3, Jonesboro, Tennessee 37659
Recording Secretary .... Mrs. Carol Schubert
Treasurer .... William Haworth

Stud Dog Class, Dalmatian Club of America National Specialty 1977. *Left to right,* Ch. Coachman's Canicula, Ch. Deltalyn Decoupage, and Ch. Tuckaway Jason James. Canicula, the sire, is owned by Tuckaway Kennels, Dr. Sidney Remmele, Lexington, Kentucky. Mrs. Alan Robson, owner of the famed Albelarm Dals, is judging.

In addition to the Parent Club, there are numerous Regional Specialty Clubs devoted to the breed situated in practically every area of the United States.

Anyone owning a Dalmatian, especially with the thought in mind of showing this dog, training and working it in obedience, or eventually becoming a breeder, will benefit in both pleasure and learning by becoming a member of a Dalmatian Specialty Club. At first, probably joining a Regional one would be the most satisfying, especially if you are able to become a member of one whose "field of action" is within your range, enabling you to attend meetings and any educational features (symposiums, obedience training classes, match shows or handling classes to name a few of the most popular). This way you have the opportunity of becoming acquainted with the other folks in your area with mutual Dalmatian interests.

A note to the corresponding secretary of the Dalmatian Club of America should bring you the name and address of the Regional Club nearest you. This information also can be obtained by contacting the American Kennel Club, 51 Madison Avenue, New York, NY 10010. If you purchased your puppy from a breeder in your area, undoubtedly that breeder can, and will gladly, put you in touch with the local Regional Club, perhaps introducing you and sponsoring you for membership.

As one becomes more involved with the breed, one will wish to join the National as well, since this is the Parent Club and offers many advantages to its members. They will wish to know a bit about you before membership application is accepted. If you are already a member of a Regional, and have friends there who will sponsor you for the National, so much the better.

This is Ch. Roadcoach Roadster, one of the greatest Dals in the history of the breed who was listed in "Who's Who in American Dogdom" published back in 1958. Roadster was bred by Roadcoach Kennels, sired by Wendell Sammet's Ch. Boot Black From Dalmatia ex Ch. Roadcoach Kittereen. Born February 16, 1954, Roadster's outstanding ring record included 17 times Best in Show. Among them the huge Morris and Essex K.C. event in 1956. Owned by Mrs. S.K. Allman, Jr., Doylestown, Pa., handled by Charley Meyer.

Chapter 6

Dalmatians in Canada

The Dalmatian enjoys sound popularity in Canada, where we have noted many outstanding members of this breed as we have attended various dog shows. Canadian breeders have imported, and presently work with, the finest American bloodlines which they have incorporated into their own breeding programs; and they are producing very noteworthy Dalmatians who are making good records in keen competition.

ALFREDRICH

Alfredrich Dalmatians, one of Canada's most outstanding kennels in this breed, are owned by Mr. Jean-Richard Millaire and are located at Casselman in Ontario.

It was a puppy intended to be a pet who became a show dog that started Mr. Millaire on his way in the Fancy. Trying his luck at the shows, this splendid young Dal truly did his owner proud, becoming American and Canadian Champion Evomack's Tsar of Carlsbad. He won the Dalmatian Club of Canada National Specialty in 1980, then stood proudly by as his daughter, American and Canadian Champion Ravensglen Midnight Cowgirl made it a double victory by taking Best of Opposite Sex to her sire's Best of Breed. To date Tsar has sired 12 champions, American or Canadian, and become winner of numerous Bests of Breed and Bests in Group and Group placements. Tsar is Canadian-bred with the Colonsay and Green Starr lines behind him.

The breeding program at Alfredrich includes some of Tsar's daughters, most particularly American and Canadian Champion

Am. and Can. Ch. Coachman's Chocolate Soldier, by Ch. Blackpool Copper Courier ex Coachman's Coffee Break, bred by William H. and Jean W. Fetner. Owned by Pauline L. Masaschi and Helene R. Masaschi, Sandwich, Mass.

Sunkist Singalong who is from the great bitch International Champion American and Mexican Champion Melody Penny Lane. Singalong is a Group winner and a Specialty Winners Bitch. She was bred to the noted Champion Count Miguel of Tuckaway, from which litter two of the puppies became Canadian Champion Alfredrich Handsome Tall 'n' Dark and Canadian Champion Alfredrich Happy Hour, both of whom are now being shown in the States (summer 1985) working on their American titles.

Another important acquisition to this kennel was that of Canadian Champion Beachcomber's Liberty Belle, a daughter of the well-known American and Canadian Champion Deltalyn Decoupage owned by the Rivards in New England. Also there has recently been added a young bitch who is now Canadian Champion Alfredrich Fantastica who has a litter by the Texas dog American Champion Rolenet's Radcliffe, whose bloodlines complement the Coachman-Colonsay background at Alfredrich.

COUNTRYROAD

Countryroad Dalmatians are owned by Mr. and Mrs. Charles Cyopik at Puslinch, Ontario, Canada. This couple has been active in the Dalmatian world since 1970, during which time they have attained 30 Canadian Champions and eight American Champions. Surely a record in which to take pride.

The first Dalmatian at Countryroad was bred by G. Arthur Davidson of Paris, Ontario, and was shown in obedience by both the Cyopiks. He became Canadian Obedience Trial Champion Diamond Jim of Woodridge, Canadian U.D. and American C.D.X. In 1973, to complete his American C.D., he earned a High in Trial at the Conewango Valley Kennel Club Show and Obedience Trial with a score of 198½ from the Novice "B" Class.

The first of the Cyopiks' many homebred champions was Canadian Champion Countryroad Betty Boop, by American and Canadian Champion Willowmount Baron Brown ex Canadian Champion Limestone Irish Lace, C.D.

The most famous of the homebreds at this kennel to date is Canadian and American Champion Countryroad Cool Million, son of American and Canadian Champion Colonial Coach Caballero ex Willowmount Go Go Dancer. Whelped in 1976, he was Winners

Can. Obedience Trial Champion Diamond Jim of Woodridge, Can. U.D. and Am. C.D.X. owned by Countryroad Dalmatians, Charles and Linda Cyopik.

Am. and Can. Ch. Countryroad Brief Bikini, by Am. and Can. Ch. Countryroad Cool Million, was Best of Winners at the 1981 Dalmatian Club of Southern New England Specialty. Homebred owned by Mr. and Mrs. Charles Cyopik.

Dog at the Pittsburgh Dalmatian Club Specialty, and Best of Winners at the Western Reserve Dalmatian Specialty, both from the Bred-by Exhibitor Class, both wins during 1977. In 1981 he was Best of Breed at the Detroit Dalmatian Specialty and Best of Breed at the Davenport Dalmatian Specialty, as well as being the No. 2 Dalmatian in Canada. Always breeder-owner-handled, in 1982 he won an all-breed Best in Show in Ontario and was retired. "Clancy," as he is known, is the sire of 22 American and 20 Canadian Champions, which numbers undoubtedly will grow as numerous others of his offspring are major pointed.

American and Canadian Champion Countryroad Brief Bikini, by Cool Million ex American and Canadian Champion Limestone Nell of Raintree, is a bitch who has done well for the kennel in the show ring, having been Best of Winners at the 1981 Dalmatian Club of Southern New England Specialty.

American and Canadian Champion Countryroad Cool Classic is another by Cool Million distinguishing himself at the important shows. His dam is Countryroad Alexander's Oma, and he was bred by the Cyopiks but is now owned by Linda Bartley of Hawleyville, Connecticut. He was Winners Dog over 90 class dogs at the 1981 Dalmatian Club of America National Specialty. In 1982, "Buddy" was Best of Breed at the Dalmatian Club of Detroit Specialty, which win he repeated in 1983. Also in 1983 he was Best of Breed at the Dalmatian Club of Greater Atlanta Specialty, and he is a multi-Group winner in the United States.

American and Canadian Champion Countryroad Pippi Longstocking, by American Champion Tuckaway Traveler Indalane ex American and Canadian Champion Countryroad Brief Bikini, a Futurity winner at the National in California during 1983, is now one of the leading Countryroad brood bitches.

It is interesting to note that the Cyopiks are avid collectors of Dalmatian figurines, having by now a very exciting assortment of them in which they take justifiable pride. This started almost simultaneously with the purchase of their first "real" Dal, and has continued through the years. Among their "goodies" are such rarities as a handsome Nymphenberg Dalmatian, this lovely German-crafted piece holding "pride of place" in the special antique cabinet where Linda Cyopik displays her most treasured pieces. Also there is the discontinued smallest size Dal in the Royal Doulton line, a Royal Belvedere Dal from Vienna, a family of Dals from the Morten's Studio, and many other treasures.

IRENE (MEISTER) MEXIC

A most enthusiastic Dalmatian owner and her very famous winner have recently moved from the southern United States to Oakville, Ontario, Canada, owing to the owner's re-marriage. She is now Irene Meister Mexic and the Dal the multiple all-breed and Specialty Best in Show winner, Champion Rolenet's Ragtime Dandy, whom Ann Schwartz piloted throughout his exciting career here.

Ragtime Dandy is a son of American Champion Blackpool Ironstone ex Champion Rolenet's Blackberry, and he was bred by Jorge A. Campero and Robert W. Liggett.

Dandy won his first Non-Sporting Group at the tender age of seven months, and his first Specialty at just under one year of age.

Am. and Can. Ch. Coachmaster's Ringmaster, black and white, completed his championship at the Greater Pittsburgh Dalmatian Club with a 4-point major. Bred by Robert and Shirley Hayes, Coachmaster Dalmatians, El Cajon, Cal. Owned by Pauline and Helene Masaschi, Canal-Side Dalmatians, Sandwich, Mass.

He went on to win six Specialty Shows, eight all-breed Bests in Show, and about 140 additional Group placements in the United States. He retired at age six years with his eighth Best in Show at Galveston, Texas. He was in the Top Three Dalmatians for three years, and always in the Top Ten so long as he was being shown.

Although no longer in the ring at dog shows, Dandy has not forgotten about showmanship, having switched his talents to making T.V. commercials in New Orleans, for the Children's Hospital, for the Fire Marshalls, Fire Alarms, and struts his stuff with his owner in commercials for clothes. Also he is the Dalmatian on bumper stickers sold around the world.

Dandy has some excellent progeny in the ring carrying on for him with Best of Breed and Group awards. Also I have a feeling he will attend some Canadian dog shows now that he lives there, which obviously he will enjoy.

It is interesting to know that Dandy works for Walt Disney movies in his spare time, as a "promotion dog" for the picture *101 Dalmatians*. Included in his activities in this regard are personal appearances (accompanied by Candy) at specified performances, where those who view the movie are invited to bring their cameras and take pictures of the dogs or be photographed with them.

201

Aust. Ch. Kirindal Evo's Escort, by Eng., Aust., and N.Z. Ch. Clydevale Mastermind (U.K. import.) ex Aust. Ch. Kirindal Apple Dancer, owned by Kirindal Kennels, Mrs. Jan Kirin, Higgins, A.C.T., Australia.

Aust. Ch. Swiftgait Excelsior, by Aust. Ch. Swiftgait Just In Time ex Swiftgait Nardia, owner-handled by Dianne Besoff, Abermain, N.S.W., Australia.

Chapter 7

Dalmatians in Australia

We are very much impressed by the beauty and quality of the Dalmatians owned and produced in Australia, and are proud at having so representative a group of breeders to tell you about in these pages. A study of the accompanying illustrations will back up the reasons for my admiration of these dogs and the many words of praise for the Dalmatians from "down under" which have reached my ears from American judges returning home after fulfilling assignments in that country.

Considerable rapport exists between the Australian fancy and ours here in the United States. It is quite usual nowadays for at least several judges each year from here to go there and vice versa. This is good both ways, as it enlarges our true scope of what is taking place world-wide within the breeds of interest to us, and the exchange of ideas and opinions is certainly beneficial to all concerned.

Australian breeders are using bloodlines from both England and the United States in their breeding programs, combining them judiciously and advantageously with their own. Achievement of a championship title in Australia is far from easy owing to the many top grade dogs and keen competition found there.

Following is a resume of some of the leading Australian Dalmatian kennels.

DUMBLEDEER

Dumbledeer Dalmatians are owned by Mary Young and her family at Dumbledeer Cottage in Elanora Heights, New South Wales. The kennel was established in 1954 by Reg and Mary Young whose daughter, Pamela, later became involved as well.

Aust. Ch. Dumbledeer Jake, U.D., by Aust. Ch. Karnang Prince Monford, C.D. ex Aust. Ch. Dubrovnik Mescal, was the start of the Dumbledeer line. Owned by Mary Young, Dumbledeer Dalmatians, Elanora Heights, N.S.W.

As of 1985, the Youngs have bred 41 Australian Champions. Their foundation bitch, Australian Champion Dubrovnik Mescal, was purchased from Mr. and Mrs. Cuth. Mathews. This bitch was Welfield (U.K.) and Dubrovnik (Aust.) lines, and mated to Australian Champion Karnang Prince Monford, C.D., of Beaudalla (Aust. lines) for five litters she produced 11 champions, thereby establishing the Dumbledeer bloodlines.

Over the years the Youngs have introduced the English bloodlines of Northpleck, Roadster, Berricutt, Greenmount, and more recently Buffrey. Currently they are linebreeding to Brackleigh Aquarius, their two stud dogs being a son and a grandson of Aquarius, and their five bitches are granddaughters and great granddaughters of this superb dog.

Mrs. Young tells us that "Dumbledeer" is a very old thatched cottage in the fields near Watchet, Somerset, England. This was Mr. Young's birthplace, and the name was selected by the Youngs for their kennel prefix.

The oldest of the Dalmatians of Dumbledeer Kennels is Australian Champion Dumbledeer Bridgette, who was born in 1969 and still going strong as of May 1985. She was bred by the Youngs and is owned by D. and N. Irwin. A champion at only ten months' age, this daughter of Australian Champion Tchachonia Flash Jack ex Australian Champion Dumbledeer Ontanna, C.D.X., had Challenge wins at all major all breed shows from 1970 to 1977, including the Melbourne Royal in 1970 and 1974; Sydney Royal in 1972 and 1974; and Best Puppy in Show at the Melbourne Royal in 1970; plus three Dalmatian Club of New South Wales Challenges; a Club Championship from there in 1971 and 1974.

Aust. Ch. Connaught Cassandra, by Aust. Ch. Brackleigh Aquarius ex Dumbledeer Baroness. This lovely bitch, born in 1972, lived to be only four years old. During her short lifetime she was a Challenge winner at Specialty and all-breed shows including the Spring Fair, and has two Dalmatian Specialty Bests in Show to her credit. She was bred by Mrs. C. Abbott. Owned by M. and P. Young.

Additionally, she was top Dalmatian Bitch in N.S.W., 1970 through 1974.

Australian Champion Dumbledeer Jake, U.D., 1961-1975, was highly instrumental in the start of the Dumbledeer line. By Australian Champion Karnang Prince Monford, C.D. ex Australian Champion Dubrovnik Mescal, Jake was the Top Dalmatian in New South Wales in 1967, was the No. 1 Dalmatian Stud Dog of the 1960's in Australia, siring 12 champions, a record at that stage which has since been broken by his grandson, Aquarius,

Jake was the first Dalmatian in Australia to achieve the Utility Obedience title. He also was famous as having been featured in nine television commercials and participated in many obedience demonstrations. His show wins included three times Reserve Challenge at the Sydney Royal shows.

Jake had an older sister, Australian Champion Dumbledeer Wahadia, 1958-1972 who was owned and shown by Mr. H. Caldwell. She was the winner of 24 Bests in Show awards, all-breeds, which in 1985 still stands as an Australian record for Dalmatians.

Australian Champion Brackleigh Aquarius, 1969-1982, was by Australian Champion Kayell Bunting ex Lady Lollipop of Exhurst (U.K. import). He was linebred on Berricot and Greenmount from the United Kingdom, incorporating the Australian Dumbledeer line. This dog holds the record as Australia's No. 1 Dalmatian Stud Dog with 37 champions to his credit as a sire.

Australian Champion Dumbledeer Glenn, A.O.C.C.D., C.D.X., U.D., T.D., T.D.X., was born in December 1970 by Australian Champion Tchachonia Flash Jack ex Australian Champion Hansom Pollyanna, C.D.X., imported from U.K. as a puppy by Jane Harris and Mary Young.

Jane Harris's achievements with Glenn are truly notable. She made this dog a breed Champion at 14 months' age; the first Dalmatian Obedience Champion in Australia; the first Dual Champion Dalmatian in Australia, and with him won an Award of Creative Excellence for Glenn's leading role in the film *Led Astray*. He made numerous obedience appearances for charity, principally "Guide Dogs for the Blind." He received the Honorary Registration Dog Tag No. 1 from the Mayor of Willoughby in recognition of his achievements. Glenn was linebred to English Champion Merithew Hey Presto through Northpleck and Hansom lines. He belongs to Mrs. Jane Harris and was bred by M. and P. Young.

Young bitches at Dumbledeer in July 1985 include the full sisters Australian Champion Dumbledeer Odella and Australian Champion Dumbledeer Razzamataz, born in 1982 and 1983 respectively. These two are homebred by Australian Champion Kronborg Capias (an Aquarius son) ex Australian and New Zealand Champion Buffrey Isabella (U.K. import).

Odella, at age two and a half is a champion four times over, and has Best Puppy and Minor Puppy and Junior in Show awards at both all-breed and Specialty shows. She won the Reserve Challenge at Sydney Royal in 1985, beaten only by her younger full sister, Razzamataz, who went on then to Best of Breed. The latter bitch is the first liver the Youngs ever have kept for themselves.

Then there is Champion Vickma Althorpe, born in 1982, by Australian Champion Kronborg Capias ex Aust. Ch. Vickma Phoebes Joy, bred by Mrs. M. Vickery, who is basically of Dumbledeer bloodlines. She obtained her championship at 14 months, has an all-breed Best in Show, and is running first for Best Dalmatian Bitch in the New South Wales Club's point score for 1985.

KIRINDAL

Kirindal Dalmatians at Canberra, Australia, are owned by Mrs. Jan Kirin and are among Australia's most outstanding for this breed. Established in 1973, Kirindal has produced 12 Australian Champion Dalmatians, three of them being multiple Best Exhibit in Show winners.

Founded on English bloodlines of imported stud dogs (Champion Chasecourt Cheers owned by Phil and Brian Beneridge of Victoria; and English, Australian, and New Zealand Champion Clydevale Mastermind, owned by Anita and Pat Easton of Surfer's Paradise, Queensland, (both dogs from U.K.), Kirindal really surged ahead when its owner imported a bitch, Sidlaw Happy Hogmanay, from the U.K. from Mrs. Jeanette Steen. This bitch is a daughter of the famous Junior Warrant English Champion Leagarth Northern Escort, a Crufts Best of Breed winner, owned by Mr. Jim Halley of Scotland. Progeny from this bitch includes multiple Best in Show winning daughter, Champion Kirindal Fancy Free and multiple Best in Show winning son, Champion Kirindal Kingsman, liver and black respectively.

Best Exhibit in Group winning grandchildren include Australian Champion Kirindal Quicksilver (liver); Australian Champion

The baby puppy Kirindal Crown Jewels at seven weeks of age. Kirindal Kennels, Canberra, Australia.

Kirindal Quintello (liver); and Australian Champion Kirindal Quality (black). Then there is the multiple In Show winning grandson, Kirindal Rolls Royce (black) and the Class in Group winning great-granddaughter, Kirindal Vanity (liver).

Another leading Dalmatian winner produced at this kennel is Australian Champion Kirindal Gay Grenadier (liver), sired by Australian Champion Kirindal Evo's Escort (liver) ex Australian Champion Kirindal Regency Belle. Grenadier was the sire of Australian Champion Kirindal Kingsman and current winner, six-month-old Kirindal Unique (liver) who has already had four Best Class in Group 6 awards, plus a Best Baby in Show and a Best Minor Puppy in Show and looks all set to become another top winner for this kennel.

208

Aust. Ch. Kirindal Quick Silver with handler Kaylene Zakiharoff of Canberra after winning 1st place in the Junior Showmanship, February 1985. Quick Silver bred by Kirindal Kennels.

Jan Kirin with her foundation bitch, Aust. Ch. Kirindal April Dancer, who has produced a number of Australian Champions. This imported daughter of Ch. Chasecourt Cheers gained her Australian title at age 11½ months, and has produced a number of Australian Champions.

SWIFTGAIT

Swiftgait Dalmatian Kennels were founded in 1972 by Ron and Dianne Besoff, both of whom are licensed championship show judges for Groups 6 and 7. This kennel, located at Abermain in New South Wales, has bred 18 champions in addition to making up an extra seven Dalmatians to championship titles. Dogs from this kennel have been exported to New Zealand, Singapore, Hong Kong, and the Philippines.

Some of the foundation bitches here include Australian Champion Cattai Cassandra, Australian Champion Clover of Farley Green (imported from New Zealand), and Australian and New Zealand Champion Buffrey Isabella, imported from the U.K.

N.Z. and Aust. Ch. Korrandulla Twist N'Time (N.Z. import), by Ch. Roadstar Royal Star ex Tanagra of Terra Nova, owned by R. and D. Besoff, Abermain, N.S.W.

Two of Australia's all-time great dogs have been exhibited and owned by this kennel: New Zealand and Australian Champion Korrandulla Twist N' Time (N.Z. import) and Australian Champion Paceaway Nutcracker.

All of the above dogs as well as others have been incorporated into a very successful breeding program, and the future looks bright with many handsome young dogs well on their way to their titles and winning numerous in Group and in Show awards.

Australian Champion Paceaway Nutcracker (liver and white) is by Australian Champion Chasecourt Cheers, who was imported from the United Kingdom. His dam is Australian Champion Checkerboard Debra, and Cracker was born in March 1976.

Cracker, as Nutcracker is known to friends, is the greatest winning Dalmatian dog of all time in Australia. He has won 20 Bests in Show awards, more than any other Dalmatian dog in Australian showing history. Also, he has six Dalmatian Specialty Bests in Show; 55 Best in Group awards, plus numerous class, in Group and in Show awards. He was the New South Wales Dalmatian Club's Club Champion in 1983 and 1984, N.S.W. Top Country Dog 1983, and Best liver Dalmatian 1984.

Cracker was bred by Mrs. F.E.L. Chandler in South Australia, and had an outstanding career as a young dog winning Royal Challenges in almost every state in Australia. He came to Dianne and Ron Besoff at five years of age, adding to his already famous name with an outstanding number of distinguished Best in Show and Runner-Up in Show placements. Cracker has been shown by Dianne Besoff in partnership with Mrs. F.E.L. Chandler until being retired just before his ninth birthday. His last Best in Show was at age eight-and-a-half years winning the New South Wales Dalmatian Club Specialty under judge Dr. Spira. Cracker has sired numerous champions throughout Australia, and Best in Show winners in almost every state.

New Zealand and Australian Champion Korrandulla Twist N' Time was the first champion imported to Australia. He was the New Zealand Dalmatian Club's "Top Dalmatian" in 1974, 1975, and 1976 and the Australian Dalmatian Club's Top Dalmatian "Club Champion" 1976, 1977, and 1978.

"Max" retired at six-and-a-half years, having held the title of "Top Dog" three years in each of the two countries. He was bred by Glennis and Lloyd Hatton of Shannon, New Zealand. His was

Aust. Ch. Swiftgait Stargazer, age 14 months, by Ch. Swiftgait Just N'Time ex Aust. Ch. Clover of Farley Green (N.Z. import). Owners R. and D. Besoff.

Aust. Ch. Swiftgait Chariot o'Fyr, by Ch. Swiftgait Just N'Time ex Ch. Clover of Farley Green, is a N.Z. import. Owner, Mrs. C. Staples, New South Wales.

an illustrious show career in New Zealand with the Hattons until purchased and imported to Australia by Ron and Dianne Besoff in March 1976. He very handily took over the show scene, then, in Australia, winning his first Specialty Show in April 1976 under U.K. Dalmatian specialist judge and owner of Great Britain's famed Greenmount Kennels, Mrs. P. Piper. He went on to win six Specialty Bests in Show. Then he went on to sire many champions including the famous Australian Champion Dizzidot Fame N' Fortune in Queensland, Champion Swiftgait Lyndall (New South Wales) who now resides in Hong Kong, Champion Almanzer Timely Allure (Victoria), and Champion Bhowani Al Capone (New South Wales).

Australian Champion Swiftgait Lyndall, by Twist N' Time ex Swiftgait Gabriella, is a Best in Group and Specialty show winner. She was the Dalmatian Club of New South Wales Top Bitch for 1983 and was exported to Hong Kong the following year along with young liver and white dog Swiftgait Firebrand, who was the Dalmatian Club of New South Wales Junior of the Year 1984.

Australian Champion Swiftgait Stargazer, by Just N' Time from the New Zealand import Champion Clover of Farley Green was Challenge Dog and Runner-Up to Best in Show at A.C.T. Dalmatian Club Specialty Show when only seven-and-a-half months of age, the judge, Dalmatian specialist from the United States, Mrs. Esme Treen. At age 15 months, "Star" has won four times First in Group 6 and four times Runner-Up to Best in Show, plus numerous class, in-group, and in-show awards. He also accounted for the Dalmatian Club of New South Wales Top Country Dalmatian in 1984, Best Puppy, and Best Junior of the Year, as well as pointscore winner of the Roadmaster Shield for dog with most points at shows throughout New South Wales.

Miss M. Reid of Weston in Australia owns a smashing young dog in Australian Champion Swiftgait My Lord Duke, by Nutcracker ex Swiftgait Sugar N' Spice. This liver male was bred by the Besoffs, and has won a Best in Show all breeds, four times Runner-Up, six times Best in Group 6, and many other honors. He took Reserve Challenge Certificate under Mrs. Treen at the A.C.T. Dalmatian Specialty, handled by Mrs. Dianne Besoff, was reserve Challenge Certificate at Victorian Dalmatian Specialty 1984, again handled by Mrs. Besoff, Reserve Challenge Certificate at the Sydney Royal in 1985 handled by owner Miss M. Reid.

Top left: This is a handsomely correct Dalmatian rear view. The model Ch. Sugarfrost Melody Commander. *Top right:* And this is the front as it should look, again our model being Ch. Sugarfrost Melody Commander. *Bottom left:* Ch. Sugarfrost Melody Commander in profile. Janet Ashbey owner-handler of this fine dog.

Chapter 8

Standards of the Breed

The *standard of the breed* to which one sees and hears such frequent reference wherever purebred dogs are written of or discussed, is the word picture of what is considered to be the ideal specimen of the breed in question. It outlines, in minute detail, each and every feature of that breed, both in physical characteristics and in temperament, accurately describing the dog from whisker to tail, creating a clear impression of what is to be considered correct or incorrect, the features comprising *breed type*, and the probable temperament and behavior patterns of typical members of that breed.

The standard is the guide for breeders endeavoring to produce quality dogs and for fanciers wishing to learn what is considered beautiful in these dogs; and it is the tool with which judges evaluate and make their decisions in the ring. The dog it describes is the one which we seek, and to which we compare in making our evaluations. It is the result of endless hours spent in dedicated work by knowledgeable members of each breed's parent Specialty Club, resulting from the combined efforts of the club itself, its individual members, and finally the American Kennel Club, by whom official approval must be granted prior to each standard's acceptance, or that of any amendments or changes to it, in the United States. Breed standards are based on intensive study of breed history, earlier standards in the States or in the countries where the dogs originated, or were recognized, prior to introduction to the United States, and the purposes for which the breed was originally created and developed. All such factors have played their part in the drawing up of our present standards.

215

THE AMERICAN KENNEL CLUB STANDARD FOR DALMATIANS

The Dalmatian should represent a strong, muscular and active dog; poised and alert; free of shyness; intelligent in expression; symmetrical in outline; and free from coarseness and lumber. He should be capable of great endurance, combined with a fair amount of speed.

HEAD: Head should be of a fair length, the skull flat, proportionately broad between the ears, and moderately well defined at the temples, and not in one straight line from the nose to the occiput bone as required in a Bull Terrier. It should be entirely free from wrinkle. *Muzzle* should be long and powerful—the lips clean. The mouth should have a scissors bite. Never undershot or overshot. It is permissible to trim whiskers. *Eyes* should be set moderately well apart, and of medium size, round, bright and sparkling, with an intelligent expression; their color greatly depending on the markings of the dog. In the black-spotted variety the eyes should be dark (black or brown or blue). In the liver-spotted variety they should be lighter than in the black-spotted variety (golden or light brown or blue). The rim around the eyes in the black-spotted variety should be black; in the liver-spotted variety, brown. Never flesh-colored in either. Lack of pigment is a major fault. *Ears* should be set rather high, of moderate size, rather wide at the base and gradually tapering to a rounded point. They should be carried close to the head, be thin and fine in texture, and preferably spotted. *Nose.* In the black-spotted variety should always be black; in the liver-spotted variety, always brown. A butterfly or flesh colored nose is a major fault.

NECK AND SHOULDERS: The neck should be fairly long, nicely arched, light and tapering, and entirely free from throatiness. The shoulder should be oblique, clean and muscular, denoting speed.

BODY, BACK, CHEST AND LOINS: The chest should not be too wide, but very deep and capacious, ribs well sprung but never rounded like barrel hoops (which would indicate want of speed). Back powerful; loin strong, muscular and slightly arched.

LEGS AND FEET: Of great importance. The forelegs should be straight, strong and heavy in bone; elbows close to the body;

feet compact, well-arched toes, and tough, elastic pads. In the hind legs the muscles should be clean, though well defined; the hocks well let down. Dewclaws may be removed from legs. *Nails.* In the black-spotted variety, black or white; or a nail may be both black and white. In the liver-spotted variety, brown or white or a nail may be both brown and white.

GAIT: Length of stride should be in proportion to the size of the dog, steady in rhythm of 1, 2, 3, 4 as in the cadence count in military drill. Front legs should not paddle, nor should there be a straddling appearance. Hind legs should neither cross nor weave; judges should be able to see each leg move with no interference of another leg. Drive and reach are most desirable. Cowhocks are a major fault.

TAIL: Should ideally reach the hock joint, strong at the insertion and tapering toward the end, free from coarseness. It should not be inserted too low down, but carried with a slight curve upwards, and never curled.

COAT: Should be short, hard, dense, and fine, sleek and glossy in appearance but neither woolly nor silky.

COLOR AND MARKINGS: Are most important points. The ground color in both varieties should be pure white, very decided, and not intermixed. The color of the spots in the black-spotted variety should be dense black; in the liver-spotted variety they should be liver brown. The spots should not intermingle but should be as round and well defined as possible, the more distinct the better. In size they should be from that of a dime to a half-dollar. The spots on the face, head, ears, legs, and tail to be smaller than those on the body. Patches, tri-colors, and any color markings other than black or liver constitute a disqualification. A true patch is a solid, sharply defined mass of black or liver that is appreciably larger than any of the markings on the dog. Several spots that are so adjacent that they actually touch one another at their edges do not constitute a patch.

SIZE: The desirable height of dogs and bitches is between 19 and 23 inches at the withers, and any dog or bitch over 24 inches at the withers is to be disqualified.

MAJOR FAULTS

Butterfly or flesh-colored nose. Cowhocks. Flat feet. Lack of pigment in eye rims. Shyness. Trichiasis (abnormal position or direction of the eyelashes).

FAULTS
Ring or low-set tail. Undersize or oversize.

SCALE OF POINTS

Body, back, chest and loins	10
Coat	5
Color and markings	25
Ears	5
Gait	10
Head and eyes	10
Legs and feet	10
Neck and shoulders	10
Size, symmetry, etc.	10
Tail	5
Total	100

DISQUALIFICATIONS
Any color markings other than black or liver. Any size over 24 inches at the withers. Patches. Tri-colors. Undershot or overshot bite.

Approved December 11, 1962

THE KENNEL CLUB (GREAT BRITAIN) VARIATION TO STANDARD
Size: ideal height: 23 to 24 inches for dogs; 22 to 23 inches for bitches.
Fault: blue eyes.

INTERPRETATION OF THE STANDARD
Anyone planning to become an owner of a purebred dog owes it to himself to immediately make a thorough study of that breed's standard and of the application of the standard to the dogs themselves. Dalmatian fanciers are fortunate in that their standard is concise, well written, has a "scale of points" (a tremendously useful guide in teaching the proper perspective in which features of the dog should be placed) and three degrees of faults, ranging from minor to major and on to disqualifications. With these guides, students of the breed are off to a head start on what is correct and desirable and which faults are the lesser, or greater, evils.

As with any show dog, the first things to concern a judge examining a class in the show ring is the general balance, style, and showmanship of the entrants. This becomes evident as the dogs make their initial move around the ring; and first impressions being important, it is well to try to present your dog to its best possible advantage at this time. A bit of "pre-show schooling" such as training classes (for shows) and some match show experiences set you off to a better start here than just leading the dog cold into the show ring.

The Dalmatian should travel in a steady, rhythmic gait, forelegs reaching out well and hindquarters flexing powerfully. The forelegs should be set sufficiently under the dog to indicate proper shoulder angulation, while the hindquarters should be well bent at the stifle with the hock joint low to the ground; in profile hock straight from joint to paw. It is atypical for a Dalmatian to break into a gallop (handlers, remember this in gaiting your dogs). The breed is a *coach* dog, intended to travel beneath the carriage at a steady gait and capable of doing so for distances of 10 or 15 miles at a clip. Intermittent bursts of speed would not be desirable for this work, and would cause the dog to soon tire.

Size is also important in the Dalmatian, again because of his coaching work. Too tall a dog would hardly fit well beneath the carriage axle; thus size specifications should be strictly enforced.

The standard makes abundantly clear the importance of correct color and markings when it allots 25 points, one fourth of the entire dog, to this feature. This is only as it should be, as the Dalmatian's distinctive and striking spotting is the feature which most instantly makes the dog recognizable to the layman as being of that breed. Great emphasis must be placed on the depth of color, size, shape, and placement of the spots. Ideally, *all* parts of the dog should be spotted, including the ears. However, in the case of a truly exceptionally high quality dog in other respects, some allowance is generally made for lack of spotting on the ears, which do have a tendency sometimes to be solid color (the black or the liver) or very nearly so.

In early times, we have read, Dalmatians were seen in spots of colors other than those now allowed, and even as tri-colors (both black and liver spots on the same dog). You will note that neither of these conditions is permissible in our present day Dalmatian.

One of the most troublesome areas of the standard for newer fanciers of the breed is that provided by the disqualification for

Ch. Roadcoach Roadster winning Best of Breed at Westminster in 1955, owner-handled by his breeder Mary Barrett. Roadster was born in 1954, by Ch. Boot Black from Dalmatia ex Ch. Roadcoach Kittereen. His 17 all-breed Bests in Show included the Morris and Essex event in 1956. Sire of champions including Tioga Sportscar, Roadcoach Random, and Kiss and Tell From Dalmatia. Roadster was sold to Mrs. S.K. Allman, Jr., Doylestown, Pa., for whom, under Charley Meyers' handling, he made outstanding wins.

"patches." Many people simply do not understand, and judges have been known to disqualify as "patched" dogs on whom the *effect* of a patch is created by the intermingling of several (or more) spots. A true patch can be *felt*, as the texture of the hair is different than the rest of the coat. It has a suede-like feeling to your fingers, therefore can be *felt* as distinctly as *seen*.

Uniformly sized, well shaped and well placed spots are a tremendous asset to a show Dalmatian. Unfortunately, all show dogs do not fall in this classification, some of them being too heavily spotted, others not heavily enough. In evaluating such dogs, one must balance the over-all quality of the dog's conformation against that of his perhaps better marked competitors, with penalization scored according to the degree of deviation from ideal markings and their effect on the dog's *overall* quality, as other features of the dog are balanced against the overall quality of each competitor. In other words, let us never forget, in applying the standard to the dog, that it is the *total* dog we are scoring, not just any single feature.

The Dalmatian should be a sturdy dog, strong boned and muscular, but never "cloddy" in appearance. His refinement and well balanced head; strong and well arched neck; deep chest; and correctly carried tail *slightly* curved upwards give an elegant distinction to the breed. On the subject of tail, handlers should not *ever* hold it *straight upright*, but bear in mind the *"curved slightly upwards"* words of the standard.

Correct pigmentation in Dalmatians is of tremendous importance, and pink spotting on the eyerims or nose leather is definitely to be discouraged.

In examining for bite, the correct scissors bite is one in which the tips of the upper incisors just slightly overlap the tips of the lower incisors. An overshot bite (disqualification in the breed) is the condition where the upper incisors extend beyond the lower incisors, referred to by some people as a "fish mouth." An undershot bite, also a disqualification, refers to the condition when the lower jaw protrudes beyond the upper jaw. In evaluating young puppies, it should be noted that an overshot mouth in a puppy may correct as the puppy matures; an undershot jaw usually does not.

Monorchidism, cryptorchidism, blindness, and deafness are disqualifications under American Kennel Club rules, and such dogs must be dismissed from the ring. Also dogs which have been castrated or bitches which have been spayed are ineligible to compete in A.K.C. competition *excepting* in the Stud Dog Class and the Brood Bitch Class.

Special care in judging Dalmatians should be taken in checking for deafness, since this is a sometimes-problem in the breed.

Ch. Coachman's Circus Wonder with Jennifer Fetner.

Lot's 'n' Lots o'Polka Dots is Anne Nicholson's caption for this photo of some of her Dals relaxing together. These handsome fellows are from Short Acre Kennels, Greenwood Lake, N.Y.

Chapter 9

The Dalmatian as a Family Dog

Dalmatians make superb family companions, and are dogs to be owned with constant pleasure. This is a breed which will fit in nicely whatever your way of life, being medium in size, thus not too large for an apartment, while at the same time a true sporting dog at heart, therefore a superb addition to your country or suburban home.

One of the first things people consider nowadays in thinking of the purchase of a dog is whether or not said dog will make a watchdog. In the case of the Dalmatian, definitely *yes*. A very sensible and alert one, who is not an hysterical "yapper" and therefore a dog whose bark is to be respected—and investigated! If your Dalmatian sounds a "danger alarm," it is quite certain to be for a reason, such as the approach of a stranger. Dalmatians are not automatically everyone's friend. They greet visitors to your home with quiet dignity (they have frequently been referred to as "courteous" dogs by those familiar with their personalities), but at the same time with reserve. Their friendship is not automatic—it must be earned!

Classifying Dalmatians as Non-Sporting Dogs seems to us a bit misleading. For actually, as many have discovered, they are excellent bird dogs, have strong scent hound tendencies, and are efficient retrievers. Tough and soundly built, they are capable of many miles in "road work" (remember, they are the one and only true coach dog), and in early days were often used for herding duties. In other words, their talents are truly diversified.

In addition to being a wonderful companion, a Dalmatian is a most decorative dog to have around with his clean lines and spot-

A Dalmatian coaching under the axle in the traditional manner for the breed. This is Group winning Ch. Coachman's Cake Walk owned by Mr. and Mrs. William Fetner, Coachman Kennels, St. Louis, Mo.

Am. and Can. Ch. Coachman's Chocolate Soldier pictured with his pony friend. Owned by Canal-Side Stables and Kennels, Pauline and Helene Masaschi, Sandwich, Mass.

ted markings giving him a smart appearance and "eye appeal."

If you are a family who enjoys spending time doing things with your dog, this is a superb breed with which to work in obedience: keenly intelligent, thus quick to learn; anxious to please, thus sharing your pleasure in his performing well.

Should showing dogs interest you, again Dalmatians are a suitable choice of breed as they enjoy being in the dog show limelight (perhaps a throwback to their use as circus performers), and are seldom difficult to teach show routine. Also with their short coats they require a minimum amount of grooming.

If you have a budding Junior Showmanship enthusiast in the family, here again the Dalmatian is easily handled by a youngster, and a nice dog for one to manage.

Dalmatians are fond of children, sharing their games with enthusiasm. They are not quarrelsome with other animals, and if properly introduced to one another, there should be no problems.

A word of caution to you who may be about to purchase a Dalmatian puppy: there is a tendency towards deafness in the breed, one which reliable breeders are making every effort to correct within their breeding programs, and this is a fact of which one should be aware in selecting the new family member. It is therefore especially important that you purchase your Dalmatian from a *reputable Dalmatian breeder* who will be aware of and anxious to avoid for the new owner of the breed the heartache of becoming attached to a dog, then discovering the existence of a problem with hearing. When you shop for your dog, be alert for signs that it does not hear. Test for keenness of hearing by talking to the puppy, snapping your fingers, chirping at it from behind or off to the side, to make certain that you are being heard and reacted to properly. It is not difficult to ascertain that the puppy's hearing is normal, but be alert and watchful as you make your selection. I know of owners who have accomplished wonders with a dearly loved Dalmatian despite hearing problems, having taken the dog through obedience and taught it to respond to hand signals almost as effectively as some do to the sound of the master's voice! But one should never stumble into this situation unaware, which is why I call to the attention of our readers the possibility of deafness. To be forewarned is to be forearmed, and while you may actually never meet up with a deaf Dalmatian, we want you to realize that it *could* happen.

Chapter 10

The Purchase of Your Dalmatian

Careful consideration should be given to what breed of dog you wish to own prior to your purchase of one. If several breeds are attractive to you, and you are undecided as to which you prefer, learn all you can about the characteristics of each before making your decision. As you do so, you are thus preparing yourself to make an intelligent choice; and this is very important when buying a dog who will be, with reasonable luck, a member of your household for at least a dozen years or more. Obviously since you are reading this book, you have decided on the breed—so now all that remains is to make a good choice.

It is never wise to just rush out and buy the first cute puppy who catches your eye. Whether you wish a dog to show, one with whom to compete in obedience, or one as a family dog purely for his (or her) companionship, the more time and thought you invest as you plan the purchase, the more likely you are to meet with complete satisfaction. The background and early care behind your pet will reflect in the dog's future health and temperament. Even if you are planning the purchase purely as a pet, with no thoughts of showing or breeding in the dog's or puppy's future, it is essential that if the dog is to enjoy a trouble-free future you assure yourself of a healthy, properly raised puppy or adult from sturdy, well-bred stock.

Throughout the pages of this book you will find the names and locations of many well-known and well-established kennels in various areas. Another source of information is the American Kennel Club (51 Madison Avenue, New York, New York 10010) from whom you can obtain a list of recognized breeders in the vicinity of your home. If you plan to have your dog campaigned by a professional handler, by all means let the handler help you locate and select a good dog. Through their numerous clients, handlers have access to a variety of interesting show prospects; and the usual arrangement is that the handler re-sells the dog to you for what his cost has been, with the agreement that the dog be campaigned for you by him throughout the dog's career. It is most strongly recommended that prospective purchasers follow these suggestions, as you thus will be better able to locate and select a satisfactory puppy or dog.

Your first step in searching for your puppy is to make appointments at kennels specializing in the chosen breed, where you can visit and inspect the dogs, both those available for sale and the kennel's basic breeding stock. You are looking for an active, sturdy puppy with bright eyes and intelligent expression and who is friendly and alert; avoid puppies who are hyperactive, dull, or listless. The coat should be clean and thick, with no sign of parasites. The premises on which he was raised should look (and smell) clean and be tidy, making it obvious that the puppies and their surroundings are in capable hands. Should the kennels featuring the breed you intend owning be sparse in your area or not have what you consider attractive, do not hesitate to contact others at a distance and purchase from them if they seem better able to supply a puppy or dog who will please you *so long as it is a recognized breeding kennel of that breed.* Shipping dogs is a regular practice nowadays, with comparatively few problems when one considers the number of dogs shipped each year. A reputable, well-known breeder wants the customer to be satisfied; thus he will represent the puppy fairly. Should you not be pleased with the puppy upon arrival, a breeder such as described will almost certainly permit its return. A conscientious breeder takes real interest and concern in the welfare of the dogs he or she causes to be brought into the world. Such a breeder also is proud of a reputation for integrity. Thus on two counts, for the sake of the dog's future and the breeder's reputation, to such a person a *satisfied* customer takes precedence over a sale at any cost.

If your puppy is to be a pet or "family dog," the earlier the age at which it joins your household the better. Puppies are weaned and ready to start out on their own, under the care of a sensible new owner, at about six weeks old; and if you take a young one, it is often easier to train it to the routine of your household and to your requirements of it than is the case with an older dog which, even though still a puppy technically, may have already started habits you will find difficult to change. The younger puppy is usually less costly, too, as it stands to reason the breeder will not have as much expense invested in it. Obviously, a puppy that has been raised to five or six months old represents more in care and cash expenditure on the breeder's part than one sold earlier and therefore should be and generally is priced accordingly.

There is an enormous amount of truth in the statement that "bargain" puppies seldom turn out to be that. A "cheap" puppy, cheaply raised purely for sale and profit, can and often does lead to great heartbreak including problems and veterinarian's bills which can add up to many times the initial cost of a properly reared dog. On the other hand, just because a puppy is expensive does not assure one that is healthy and well reared. There have been numerous cases where unscrupulous dealers have sold for several hundred dollars puppies that were sickly, in poor condition, and such poor specimens that the breed of which they were supposedly members was barely recognizable. So one cannot always judge a puppy by price alone. Common sense must guide a prospective purchaser, plus the selection of a *reliable*, well-recommended dealer whom you know to have well satisfied customers or, best of all, a specialized breeder. You will probably find the fairest pricing at the kennel of a breeder. Such a person, experienced with the breed in general and with his or her own stock in particular, through extensive association with these dogs has watched enough of them mature to have obviously learned to assess quite accurately each puppy's potential—something impossible where such background is non-existent.

One more word on the subject of pets. Bitches make a fine choice for this purpose as they are usually quieter and more gentle than the males, easier to house train, more affectionate, and less inclined to roam. If you do select a bitch and have no intention of breeding or showing her, by all means have her spayed, for your sake and for hers. The advantages to the owner of a spayed bitch include avoiding the nuisance of "in season" periods which normally occur twice yearly, with the accompanying eager canine swains haunting your premises in an effort to get close to your female, plus the unavoidable messiness and spotting of furniture and rugs at this time, which can be annoying if she is a household companion in the habit of sharing your sofa or bed. As for the spayed bitch, she benefits as she grows older because this simple operation almost entirely eliminates the possibility of breast cancer ever occurring. It is recommended that all bitches eventually be spayed—even those used for show or breeding when their careers have ended—in order that they may enjoy a happier, healthier old age. Please take note, however, that a bitch who has been spayed (or an altered dog) *cannot be shown at American Kennel Club dog shows once this operation has been performed.* Be certain that you are *not* interested in showing her before taking this step.

Also, in selecting a pet, never underestimate the advantages of an older dog, perhaps a retired show dog or a bitch no longer needed for breeding, who may be available quite reasonably priced by a breeder anxious to place such a dog in a loving home. These dogs are settled and can be a delight to own, as they make wonderful companions, especially in a household of adults where raising a puppy can sometimes be a trial.

Everything that has been said about careful selection of your pet puppy and its place of purchase applies, but with many further considerations, when you plan to buy a show dog or foundation stock for a future breeding program. Now is the time for an in-depth study of the breed, starting with every word and every illustration in this book and all others you can find written on the subject. The Standard of the breed now has become your guide, and you must learn not only the words but also how to interpret them and how they are applicable in actual dogs before you are ready to make an intelligent selection of a show dog.

If you are thinking in terms of a dog to show, obviously you must have learned about dog shows and must be in the habit of attending them. This is fine, but now your activity in this direction should be increased, with your attending every single dog show within a reasonable distance from your home. Much can be learned about a breed at ringside at these events. Talk with the breeders who are exhibiting. Study the dogs they are showing. Watch the judging with concentration, noting each decision made, and attempt to follow the reasoning by which the judge has reached it. Note carefully the attributes of the dogs who win and, for your later use, the manner in which each is presented. Close your ears to the ringside know-it-alls, usually novice owners of only a dog or two and very new to the Fancy, who have only derogatory remarks to make about all that is taking place unless they happen to win. This is the type of exhibitor who "comes and goes" through the Fancy and whose interest is usually of very short duration owing to lack of knowledge and dissatisfaction caused by the failure to recognize the need to learn. You, as a fancier it is hoped will last and enjoy our sport over many future years, should develop independent thinking at this stage; you should learn to draw your own conclusions about the merits, or lack of them, seen before you in the ring and, thus, sharpen your own judgement in preparation for choosing wisely and well.

Note carefully which breeders campaign winning dogs, not just an occasional isolated good one but consistent, homebred winners. It is from one of these people that you should select your own future "star."

If you are located in an area where dog shows take place only occasionally or where there are long travel distances involved, you will need to find another testing ground for your ability to select a worthy show dog. Possibly, there are some representative kennels raising this breed within a reasonable distance. If so, by all means ask permission of the owners to visit the kennels and do so when permission is granted. You may not necessarily buy then and there, as they may not have available what you are seeking that very day, but you will be able to see the type of dog being raised there and to discuss the dogs with the breeder. Every time you do this, you add to your knowledge. Should one of these kennels have dogs which especially appeal to you, perhaps you could reserve a show-prospect puppy from a coming litter. This is frequently done, and it is often worth waiting for a puppy, unless you have seen a dog with which you truly are greatly impressed and which is immediately available.

The purchase of a puppy has already been discussed. Obviously this same approach applies in a far greater degree when the purchase involved is a future show dog. The only place at which to purchase a show prospect is from a breeder who raises show-type stock; otherwise, you are almost certainly doomed to disappointment as the puppy matures. Show and breeding kennels obviously cannot keep all of their fine young stock. An active breeder-exhibitor is, therefore, happy to place promising youngsters in the

Dymondee Dalmatian puppies playing with riding hat and boots. Owned by Mr. and Mrs. C.F. Lester, Jr., Itasca, Ill.

hands of people also interested in showing and winning with them, doing so at a fair price according to the quality and prospects of the dog involved. Here again, if no kennel in your immediate area has what you are seeking, do not hesitate to contact top breeders in other areas and to buy at long distance. Ask for pictures, pedigrees, and a complete description. Heed the breeder's advice and recommendations, after truthfully telling exactly what your expectations are for the dog you purchase. Do you want something with which to win just a few ribbons now and then? Do you want a dog who can complete his championship? Are you thinking of the real "big time" (*i.e.*, seriously campaigning with Best of Breed, Group wins, and possibly even Best in Show as your eventual goal)? Consider it all carefully in advance; then hon-

231

estly discuss your plans with the breeder. You will be better satisfied with the results if you do this, as the breeder is then in the best position to help you choose the dog who is most likely to come through for you. A breeder selling a show dog is just as anxious as the buyer for the dog to succeed, and the breeder will represent the dog to you with truth and honesty. Also, this type of breeder does not lose interest the moment the sale has been made but when necessary will be right there ready to assist you with beneficial advice and suggestions based on years of experience.

As you make inquiries of at least several kennels, keep in mind that show-prospect puppies are less expensive than mature show dogs, the latter often costing close to four figures, and sometimes more. The reason for this is that, with a puppy, there is always an element of chance, the possibility of its developing unexpected faults as it matures or failing to develop the excellence and quality that earlier had seemed probable. There definitely is a risk factor in buying a show- prospect puppy. Sometimes all goes well, but occasionally the swan becomes an ugly duckling. Reflect on this as you consider available puppies and young adults. It just might be a good idea to go with a more mature, though more costly, dog if one you like is available.

When you buy a mature show dog, "what you see is what you get," and it is not likely to change beyond coat and condition which are dependent on your care. Also advantageous for a novice owner is the fact that a mature dog of show quality almost certainly will have received show-ring training and probably match-show experience, which will make your earliest handling ventures far easier.

Frequently it is possible to purchase a beautiful dog who has completed championship but who, owing to similarity in bloodlines, is not needed for the breeder's future program. Here you have the opportunity of owning a champion, usually in the two-to-five-year-old range, which you can enjoy campaigning as a special (for Best of Breed competition) and which will be a settled, handsome dog for you and your family to enjoy with pride.

If you are planning foundation for a future kennel, concentrate on acquiring one or two really superior bitches. These need not necessarily be top show-quality, but they should represent your breed's finest producing bloodlines from a strain noted for producing quality, generation after generation. A proven matron who

232

is already the dam of show-type puppies is, of course, the ideal selection; but these are usually difficult to obtain, no one being anxious to part with so valuable an asset. You just might strike it lucky, though, in which case you are off to a flying start. If you cannot find such a matron available, select a young bitch of finest background from top-producing lines who is herself of decent type, free of obvious faults, and of good quality.

Great attention should be paid to the pedigree of the bitch from whom you intend to breed. If not already known to you, try to see the sire and dam. It is generally agreed that someone starting with a breed should concentrate on a fine collection of topflight bitches and raise a few litters from these before considering keeping one's own stud dog. The practice of buying a stud and then breeding everything you own or acquire to that dog does not always work out well. It is better to take advantage of the many noted sires who are available to be used at stud, who represent all of the leading strains, and in each case to carefully select the one who in type and pedigree seems most compatible to each of your bitches, at least for your first several litters.

To summarize, if you want a "family dog" as a companion, it is best to buy it young and raise it according to the habits of your household. If you are buying a show dog, the more mature it is, the more certain you can be of its future beauty. If you are buying foundation stock for a kennel, then bitches are better, but they must be from the finest *producing* bloodlines.

When you buy a pure-bred dog that you are told is eligible for registration with the American Kennel Club, you are entitled to receive from the seller an application form which will enable you to register your dog. If the seller cannot give you the application form you should demand and receive an identification of your dog consisting of the name of the breed, the registered names and numbers of the sire and dam, the name of the breeder, and your dog's date of birth. If the litter of which your dog is a part is already recorded with the American Kennel Club, then the litter number is sufficient identification.

Do not be misled by promises of papers at some later date. Demand a registration application form or proper identification as described above. If neither is supplied, do not buy the dog. So warns the American Kennel Club, and this is especially important in the purchase of show or breeding stock.

Chapter 11

The Care of Your Dalmatian

The moment you decide to be the new owner of a puppy is not one second too soon to start planning for the puppy's arrival in your home. Both the new family member and you will find the transition period easier if your home is geared in advance of the arrival.

The first things to be prepared are a bed for the puppy and a place where you can pen him up for rest periods. Every dog should have a crate of its own from the very beginning, so that he will come to know and love it as his special place where he is safe and happy. It is an ideal arrangement, for when you want him to be free, the crate stays open. At other times you can securely latch it and know that the pup is safely out of mischief. If you travel with him, his crate comes along in the car; and, of course, in traveling by plane there is no alternative but to have a carrier for the dog. If you show your dog, you will want him upon occasion to be in a crate a good deal of the day. So from every consideration, a crate is a very sensible and sound investment in your puppy's future safety and happiness and for your own peace of mind.

The crates most desirable are the wooden ones with removable side panels, which are ideal for cold weather (with the panels in place to keep out drafts) and in hot weather (with the panels removed to allow better air circulation). Wire crates are all right in the summer, but they give no protection from cold or drafts. Aluminum crates, due to the manner in which the metal reflects surrounding temperatures, are not recommended. If it is cold, so is the metal of the crate; if it is hot, the crate becomes burning hot.

When you choose the puppy's crate, be certain that it is roomy enough not to become outgrown. The crate should have sufficient height so the dog can stand up in it as a mature dog and sufficient area so that he can stretch out full length when relaxed. When the puppy is young, first give him shredded newspaper as a bed; the papers can be replaced with a mat or turkish towels when the dog is older. Carpet remnants are great for the bottom of the crate, as they are inexpensive and in case of accidents can be quite easily replaced. As the dog matures and is past the chewing age, a pillow or blanket in the crate is an appreciated comfort.

Sharing importance with the crate is a safe area in which the puppy can exercise and play. If you are an apartment dweller, a baby's playpen for a young puppy works out well; for an older puppy use a portable exercise pen which you can use later when traveling with your dog or for dog shows. If you have a yard, an area where he can be outside in safety should be fenced in prior to the dog's arrival at your home. This area does not need to be huge, but it does need to be made safe and secure. If you are in a suburban area where there are close neighbors, stockade fencing works out best as then the neighbors are less aware of the dog and the dog cannot see and bark at everything passing by. If you are out in the country where no problems with neighbors are likely to occur, then regular chain-link fencing is fine. For added precaution in both cases, use a row of concrete blocks or railroad ties inside against the entire bottom of the fence; this precludes or at least considerably lessens the chances of your dog digging his way out.

Be advised that if yours is a single dog, it is very unlikely that it will get sufficient exercise just sitting in the fenced area, which is what most of them do when they are there alone. Two or more dogs will play and move themselves around, but one by itself does little more than make a leisurely tour once around the area to check things over and then lie down. You must include a daily walk or two in your plans if your puppy is to be rugged and well. Exercise is extremely important to a puppy's muscular development and to keep a mature dog fit and trim. So make sure that those exercise periods, or walks, a game of ball, and other such activities, are part of your daily program as a dog owner.

If your fenced area has an outside gate, provide a padlock and key and a strong fastening for it, and use them, so that the gate cannot be opened by others and the dog taken or turned free. The ultimate convenience in this regard is, of course, a door (unused for other purposes) from the house around which the fenced area can be enclosed, so that all you have to do is open the door and out into his area he goes. This arrangement is safest of all, as then you need not be using a gate, and it is easier in bad weather since then you can send the dog out without taking him and becoming soaked yourself at the same time. This is not always possible to manage, but if your house is arranged so that you could do it this way, you would never regret it due to the convenience and added safety thus provided. Fencing in the entire yard, with gates to be opened and closed whenever a caller, deliveryman, postman, or some other person comes on your property, really is not safe at all because people not used to gates and their importance are frequently careless about closing and latching gates *securely*. Many heartbreaking incidents have been brought about by someone carelessly only half closing a gate which the owner had thought to be firmly latched and the dog wandering out. For greatest security a fenced *area* definitely takes precedence over a fenced *yard*.

The puppy will need a collar (one that fits now, not one to be grown into) and lead from the moment you bring him home. Both should be an appropriate weight and type for his size. Also needed are a feeding dish and a water dish, both made preferably of unbreakable material. Your pet supply shop should have an interesting assortment of these and other accessories from which you can choose. Then you will need grooming tools of the type the breeder recommends and some toys. One of the best toys is a beef bone, either rib, leg, or knuckle (the latter type you can purchase to make soup), cut to an appropriate size for your puppy dog. These are absolutely safe and are great exercise for the teething period, helping to get the baby teeth quickly out of the way with no problems. Equally satisfactory is Nylabone®, a nylon bone that does not chip or splinter and that "frizzles" as the puppy chews, providing healthful gum massage. Rawhide chews are safe, too, *if made in the United States*. There was a problem a few years back, owing to the chemicals with which some foreign rawhide toys had been treated. Also avoid plastics and any sort of rubber toys, *particularly those with squeakers* which the puppy may remove and swallow. If you want a ball for the puppy to use when playing with him, select one of very hard construction made for this pur-

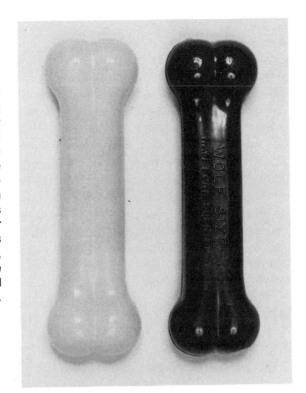

Your Dalmatian's craving for chewing can be satisfied by giving him Nylabones.® In addition to the traditional bone-shaped type shown here, Nylabones come in other shapes as well as (rings, knots, balls, etc.). You also have a choice of sizes and flavors.

pose and do not leave it alone with him because he may chew off and swallow bits of the rubber. Take the ball with you when the game is over. This also applies to some of those "tug of war" type rubber toys which are fun when used with the two of you for that purpose but again should *not* be left behind for the dog to work on with his teeth. Bits of swallowed rubber, squeakers, and other such foreign articles can wreak great havoc in the intestinal tract—do all you can to guard against them.

Too many changes all at once can be difficult for a puppy. For at least the first few days he is with you, keep him on the food and feeding schedule to which he is accustomed. Find out ahead of time from the breeder what he feeds his puppies, how frequently, and at what times of the day. Also find out what, if any, food supplements the breeder has been using and recommends. Then be prepared by getting in a supply of the same food so that you will have it there when you bring the puppy home. Once the puppy is accustomed to his new surroundings, then you can switch the type of food and schedule to fit your convenience, but for the first several days do it as the puppy expects.

Your selection of a veterinarian also should be attended to before the puppy comes home, because you should stop at the vet's office for the puppy to be checked over as soon as you leave the breeder's premises. If the breeder is from your area, ask him for recommendations. Ask you dog-owning friends for their opinions of the local veterinarians, and see what their experiences with those available have been. Choose someone whom several of your friends recommend highly, then contact him about your puppy, perhaps making an appointment to stop in at his office. If the premises are clean, modern, and well equipped, and if you like the veterinarian, make an appointment to bring the puppy in on the day of purchase. Be sure to obtain the puppy's health record from the breeder, including information on such things as shots and worming that the puppy has had.

JOINING THE FAMILY

Remember that, exciting and happy an occasion as it is for you, the puppy's move from his place of birth to your home can be, for him, a traumatic experience. His mother and littermates will be missed. He quite likely will be awed or frightened by the change of surroundings. the person on whom he depended will be gone. Everything should be planned to make his arrival at your home pleasant—to give him confidence and to help him realize that yours is a pretty nice place to be after all.

Never bring a puppy home on a holiday. There just is too much going on with people and gifts and excitement. If he is in honor of an "occasion," work it out so that his arrival will be a few days earlier, or perhaps even better, a few days later than the "occasion." Then your home will be back to it normal routine and the puppy can enjoy your undivided attention. Try not to bring the puppy home in the evening. Early morning is the ideal time, as then he has the opportunity of getting acquainted and the initial strangeness should wear off before bedtime. You will find it a more peaceful night that way. Allow the puppy to investigate as he likes, under your watchful eye. If you already have a pet in the household, keep a careful watch that the relationship between the two gets off to a friendly start or you may quickly find yourself with a lasting problem. Much of the future attitude of each toward the other will depend on what takes place that first day, so keep your mind on what they are doing and let your other activities

238

Ch. Dalquest Rhythm of Dalmatia, a great show and producing bitch who was the dam of Ch. Boot Black of Dalmatia. Wendell J. Sammet, owner, Dalmatia Kennels, Bryantville, Mass.

slide for the moment. Be careful not to let your older pet become jealous by paying more attention to the puppy than to him, as that will start a bad situation immediately.

If you have a child, here again it is important that the relationship start out well. Before the puppy is brought home, you should have a talk with the youngster about puppies so that it will be clearly understood that puppies are fragile and can easily be injured; therefore, they should not be teased, hurt, mauled, or overly rough-housed. A puppy is not an inanimate toy; it is a living thing with a right to be loved and handled respectfully, treatment which will reflect in the dog's attitude toward your child as both mature together. Never permit your children's playmates to mishandle the puppy, tormenting the puppy until it turns on the children in self-defense. Children often do not realize how rough is too rough. You, as a responsible adult, are obligated to assure that your puppy's relationship with children is a pleasant one.

Do not start out by spoiling your puppy. A puppy is usually pretty smart and can be quite demanding. What you had considered to be "just for tonight" may be accepted by the puppy as "for keeps." Be firm with him, strike a routine, and stick to it. The puppy will learn more quickly this way, and everyone will be happier at the result. A radio playing softly or a dim night light are often comforting to a puppy as it gets accustomed to new surroundings and should be provided in preference to bring the puppy to bed with you—unless, of course, you intend him to share the bed as a permanent arrangement.

SOCIALIZING AND TRAINING

Socialization and training of your puppy should start the very day of his arrival in your home. Never address him without calling him by name. A short, simple name is the easiest to teach as it catches the dog's attention quickly, so avoid elaborate call names. Always address the dog by the same name, not a whole series of pet names; the latter will only confuse the puppy.

Use his name clearly, and call the puppy over to you when you see him awake and wandering about. When he comes, make a big fuss over him for being such a good dog. He thus will quickly associate the sound of his name with coming to you and a pleasant happening.

Several hours after the puppy's arrival is not too soon to start accustoming him to the feel of a light collar. He may hardly notice it; or he may struggle, roll over, and try to rub it off his neck with his paws. Divert his attention when this occurs by offering a tasty snack or a toy (starting a game with him) or by petting him. Before long he will have accepted the strange feeling around his neck and no longer appear aware of it. Next comes the lead. Attach it and then immediately take the puppy outside or otherwise try to divert his attention with things to see and sniff. He may struggle against the lead at first, biting at it and trying to free himself. Do not pull him with it at this point; just hold the end loosely and try to follow him if he starts off in any direction. Normally his attention will soon turn to investigating his sourroundings if he is outside or you have taken him into an unfamiliar room in your house; curiosity will take over and he will become interested in sniffing around the surroundings. Just follow him with the lead slackly held until he seems to have completely forgotten about it; then try

Note the classic head on Coachman's Crazy Jacks, age eight months, current young hopeful owned by the Fetners, Coachman Kennels, already a Group winner at a large all-breed match the first time shown.

with gentle urging to get him to follow you. Don't be rough or jerk at him; just tug gently on the lead in short quick motions (steady pulling can become a battle of wills), repeating his name or trying to get him to follow your hand which is holding a bite of food or an interesting toy. If you have an older lead-trained dog, then it should be a cinch to get the puppy to follow along after *him*. In any event the average puppy learns quite quickly and will soon be trotting along nicely on the lead. Once that point has been reached, the next step is to teach him to follow on your left side, or heel. Of course this will not likely be accomplished all in one day but should be done with short training periods over the course of several days until you are satisfied with the result.

During the course of house training your puppy, you will need to take him out frequently and at regular intervals: first thing in the morning directly from the crate, immediately after meals, after the puppy has been napping, or when you notice that the puppy is looking for a spot. Choose more or less the same place to take the puppy each time so that a pattern will be established. If he does not go immediately, do not return him to the house as he will probably relieve himself the moment he is inside. Stay out with him until he has finished; then be lavish with your praise for his good behavior. If you catch the puppy having an accident indoors, grab him firmly and rush him outside, sharply saying "No!" as you pick him up. If you do not see the accident occur, there is little point in doing anything except cleaning it up, as once it has happened and been forgotton, the puppy will most likely not even realize why you are scolding him.

Especially if you live in a big city or are away many hours at a time, having a dog that is trained to go on paper has some very definite advantages. To do this, one proceeds pretty much the same way as taking the puppy outdoors, except now you place the puppy on the newspaper at the proper time. The paper should always be kept in the same spot. An easy way to paper train a puppy if you have a playpen for it or an exercise pen is to line the area with newspapers; then gradually, every day or so, remove a section of newspaper until you are down to just one or two. The puppy acquires the habit of using the paper; and as the prepared area grows smaller, in the majority of cases the dog will continue to use whatever paper is still available. It is pleasant, if the dog is along for an excessive length of time, to be able to feel that if he needs it the paper is there and will be used.

The puppy should form the habit of spending a certain amount of time in his crate, even when you are home. Sometimes the puppy will do this voluntarily, but if not, he should be taught to do so, which is accomplished by leading the puppy over by his collar, gently pushing him inside, and saying firmly, "Down" or "Stay." Whatever expression you use to give a command, stick to the very same one each time for each act. Repetition is the big thing in training—and so is association with what the dog is expected to do. When you mean "Sit" always say exactly that. "Stay" should mean *only* that the dog should remain where he receives the command. "Down" means something else again. Do

Salimar's Napoleon, C.D., Can. C.D.X. was purchased, trained, and put through to his obedience degrees by Michael T. Manning, M.D. while Dr. Manning was attending medical school. One of the earliest of the Cavalier Dalmatians, Staten Island, N.Y.

not confuse the dog by shuffling the commands, as this will create training problems for you.

As soon as he had had his immunization shots, take your puppy with you whenever and wherever possible. There is nothing that will build a self-confident, stable dog like socialization, and it is extremely important that you plan and give the time and energy necessary for this whether your dog is to be a show dog or a pleasant, well-adjusted family member. Take your puppy in the car so that he will learn to enjoy riding and not become carsick as dogs may do if they are infrequent travelers. Take him anywhere you are going where you are certain he will be welcome: visiting friends and relative (if they do not have housepets who may resent the visit), busy shopping centers (keeping him always on lead), or just walking around the streets of your town. If someone admires him (as always seems to happen when one is out with puppies), encourage the stranger to pet and talk with him. Socialization of this type brings out the best in your puppy and helps him to grow up with a friendly outlook, liking the world and its inhabitants. The worst thing that can be done to a puppy's personality is to overly shelter him. By always keeping him at home away from things and people unfamiliar to him you may be creating a personality problem for the mature dog that will be a cross for you to bear later on.

FEEDING YOUR DOG

Time was when providing nourishing food for dogs involved a far more complicated procedure than people now feel is necessary. The old school of thought was that the daily ration must consist of fresh beef, vegetables, cereal, egg yolks, and cottage cheese as basics with such additions as brewer's yeast and vitamin tablets on a daily basis.

During recent years, however, many minds have changed regarding this procedure. Eggs, cottage cheese, and supplements to the diet are still given, but the basic method of feeding dogs has changed; and the change has been, in the opinion of many authorities, definitely for the better. The school of thought now is that you are doing your dogs a favor when you feed them some of the fine commerically prepared dog foods in preference to your own home-cooked concoctions.

The reason behind this new outlook is easily understandable. The dog food industry has grown to be a major one, participated in by some of the best known and most respected names in America. These trusted firms, it is agreed, turn out excellent products, so people are feeding their dog food preparations with confidence and the dogs are thriving, living longer, happier, and healthier lives than ever before. What more could one want?

There are at least half a dozen absolutely top-grade dry foods to be mixed with broth or water and served to your dog according to directions. There are all sorts of canned meats, and there are several kinds of "convenience foods," those in a packet which you open and dump out into the dog's dish. It is just that simple. The convenience foods are neat and easy to use when you are away from home, but generally speaking a dry food mixed with hot water or soup and meat is preferred. It is the opinion of many that the canned meat, with its added fortifiers, is more beneficial to the dogs than the fresh meat. However, the two can be alternated or, if you prefer and your dog does well on it, by all means use fresh ground beef. A dog enjoys changes in the meat part of his diet, which is easy with the canned food since all sorts of beef are available (chunk, ground, stewed, and so on), plus lamb, chicken, and even such concoctions as liver and egg, just plain liver flavor, and a blend of five meats.

There is also prepared food geared to every age bracket of your dog's life, from puppyhood on through old age, with special additions or modifications to make it particularly nourishing and beneficial. Previous generations never had it so good where the canine dinner is concerned, because these commercially prepared foods are tasty and geared to meeting the dog's gastronomic approval.

Additionally, contents and nutrients are clearly listed on the labels, as are careful instructions for feeding just the right amount for the size, weight, and age of each dog.

With these foods the addition of extra vitamins is not necessary, but if you prefer there are several kinds of those, too, that serve as taste treats as well as being beneficial. Your pet supplier has a full array of them.

Of course there is no reason not to cook up something for your dog if you would feel happier doing so. But it seems unnecessary when such truly satisfactory rations are available with so much less trouble and expense.

How often you feed your dog is a matter of how it works out best for you. Many owners prefer to do it once a day. It is generally agreed that two meals, each of smaller quantity, are better for the digestion and more satisfying to the dog, particularly if yours is a household member who stands around and watches preparations for the family meals. Do not overfeed. This is the shortest route to all sorts of problems. Follow directions and note carefully how your dog is looking. If your dog is overweight, cut back the quantity of food a bit. If the dog looks thin, then increase the amount. Each dog is an individual and the food intake should be adjusted to his requirements to keep him feeling and looking trim and in top condition.

From the time puppies are fully weaned until they are about twelve weeks old, they should be fed four times daily. From three months to six months of age, three meals should suffice. At six months of age the puppies can be fed two meals, and the twice daily feedings can be continued until the puppies are close to one year old, at which time feeding can be changed to once daily if desired. If you do feed just once a day, do so by early afternoon at the latest and give the dog a snack, a biscuit or two, at bedtime.

Remember that plenty of fresh water should always be available to your puppy or dog for drinking. This is of utmost importance to his health.

Chapter 12

The Making of a Show Dog

If you have decided to become a show dog exhibitor, you have accepted a very real and very exciting challenge. The groundwork has been accomplished with the selection of your future show prospect. If you have purchased a puppy, it is assumed that you have gone through all the proper preliminaries concerning good care, which should be the same if the puppy is a pet or future show dog with a few added precautions for the latter.

GENERAL CONSIDERATIONS

Remember the importance of keeping your future winner in trim, top condition. Since you want him neither too fat nor too thin, his appetite for his proper diet should be guarded, and children and guests should not be permitted to constantly feed him "goodies." The best treat of all is a small wad of raw ground beef or a packaged dog treat. To be avoided are ice cream, cake, cookies, potato chips, and other fattening items which will cause the dog to put on weight and may additionally spoil his appetite for the proper, nourishing, well-balanced diet so essential to good health and condition.

The importance of temperament and showmanship cannot possibly be overestimated. They have put many a mediocre dog across while lack of them can ruin the career of an otherwise outstanding specimen. From the day your dog joins your family, socialize him. Keep him accustomed to being with people and to being handled by people. Encourage your friends and relatives to "go over" him as the judges will in the ring so this will not seem a

Ch. Coachman's Hot Coffee, handled by Mrs. William Fetner, at Westminster in 1982 where she won the breed. Now owned by Canal-Side Stables and Kennels, Pauline and Helene Masaschi, Sandwich, Mass. Bred by John and Sharon Lyons.

strange and upsetting experience. Practice showing his "bite" (the manner in which his teeth meet) quickly and deftly. It is quite simple to slip the lips apart with your fingers, and the puppy should be willing to accept this from you or the judge without struggle. This is also true of further mouth examination when necessary. When missing teeth must be noted, again, teach the dog to permit his jaws to be opened wide and his side lips separated as judges will need to check them one or both of these ways.

Some judges prefer that the exhibitors display the dog's bite and other mouth features themselves. These are the considerate ones, who do not wish to chance the spreading of possible infection from dog to dog with their hands on each one's mouth—a courtesy particularly appreciated in these days of virus epidemics. But the old-fashioned judges still insist in doing it themselves, so the dog should be ready for either possibility.

Take your future show dog with you in the car, thus accustoming him to riding so that he will not become carsick on the day of a dog show. He should associate pleasure and attention with going in the car, van, or motor home. Take him where it is crowded: downtown, to the shops, everywhere you go that dogs are permitted. Make the expeditions fun for him by frequent petting and words of praise; do not just ignore him as you go about your errands.

Do not overly shelter your future show dog. Instinctively you may want to keep him at home where he is safe from germs or danger. This can be foolish on two counts. The first reason is that a puppy kept away from other dogs builds up no natural immunity against all the things with which he will come in contact at dog shows, so it is wiser actually to keep him well up to date on all protective shots and then let him become accustomed to being among dogs and dog owners. Also, a dog who never is among strange people, in strange places, or among strange dogs, may grow up with a shyness or timidity of spirit that will cause you real problems as his show career draws near.

Keep your show prospect's coat in immaculate condition with frequent grooming and daily brushing. When bathing is necessary, use a mild dog shampoo or whatever the breeder of your puppy may suggest. Several of the brand-name products do an excellent job. Be sure to rinse thoroughly so as not to risk skin irritation by traces of soap left behind and protect against soap entering the eyes by a drop of castor oil in each before you lather up. Use warm water (be sure it is not uncomfortably hot or chillingly cold) and a good spray. Make certain you allow your dog to dry thoroughly in a warm, draft-free area (or outdoors, if it is warm and sunny) so that he doesn't catch cold. Then proceed to groom him to perfection.

Toenails should be watched and trimmed every few weeks. It is important not to permit nails to grow excessively long, as they will ruin the appearance of both the feet and pasterns.

A show dog's teeth must be kept clean and free of tartar. Hard dog biscuits can help toward this, but if tartar accumulates, see that it is removed promptly by your veterinarian. Bones for chewing are not suitable for show dogs as they tend to damage and wear down the tooth enamel.

Assuming that you will be handling the dog yourself, or even if he will be professionally handled, a few moments each day of dog show routine is important. Practice setting him up as you have seen the exhibitors do at the shows you've attended, and teach him to hold this position once you have him stacked to your satisfaction. Make the learning period pleasant by being firm but lavish in your praise when he responds correctly. Teach him to gait at your side at a moderate rate on a loose lead. When you have mastered the basic essentials at home, then hunt out and join a training class for future work. Training classes are sponsored by show-giving clubs in many areas, and their popularity is steadily increasing. If you have no other way of locating one, perhaps your veterinarian would know of one through some of his other clients; but if you are sufficiently aware of the dog show world to want a show dog, you will probably be personally acquainted with other people who will share information of this type with you.

Accustom your show dog to being in a crate (which you should be doing with a pet dog as well). He should relax in his crate at the shows "between times" for his own well being and safety.

MATCH SHOWS

Your show dog's initial experience in the ring should be in match show competition for several reasons. First, this type of event is intended as a learning experience for both the dog and the exhibitor. You will not feel embarrassed or out of place no matter how poorly your puppy may behave or how inept your attempts at handling may be, as you will find others there with the same type of problems. The important thing is that you get the puppy out and into a show ring where the two of you can practice together and learn the ropes.

Only on rare occasions is it necessary to make match show entries in advance, and even those with a pre-entry policy will usually accept entries at the door as well. Thus you need not plan several weeks ahead, as is the case with point shows, but can go when the mood strikes you. Also there is a vast difference in the cost, as match show entries only cost a few dollars while entry fees for the point shows may be over ten dollars, an amount none of us needs to waste until we have some idea of how the puppy will behave or how much more pre-show training is needed.

Match shows very frequently are judged by professional handlers who, in addition to making the awards, are happy to help new exhibitors with comments and advice on their puppies and their presentation of them. Avail yourself of all these opportunities before heading out to the sophisticated world of the point shows.

POINT SHOWS

As previously mentioned, entries for American Kennel Club point shows must be made in advance. This must be done on an official entry blank of the show-giving club. The entry must then

Am. and Can. Ch. Coachmaster's Ringmaster, black and white, by Ch. Coachmaster's Impressario ex Coachmaster's Black Buttons. Owned by Pauline and Helene Masaschi, Sandwich, Mass.

Am. and Can. Ch. Boot Black From Dalmatia, born Feb. 9, 1951, by Ch. Colonel Bones ex Ch. Dalquest Rhythm of Dalmatia, another of Wendell J. Sammet's outstanding homebred Dalmatian winners.

Ch. Green Starr's Major Hoolihan winning the Chicagoland Dalmatian Club 25th Anniversary Specialty Show in an entry of 140. Owner-handled by Linda Hazen Lewiṅ. Bred by Mr. and Mrs. David G. Doane. By Ch. Green Starr's Colonel Joe ex Williamsview Majorette. Born March 16, 1981.

Headstudies of two important Dalmatians. On the *left* is Ch. Melody Up Up and Away, C.D. (Pooka), the dam of 15 champions; on the *right,* Ch. Melody Crimson and Clover C.D. (Clover), the dam of eight champions. These two sisters were eight and a half years old in this photo, about to be bred for their last litters. Clover is gone now, but Pooka is well and happy at 13½ years old. Melody Kennels, Jack and Beth White.

be filed either personally or by mail with the show superintendent or the show secretary (if the event is being run by the club members alone and a superintendent has not been hired, this information will appear on the premium list) in time to reach its destination prior to the published closing date or filling of the quota. These entries must be made carefully, must be signed by the owner of the dog or the owner's agent (your professional handler), and must be accompanied by the entry fee; otherwise they will not be accepted. Remember that it is not when the entry leaves your hands that counts but the date of arrival at its destination. If you are relying on the mails, which are not always dependable, get the entry off well before the deadline to avoid disappointment.

A dog must be entered at a dog show in the name of the actual owner at the time of the entry closing date of that specific show. If a registered dog has been acquired by a new owner, it must be entered in the name of the new owner in any show for which entries close after the date of acquirement, regardless of whether the new owner has or has not actually received the registration certificate indicating that the dog is recorded in his name. State on the entry form whether or not transfer application has been mailed to the American Kennel Club, and it goes without saying that the latter should be attended to promptly when you purchase a registered dog.

In filling out your entry blank, type, print, or write clearly, paying particular attention to the spelling of names, correct registration numbers, and so on. Also, if there is more than one variety in your breed, be sure to indicate into which category your dog is being entered.

The Puppy Class is for dogs or bitches who are six months of age and under twelve months, were whelped in the United States, and are not champions. The age of a dog shall be calculated up to and inclusive of the first day of a show. For example, the first day a dog whelped on January 1st is eligible to compete in a Puppy Class at a show is July 1st of the same year; and he may continue to compete in Puppy Classes up to and including a show on December 31st of the same year, but he is *not* eligible to compete in a Puppy Class at a show held on or after January 1st of the following year.

The Puppy Class is the first one in which you should enter your puppy. In it a certain allowance will be made for the fact that they *are* puppies, thus an immature dog or one displaying less than perfect showmanship will be less severely penalized than, for instance, would be the case in Open. It is also quite likely that others in the class will be suffering from these problems, too. When you enter a puppy, be sure to check the classification with care, as some shows divide their Puppy Class into a 6-9 months old section and a 9-12 months old section.

The Novice Class is for dogs six months of age and over, whelped in the United States or Canada, who *prior to the official closing date for entries* have *not* won three first prizes in the Novice Class, any first prize at all in the Bred-by Exhibitor, American-bred, or Open Classes, or one or more points toward championship. The provisions for this class are confusing to many people, which is probably the reason exhibitors do not enter in it more frequently. A dog may win any number of first prizes in the Puppy Class and still retain his eligibility for Novice. He may place second, third, or fourth not only in Novice on an unlimited number of occasions but also in Bred-by-Exhibitor, American-bred and Open and still remain eligible for Novice. But he may no longer be shown in Novice when he has won three blue ribbons in that class, when he has won even one blue ribbon in either Bred-by-Exhibitor, American-bred, or Open, or when he has won a single championship point.

In determining whether or not a dog is eligible for the Novice Class, keep in mind the fact that previous wins are calculated according to the official published date for closing of entries, not by the date on which you may actually have made the entry. So if in the interim, between the time you made the entry and the official closing date, your dog makes a win causing him to become ineligible for Novice, change your class *immediately* to another for which he will be eligible, preferably either Bred-by-Exhibitor or American-bred. To do this, you must contact the show's superintendent or secretary, at first by telephone to save time and at the same time confirm it in writing. The Novice Class always seems to have the fewest entries of any class, and therefore it is a splendid "practice ground" for you and your young dog while you are getting the "feel" of being in the ring.

Bred-by-Exhibitor Class is for dogs whelped in the United States or, if individually registered in the American Kennel Club Stud Book, for dogs whelped in Canada who are six months of age

253

or older, are not champions, and are owned wholly or in part by the person or by the spouse of the person who was the breeder or one of the breeders of record. Dogs entered in this class must be handled in the class by an owner or by a member of the immediate family of the owner. Members of an immediate family for this purpose are husband, wife, father, mother, son, daughter, brother, or sister. This is the class which is really the "breeders' showcase," and the one which breeders should enter with particular pride to show off their achievements.

The American-bred Class is for all dogs excepting champions, six months of age or older, who were whelped in the United States by reason of a mating which took place in the United States.

The Open Class is for any dog six months of age or older (this is the only restriction for this class). Dogs with championship points compete in it, dogs who are already champions are eligible to do

Ch. Sparkling Rhythm of Dalmatia, born June 8, 1957, by Ch. Colonel Boots From Dalmatia ex Ch. Dalquest Rhythm of Dalmatia. One of the famous and important Dalmatians of the 1950's owned by Wendell J. Sammet, Dalmatia Kennels, Bryantville, Mass.

Noted professional handler Russ Petruzzo illustrating how a good Dalmatian can be shown. The dog is Ch. Sugarfrost Flying Parson owned by Janet Ashbey, Sugarfrost, Stewartsville, N.J.

so, dogs who are imported can be entered, and, of course, American-bred dogs compete in it. This class is, for some strange reason, the favorite of exhibitors who are "out to win." They rush to enter their pointed dogs in it, under the false impression that by doing so they assure themselves of greater attention from the judges. This really is not so, and some people feel that to enter in one of the less competitive classes, with a better chance of winning it and thus earning a second opportunity of gaining the judge's approval by returning to the ring in the Winners Class, can often be a more effective strategy.

One does not enter the Winners Class. One earns the right to compete in it by winning first prize in Puppy, Novice, Bred-by-Exhibitor, American-bred, or Open. No dog who has been defeated on the same day in one of these classes is eligible to compete for Winners, and every dog who has been a blue-ribbon winner in one of them and not defeated in another, should he have been entered in more than one class (as occasionally happens), *must* do so. Following the selection of the Winners Dog or the Winners Bitch, the dog or bitch receiving that award leaves the ring. Then the dog or bitch who placed second in that class, unless previously beaten by another dog or bitch in another class at the same show, re-enters the ring to compete against the remaining first-prize winners for Reserve. The latter award indicates that the dog or bitch selected for it is standing "in reserve" should the one who received Winners be disqualified or declared ineligible' through any technicality when the awards are checked at the American Kennel Club. In that case, the one who placed Reserve is moved up to Winners, at the same time receiving the appropriate championship points.

Winners Dog and Winners Bitch are the awards which carry points toward championship with them. The points are based on the number of dogs or bitches actually in competition, and the points are scaled one through five, the latter being the greatest number available to any one dog or bitch at any one show. Three-, four-, or five-point wins are considered majors. In order to become a champion, a dog or bitch must have won two majors under two different judges, plus at least one point from a third judge, and the additional points necessary to bring the total to fifteen. When your dog has gained fifteen points as described above, a championship certificate will be issued to you, and your dog's name will be published in the champions of record list in the *Pure-Bred Dogs/American Kennel Gazette*, the official publication of the American Kennel Club.

The scale of championship points for each breed is worked out by the American Kennel Club and reviewed annually, at which time the number required in competition may be either changed (raised or lowered) or remain the same. The scale of championship points for all breeds is published annually in the May issue of the *Gazette*, and the current ratings for each breed within that area are published in every show catalog.

When a dog or bitch is adjudged Best of Winners, its championship points are, for that show, compiled on the basis of which sex had the greater number of points. If there are two points in dogs

Ch. Coachman's Circus Wonder owned by the William Fetners, Coachman Kennels, St. Louis, Mo.

and four in bitches and the dog goes Best of Winners, then *both* the dog and the bitch are awarded· an equal number of points, in this case four. Should the Winners Dog or the Winners Bitch go on to win Best of Breed or Best of Variety, additional points are accorded for the additional dogs and bitches defeated by so doing, provided, of course, that there were entries specifically for Best of Breed competition or Specials, as these specific entries are generally called.

If your dog or bitch takes Best of Opposite Sex after going Winners, points are credited according to the number of the same sex defeated in both the regular classes and Specials competition. If Best of Winners is also won, then whatever additional points for each of these awards are available will be credited. Many a one- or two-point win has grown into a major in this manner.

Moving further along, should your dog win its Variety Group from the classes (in other words, if it has taken either Winners Dog or Winners Bitch), you then receive points based on the greatest number of points awarded to any member of any breed

257

included within that Group during that show's competition. Should the day's winning also include Best in Show, the same rule of thumb applies, and your dog or bitch receives the highest number of points awarded to any other dog of any breed at that event.

Best of Breed competition consists of the Winners Dog and the Winners Bitch, who automatically compete on the strength of those awards, in addition to whatever dogs and bitches have been entered specifically for this class for which champions of record are eligible. Since July 1980, dogs who, according to their owner's records, have completed the requirements for a championship after the closing of entries for the show, but whose championships are unconfirmed, may be transferred from one of the regular classes to the Best of Breed competition, provided this transfer is made by the show superintendent or show secretary *prior to the start of any judging at the show*.

This has proved an extremely popular new rule, as under it a dog can finish on Saturday and then be transferred and compete as a Special on Sunday. It must be emphasized that *the change must be made prior to the start of any part of the day's judging, not for just your individual breed*.

In the United States, Best of Breed winners are entitled to compete in the Variety Group which includes them. This is not mandatory; it is a privilege which exhibitors value. (In Canada, Best of Breed winners *must* compete in the Variety Group, or they lose any points already won.) The dogs winning *first* in each of the seven Variety Groups *must* compete for Best in Show. Missing the opportunity of taking your dog in for competition in its Group is foolish as it is there where the general public is most likely to notice your breed and become interested in learning about it.

Non-regular classes are sometimes included at the all-breed shows, and they are almost invariably included at Specialty shows. These include Stud Dog Class and Brood Bitch Class, which are judged on the basis of the quality of the two offspring accompanying the sire or dam. The quality of the latter two is beside the point and should not be considered by the judge; it is the youngsters who count, and the quality of *both* are to be averaged to decide which sire or dam is the best and most consistent producer. Then there is the Brace Class (which, at all-breed shows, moves up to Best Brace in each Variety Group and then Best Brace in Show), which is judged on the similarity and evenness of appearance of the two members of the brace. In other words, the two dogs should look like identical twins in size, color, and conformation and should move together almost as a single dog, one person handling with precision and ease. The same applies to the Team Class competition, except that four dogs are involved and, if necessary, two handlers.

The Veterans Class is for the older dogs, the minimum age of whom is seven years. This class is judged on the quality of the dogs, as the winner competes in Best of Breed competition and has, on a respectable number of occasions, been known to take that top award. So the point is *not* to pick out the oldest dog, as some judges seem to believe, but the best specimen of the breed, exactly as in the regular classes.

Then there are Sweepstakes and Futurity Stakes sponsored by many Specialty clubs, sometimes as part of their regular Specialty shows and sometimes as separate events on an entirely different occasion. The difference between the two stakes is that Sweepstakes entries usually include dogs from six to eighteen months age with entries made at the same time as the others for the show, while for a Futurity the entries are bitches nominated when bred and the individual puppies entered at or shortly following their birth.

If you already show your dog, if you plan on being an exhibitor in the future, or if you simply enjoy attending dog shows, there is a book which you will find to be an invaluable source of detailed information about all aspects of show dog competition. This book is *Successful Dog Show Exhibiting* (T.F.H. Publications, Inc.) and is available wherever the one you are reading was purchased.

JUNIOR SHOWMANSHIP COMPETITION

If there is a youngster in your family between the ages of ten and sixteen there is no better or more rewarding hobby than becoming an active participant in Junior Showmanship. This is a marvelous activity for young people. It teaches responsibility, good sportsmanship, the fun of competition where one's own skills are the deciding factor of success, proper care of a pet, and how to socialize with other young folks. Any youngster may experience the thrill of emerging from the ring a winner and the satisfaction of a good job well done.

259

Entry in Junior Showmanshiop Classes is open to any boy or girl who is at least ten years old and under seventeen years old on the day of the show. The Novice Junior Showmanship Class is open to youngsters who have not already won, at the time the entries close, three firsts in this class. Youngsters who have won three firsts in Novice may compete in the Open Junior Showmanship Class. Any junior handler who wins his third first-place award in Novice may participate in the Open Class at the same show, provided that the Open Class has at least one other junior handler entered and competing in it that day. The Novice and Open Classes may be divided into Junior and Senior Classes. Youngsters between the ages of ten and twelve, inclusively, are eligible for the Junior division; and youngsters between thirteen and seventeen, inclusively, are eligible for the Senior division.

Ch. Centurion Cloudburst, handled exclusively by 15-year-old Suzy Lindhorst, St. Charles, Mo.

Swiftgait Fire Brand, by Aust. Ch. Swiftgait Just n'Time ex Swiftgait Ukelele Lady, owned by R. and D. Besoff, Abermain, N.S.W., Australia.

Any of the foregoing classes may be separated into individual classes for boys and for girls. If such a division is made, it must be so indicated on the premium list. The premium list also indicates the prize for Best Junior Handler, if such a prize is being offered at the show. Any youngster who wins a first in any of the regular classes may enter the competition for this prize, provided the youngster has been undefeated in any other Junior Showmanship Class at that show.

Junior Showmanship Classes, unlike regular conformation classes in which the quality of the dog is judged, are judged solely on the skill and ability of the junior handling the dog. Which dog is best is not the point—it is which youngster does the best job with the dog that is under consideration. Eligibility requirements for the dog being shown in Junior Showmanship, and other detailed information, can be found in *Regulations for Junior Showmanship*, available from the American Kennel Club.

A junior who has a dog that he or she can enter in both Junior Showmanship and conformation classes has twice the opportunity for success and twice the opportunity to get into the ring and work with the dog, a combination which can lead to not only awards for expert handling, but also, if the dog is of sufficient quality, for making a conformation champion.

PRE-SHOW PREPARATIONS

Preparations of the items you will need as a dog show exhibitor should not be left until the last moment. They should be planned and arranged for at least several days in advance of the show in order for you to remain calm and relaxed as the countdown starts.

The importance of the crate has already been mentioned, and should already be is hoped that it is already part of your equipment. Of equal importance is the grooming table, which very likely you have also already acquired for use at home. You should take it along with you to the shows, as your dog will need last minute touches before entering the ring. Should you have not yet made this purchase, folding tables with rubber tops are made specifically for this purpose and can be purchased at most dog shows, where concession booths with marvelous assortments of "doggy" necessities are to be found, or at your pet supplier. You will also need a sturdy tack box (also available at the dog show concessions) in which to carry your grooming tools and equipment. The latter should include brushes, comb, scissors, nail clippers, whatever you use for last minute clean-up jobs, cotton swabs, first-aid equipment, and anything you are in the habit of using on the dog, including a leash or two of the type you prefer, some well-cooked and dried-out liver or any of the small packaged "dog treats" for use as bait in the ring, an atomizer in case you wish to dampen your dog's coat when you are preparing him for the ring, and so on. A large turkish towel to spread under the dog on the grooming table is also useful.

Take a large thermos or cooler of ice, the biggest one you can accommodate in your vehicle, for use by "man and beast." Take a jug of water (there are lightweight, inexpensive ones available at all sporting goods shops) and a water dish. If you plan to feed the dog at the show, or if you and the dog will be away from home more than one day, bring food for him from home so that he will have the type to which he is accustomed.

You may or may not have an exercise pen. While the shows do provide areas for exercise of the dogs, these are among tjhe most likely places to have your dog come in contact with any illnesses which may be going around, and having a pen of your own for your dog's use is excellent protection. Such a pen can be used in other ways, too, such as a place other than the crate in which to put the dog to relax (that is roomier than the crate) and a place in which the dog can exercise at motels and rest stops. These pens are available at the show concession stands and come in a variety of heights and sizes. A set of "pooper scoopers" should also be part of your equipment, along with a package of plastic bags for cleaning up after your dog.

Bring along folding chairs for the members of your party, unless all of you are fond of standing, as these are almost never provided anymore by the clubs. Have your name stamped on the chairs so that there will be no doubt as to whom the chairs belong. Bring whatever you and you family enjoy for drinks or snacks in a picnic basket or cooler, as show food, in general, is expensive and usually not great. You should always have a pair of boots, a raincoat, and a rain hat with you (they should remain permanently in your vehicle if you plan to attend shows regularly), as well as a sweater, a warm coat, and a change of shoes. A smock or big cover-up apron will assure that you remain tidy as you prepare the dog for the ring. Your overnight case should include a small sewing kit for emergency repairs, bandaids, headache and indigestion remedies, and any personal products or medications you normally use.

In your car you should always carry maps of the area where you are headed and an assortment of motel directories. Generally speaking, Holiday Inns have been found to be the nicest about taking dogs. Ramadas and Howard Johnsons generally do so cheerfully (with a few exceptions). Best Western generally frowns on pets (not always, but often enough to make it necessary to find out which do). Some of the smaller chains welcome pets; the majority of privately owned motels do not.

Have everything prepared the night before the show to expedite your departure. Be sure that the dog's identification and your judging program and other show information are in your purse or briefcase. If you are taking sandwiches, have them ready. Anything that goes into the car the night before the show will be one thing less to remember in the morning. Decide upon what you will wear and have it out and ready. If there is any question in your mind about what to wear, try on the possibilities before the day of the show; don't risk feeling you may want to change when you see yourself dressed a few moments prior to departure time!

In planning your outfit, make it something simple that will not detract from your dog. Remember that a dark dog silhouettes attractively against a light background and vice-versa. Sport clothes

Dottidale Elizabeth winning the Veteran Bitch Class at the Dalmatian Club of Greater New York Specialty with Westchester K.C. in 1980, age 12 years and 4 months. Also won Veteran Bitch Class at Dalmatian Club of Southern New England Specialty, 1975, 1976 and 1977; and the Dalmatian Club of America Specialty in 1976. By Ch. Dottidale Jo Jo ex Countess of Charbet. Bred by Phillip Pantaleo. Owned by Dottidale Kennels.

Ch. Strathglass Cricket came from the Strathglass Kennels of Mr. and Mrs. Hugh Chisholm at Port Chester, N.Y. to join the Dals at Mary Barrett's Roadcoach Kennels.

"At the show." Jan Kirin with her bitch Top Winner, Aust. Ch. Kirindal Fancy Free, being judged by Dalmatian Specialist Mr. Robert Lawson (Australia). She was awarded Bitch Challenge Certificate, Best of Opposite Sex in Show on this occasion.

Ch. Dalhalla Thunderbolt, by Ch. Dottidale Jo Jo ex Chloe's Jane of East Norwich, bred by owners, Jane and John Rauscher, handled by the latter. Winners Dog from the Puppy Class, Dalmatian Club of America Specialty 1969. Best of Breed Westminster 1972. Sire of numerous champions.

always seem to look best at dog shows, preferably conservative in type and not overly "loud" as you do not want to detract from your dog, who should be the focus of interest at this point. What you wear on your feet is important. Many types of flooring can be hazardously slippery, as can wet grass. Make it a habit to wear rubber soles and low or flat heels in the ring for your own safety, especially if you are showing a dog that like to move out smartly.

Your final step in pre-show preparation is to leave yourself plenty of time to reach the show that morning. Traffic can get amazingly heavy as one nears the immediate area of the show, finding a parking place can be difficult, and other delays may occur. You'll be in better humor to enjoy the day if your trip to the show is not fraught with panic over fear of not arriving in time!

ENJOYING THE DOG SHOW

From the moment of your arrival at the show until after your dog has been judged, keep foremost in your mind the fact that he is your reason for being there and that he should therefore be the center of your attention. Arrive early enough to have time for those last-minute touches that can make a great difference when he enters the ring. Be sure that he has ample time to exercise and that he attends to personal matters. A dog arriving in the ring and immediately using it as an exercise pen hardly makes a favorable impression on the judge.

When you reach ringside, ask the steward for your arm-card and anchor it firmly into place on your arm. Make sure that you are where you should be when your class is called. The fact that you have picked up your arm-card does not guarantee, as some seem to think, that the judge will wait for you. The judge has a full schedule which he wishes to complete on time. Even though you may be nervous, assume an air of calm self-confidence. Remember that this is a hobby to be enjoyed, so approach it in that state of mind. The dog will do better, too, as he will be quick to reflect your attitude.

Always show your dog with an air of pride. If you make mistakes in presenting him, don't worry about it. Next time you will do better. Do not permit the presence of more experienced exhibitors to intimidate you. After all, they, too, once were newcomers.

The judging routine usually starts when the judge asks that the dogs be gaited in a circle around the ring. During this period the judge is watching each dog as it moves, noting style, topline, reach and drive, head and tail carriage, and general balance. Keep your mind and your eye on your dog, moving him at his most becoming gait and keeping your place in line without coming too close to the exhibitor ahead of you. Always keep your dog on the inside of the circle, between yourself and the judge, so that the judge's view of the dog is unobstructed.

Calmly pose the dog when requested to set up for examination. If you are at the head of the line and many dogs are in the class, go all the way to the end of the ring before starting to stack the dog, leaving sufficient space for those behind you to line theirs up as well, as requested by the judge. If you are not at the head of the line but between other exhibitors, leave sufficient space ahead of your dog for the judge to examine him. The dogs should be spaced so that the judge is able to move among them to see them from all angles. In practicing to "set up" or "stack" your dog for the judge's examination, bear in mind the importance of doing so quickly and with dexterity. The judge has a schedule to meet and only a few moments in which to evaluate each dog. You will immeasurably help yours to make a favorable immpression if you are able to "get it all together" in a minimum amount of time. Practice at home before a mirror can be a great help toward bringing this about, facing the dog so that you see him from the same side that the judge will and working to make him look right in the shortest length of time.

Listen carefully as the judge describes the manner in which the dog is to be gaited, whether it is straight down and straight back; down the ring, across, and back; or in a triangle. The latter has become the most popular pattern with the majority of judges. "In a triangle" means the dog should move down the outer side of the ring to the first corner, across that end of the ring to the second corner, and then back to the judge from the second corner, using the center of the ring in a diagonal line. Please learn to do this pattern without breaking at each corner to twirl the dog around you, a senseless maneuver that has been noticed on occasion. Judges like to see the dog in an uninterrupted triangle, as they are thus able to get a better idea of the dog's gait.

It is impossible to overemphasize that the gait at which you move your dog is tremendously important and considerable study and thought should be given to the matter. At home, have some-

Ch. Roadcoach Phaeton, a splendid example of the type and quality of Mary Barrett's Dals. Roadcoach Kennels, Dover, Mass.

one move the dog for you at different speeds so that you can tell which shows him off to best advantage. The most becoming action almost invariably is seen at a moderate gait, head up and topline holding. Do not gallop your dog around the ring or hurry him into a speed atypical of his breed. Nothing being rushed appears at its best; give your dog a chance to move along at his (and the breed's) natural gait. For a dog's action to be judged accurately, that dog should move with strength and power, but not excessive speed, holding a straight line as he goes to and from the judge.

As you bring the dog back to the judge, stop him a few feet away and be sure that he is standing in a becoming position. Bait him to show the judge an alert expression, using whatever tasty morsel he has been trained to expect for this purpose or, if that works better for you, use a small squeak-toy in your hand.

When the awards have been made, accept yours graciously, no matter how you actually may feel about it. What's done is done, and arguing with a judge or stomping out of the ring is useless and a reflection on your sportsmanship. Be courteous, congratulate the winner if your dog was defeated, and try not to show your disappointment. By the same token, please be a gracious winner; this, surprisingly, sometimes seems to be still more difficult.

Chapter 13

Your Dalmatian and Obedience

For its own protection and safety, every dog should be taught, at the very least, to recognize and obey the commands "Come," "Heel," "Down," "Sit," and "Stay." Doing so at some time might save the dog's life and in less extreme circumstances will certainly make him a better behaved, more pleasant member of society. If you are patient and enjoy working with your dog, study some of the excellent books available on the subject of obedience and then teach your canine friend these basic manners. If you need the stimulus of working with a group, find out where obedience training classes are held (usually your veterinarian, your dog's breeder, or a dog-owning friend can tell you) and you and your dog can join up. Alternatively, you could let someone else do the training by sending the dog to class, but this is not very rewarding because you lose the opportunity of working with your dog and the pleasure of the rapport thus established.

If you are going to do it yourself, there are some basic rules which you should follow. You must remain calm and confident in attitude. Never lose your temper and frighten or punish your dog unjustly. Be quick and lavish with praise each time a command is correctly followed. Make it fun for the dog and he will be eager to please you by responding correctly. Repetition is the keynote, but it should not be continued without recess to the point of tedium. Limit the training sessions to ten- or fifteen-minute periods at a time.

Formal obedience training can be followed, and very frequently is, by entering the dog in obedience competition to work toward an obedience degree, or several of them, depending on the dog's aptitude and your own enjoyment. Obedience trials are held in conjunction with the majority of all-breed conformation dog shows, with Specialty shows, and frequently as separate Specialty events. If you are working alone with your dog, a list of trial dates might be obtained from your dog's veterinarian, your dog breeder, or a dog-owning friend; the AKC *Gazette* lists shows and trials to be scheduled in the coming months; and if you are a member of a training class, you will find the information readily available.

The goals for which one works in the formal AKC Member or Licensed Trials are the following titles: Companion Dog (C.D.), Companion Dog Excellent (C.D.X.), and Utility Dog (U.D.). These degrees are earned by receiving three "legs," or qualifying scores, at each level of competition. The degrees must be earned in order, with one completed prior to starting work on the next. For example, a dog must have earned C.D. prior to starting work on C.D.X.; then C.D.X. must be completed before U.D. work begins. The ultimate title attainable in obedience work is Obedience Trial Champion (O.T.Ch.)

When you see the letters C.D. following a dog's name, you will know that this dog has satisfactorily completed the following exercises: heel on leash and figure eight, heel free, stand for examination, recall, long sit, and long down. C.D.X. means that tests have been passed on all of those just mentioned plus heel free and figure eight, drop on recall, retrieve on flat, retrieve over high jump, broad jump, long sit, and long down. U.D. indicates that the dog has additionally passed tests in scent discrimination (leather article), scent discrimination (metal article), signal exercise, directed retrieve, directed jumping, and group stand for examination. The letters O.T.Ch. are the abbreviation for the only obedience title which precedes rather than follows a dog's name. To gain an obedience trial championship, a dog who already holds a Utility Dog degree must win a total of one hundred points and must win three firsts, under three different judges, in Utility and Open B Classes.

There is also a Tracking Dog title (T.D.) which can be earned at tracking trials. In order to pass the tracking tests the dog must follow the trail of a stranger along a path on which the trail was laid between thirty minutes and two hours previously. Along this track there must be more than two right-angle turns, at least two of which are well out in the open where no fences or other bound-

Ch. Atlantis Conquestador, C.D.X., AD. This is, to the owners' knowledge, the only Dalmatian champion to have earned a Schutzhund Endurance Title as well. Owners, Kathy and Lee McCoubrey, Ravenwood Dalmatians, Chuluota, Florida.

aries exist for the guidance of the dog or the handler. The dog wears a harness and is connected to the handler by a lead twenty to forty feet in length. Inconspicuously dropped at the end of the track is an article to be retrieved, usually a glove or wallet, which the dog is expected to locate and the handler to pick up. The letters T.D.X. is the abbreviation for Tracking Dog Excellent, a more difficult version of the Tracking Dog test with a longer track and more turns to be worked through.

SUCCESSFUL OBEDIENCE DALMATIANS

Dalmatians have made good in obedience with some very notable scores and honors over the years, seeming to have an aptitude for this training. Pride of place among them all must go to Obedience Trial Champion Chadis Skagit Belle, whose story we tell you a bit further along. By mid-1985, this is still the only Dalmatian to have attained the difficult and prestigious O.T.Ch. title. But, we are happy to note, there are about a dozen others on their way, the closest being Dominique's Rusty Nail, U.D. who has earned 49 of the required 100 points; Sneak Preview, U.D.T.X., follow-

271

ing up with 43, and Domino's Winter Midnight, U.D.T. with 16 points followed by Dalcroft's Lotsa Spots, U.D. with 14. Two conformation champions are also gaining points to their O.T.Ch. titles., these being Cal Dal Chocolate Chip, U.D.T. and Champion Touchstone's Yosemite Sam, U.D.

It is interesting to note the considerable number of Dalmatian breeders and owners who are working their dogs in obedience as well as taking them through their paces in the conformation ring. This we feel is excellent for the breed, and you will note numerous pictures in this book, and references to bench champions with one or more obedience titles as well.

Probably the leader in this regard is Sue MacMillan who herself is breeder of an imposing number of obedience degree holders and whose stud dog, Champion Paisley's A Change of Pace, is top sire of numerous obedience titlists at this time. Other kennels placing emphasis in this area are Indalane owned by Eleanore Hilane; Bespeckled owned by Ken Nagler; Centurion owned by Elaine Lindhorst; and Touchstone owned by Cathy Murphy. Other distinguished show dogs with multiple obedience titled progeny include Champion Tuckaway Traveler Indalane, Champion Joe Forrester of Proctor, Champion Long Last Link to Paisley, and Champion Indalane Bryan's Knockout. Not forgetting the bitches, Champion Centurion Special Edition, U.D. in both 1983 and 1984 was Top Brood Bitch among the dams of obedience titlists during that period.

Dalmatians have been involved with obedience from the earlier days right up until the present. Some of our readers will recall the days of Obedience Teams, thus should particularly enjoy the accompanying photo of the South Shore Dog Training Club Team which was taken several decades back.

A notable achievement in obedience which has taken place during the spring of 1985 has been completion of the T.D. degree on the *11-year-old* Dalmatian, Forever Embers, C.D., owned by Darleen Chirolas, Urbana, Illinois. Embers was certified for tracking at the Dog Training Club of Champaign-Urbana Tracking Match on March 31, 1985, and passed her Tracking Dog Test, doing her track in just over four minutes, at the Lyons Township Dog Training Club Tracking Test on April 28, 1985, 21 days following her 11th birthday. Which proves once again that it is, indeed, possible to teach an older dog new tricks!

O.T.C. Candis Skagit Belle, distinguished obedience Dalmatian, "in action," Owned by Rebecca J. Auker, Beaufort, S.C.

The puppy "Randi," who was to become Obedience Trial Champion Candis Skigit Belle, was purchased as a seven-month-old puppy by Rebecca Auker of Beaufort, South Carolina, who started her in obedience two weeks later. The puppy was the first Dalmatian and the first obedience dog owned by the Aukers, although Rebecca (or "Becky" as she is known to her friends) had grown up with dogs and had shown horses.

Randi's first show was five months later, in obedience, at the Seattle Kennel Club where she received first place in a class of 46 other dogs. Needless to say, Becky was thrilled, delighted, and "hooked." Randi went back out twice more in Novice, gaining scores of 192½ and 197½ for first place, completing her C.D. in October 1978. During February 1979, Becky started Randi out in Open, so successfully that she received a *Dog World* Certificate for her three scores above 195. They were 196 (third place), 197½ (second place), and 197¼ (first place and High in Trial). Her third leg on C.D.X. was received in September of 1979.

The great Ch. Panore of Watseka in an informal moment with his owner-handler Carol Schubert. A great show dog, a great sire, and a great family dog, Panore exemplifies all of the finest features of the Dal.

Am. and Can. Ch. Roughrider Koda's Kid, U.D. about to retrieve. Kathryn Braund, owner, Roughrider Dalmatians, Great Falls, Mont.

Coachman's Capricorn, C.D. takes the jumps with ease. C.D. Fetner, owner, Dallas, Texas.

This is the obedience team that represented the South Shore Dog Training Club back in the days when teams were active in obedience competition. *Left to right* are Mrs. Charles L. Thiessen, Virginia E. Lindsay, Mrs. Wm. B. Foster, and Wendell J. Sammet with their Dals.

Ch. Fobette's Fanfare, C.D.X., dumbbell in mouth, taking the jump with style during obedience competition. Owned by Mr. and Mrs. Alfred E. Treen, Brookfield, Wis.

The next challenge was Utility, which started for Randi in June of 1979. It took her seven shows in which to complete her three legs for U.D. with scores of 181 (first), 191 (second) and 194. Her third leg was earned in September 1979.

It took Randi 38 times in Open and 33 times in Utility for her to become the *first and to date only obedience trial champion* (O.T.C.) *Dalmatian on record!* She ended up having eight firsts in Open B for 60 points; one second in Open B for three points; five firsts in Utility for 26 points, and four second for 15 points, completing her degree with 104 points of which 18 points were earned at Dalmatian Specialty Shows, 86 at all-breed events. Her average Open placing scores were 197.75; and her average Utility placing scores 196.33. On the way, she got 11 thirds and two fourths. She has also earned High in Trial on seven occasions.

Needless to say, the entire Dalmatian fancy takes pride in the accomplishments of this very intelligent bitch! The Dalmatian Club of America has awarded her Fifth Place among Obedience Dals in 1978 (a tie); Second Place in 1979; and First Place in both 1980 and 1981.

The Dotted Line, the Dalmatian Obedience Newsletter, has recognized Randi as No. 1 ranked Dal for 1979; No. 2 for 1980; and No. 1 for 1981.

During November of 1981, Randi competed at the Gaines Classic and received Tenth Place in the Super Dog competition. This award and her Obedience Trial Championship are the two achievements which have brought very special pleasure to Randi's owner. But they are not her only successes. For example, she also has been the Top Dalmatian in the Schuman and Delaney Systems at times, although Becky does not have the records available at her fingertips to say in exactly which years.

In 1982 Becky's husband, Chaplain Rex Auker, was transferred to Guam where Randi was in quarantine for four months. Randi sailed through that period with no problems, but Becky found it difficult! They returned to South Carolina in 1984, and Becky has been showing Randi since then. She's been doing okay, to quote Becky, having received a couple of firsts, a second, and a third.

Becky tells us, "I have really enjoyed showing Randi, who has been quite consistent. She once had a run of 17 qualifying utility scores in a row."

In reading Randi's story, please remember that she was the *first* obedience dog ever owned by Becky Auker, which just shows what can be accomplished by an owner-trainer-handler and a smart Dalmatian!

No resume of obedience activities among Dalmatian fanciers in the United States would be complete without making mention of Mrs. Harland W. (Lois) Meistrell and her work with several breeds of dog including this one. Mrs. Meistrell, a resident of Long Island in those days who, since her retirement (or perhaps I should say semi-retirement as she is a lady who is always busy with one thing or another) has moved to Vermont where she enjoys the living.

No "old timer" in Dals could possibly fail to recall the superb performance in obedience competition of Lois's American and Canadian Champion Whiteside Sioux Oros, U.D., whose earned honors added up to an imposing array; and whose son, Oros II, C.D. carried on in his sire's pawprints. Lois Meistrell was involved in many different phases of obedience, from training to exhibition work. To say that Oros and Oros II were trail blazers for the breed would be no exaggeration. She was as well a Dalmatian exhibitor. Three of her finest in the conformation world were Champion Battered Bentley in the Valley; Champion Lady Callisto of Pine, and Champion Barney Oldfield in the Valley.

Chapter 14

Dalmatian Road Trials

We are indebted to both Janet Ashbey (Sugarfrost Kennels) and Wendell J. Sammet (Dalmatia) for their thoughtfulness in sending us information and photographs telling the story of the Dalmatian Road Trials which were held in Massachusetts following World War II. They were exciting events which created considerable interest locally in their area.

To give our readers an idea of what took place, the cast included one mounted judge on horseback; two judges on foot; and as many handlers with their dogs who cared to participate, each of them permitted to handle up to six dogs. Trials could be One-Day 15 Mile Puppy Trial; or Two-Day 25 Mile Derby Trial or All-Age Trial, these each covering a 25 Mile Distance each day.

The mounted judge would start riding with the first handler, other handlers joining in at ten minute intervals. The mounted judge rode approximately ten minutes with each handler. The foot judges were transported over the field in an automobile by someone very familiar with this course, and posted at the most difficult sections on the trail in order to observe the dogs under the hardest working conditions. When the last dog down-passed the mounted judges, the latter were picked up in an automobile and taken ahead to some part of the trail where the first handler was certain to pass.

Before running dogs, each was weighed and measured, which was repeated at the close of each day's running, giving the judge the opportunity to observe any changes in their condition.

That is the general idea of what took place. Numerous additional suggestions were made by various members of the committee, some of which were accepted. When in congested areas, the handler should road his dog or dogs as does the huntsman his Foxhounds, for safety's sake. On bridle path, the dogs were al-

Wendell Sammet and Frou Frou getting ready to go in the Dalmatian Road Races following World War II back in 1949.

lowed to run free, preferably in front of the rider, and judged for alertness and way of going. The dogs were not to be noisy, and excess noise was scored against them. They were expected to give a warning bark when pedestrians or other riders approached their own rider; and immediately come to "hock" when ordered by their rider to do so. The handler was permitted to carry a huntsman's whip for the protection of his own dogs from strays, and also to control his dogs from breaking away on rabbits, squirrels, etc.

Scoring was broken down to suit the majority in the same manner as in the Hunters' Class in a Horse Show, with consideration given to obedience, alertness, way of going, and soundness. Some dogs would start out with head and tail held high, then return with tail between their legs. But the majority, if properly conditioned, finished up with heads and tail on high and in a lot better shape than the horses.

Mrs. Lois Meistrell had obviously been consulted and asked for suggestions on improving the road trials. Among them was that, since this was then an experiment, a ten-mile ride might be sufficient for any Dalmatian, any age over six months.

279

Getting underway, Dalmatian Road Race, 1949, Dedham, Mass.

Wendell Sammet being scored with Frou Frou, the winner, at the Dalmatian Road Trial, Dedham, Mass. in 1949. The judges were Arnault B. Edgerly, mounted; Mrs. Leonard W. Bonney and Mr. C.L. Pipping, Jr., foot. Mrs. Barrett, Chairman for this event, was ably assisted by her committee consisting of Mr. Barrett, Mr. Sammet, Miss Virginia Lindsay, Mrs. Evelyn Wall, and Miss Helen Powers.

The outlined judging procedure she felt to be excellent. Her suggestions there were that a local Master of Fox Hounds be given the mounted judge assignment, with prominent Dalmatian show judges as the foot arbiters. Also she thought that a Committee might be invited to observe and make suggestions for evolving a final set of rules to become standard for such trials. Mrs. Meistrell indicated her willingness to organize trials of this type on Long Island, as did Mrs. Dewell for her section of Connecticut.

Mrs. Meistrell thought, under judging points, that barking at the approach of another rider, while in some ways a good idea, might upset or frighten a young, nervous horse or an inexperienced rider, thus causing a spill. For this reason she favored that the provisions merely state "indicate the approach of another rider or pedestrian by a bark or, preferably, such signal as coming to a stop with ears erect and body poised, head pointing in the direction of the stranger."

Mrs. Meistrell, after one or two other small suggestions, added the thought that the same foot judges and committee observe all trials, at least in the beginning, with only the mounted judge different in order that the same judges and committee thus collect a sound basis for perfecting trial rules.

It then became the task of Mrs. Alfred Barrett to take the first of the suggestions, which had been drawn up by Mr. Lloyd Reeves, consolidate them with those made by Mrs. Meistrell, and arrange an experimental trial in Dover. There was plenty of available area of woods and hunting country where only crossroads would be encountered, which became the locale.

It had evidently been suggested that these Road Trials should be part of the National Specialty, which Mrs. Barrett very wisely felt would not work out, since the Specialty and Obedience provided a very full day for all concerned. But autumn is the ideal time for such events, and that was the final choice.

The opening trial was a huge success from all the comments we have heard back there in 1949. I have not heard of similar events elsewhere, but wouldn't they be fun, in really rural areas where they could be conducted in perfect safety from traffic for "man and beast"? Wendell Sammet had the winner at this Dedham Country and Polo Club trial in his well-known Roadcoach Frou Frou, C.D.X.

Chapter 15

Tracking with Your Dalmatian

by *Janis Butler*

"Tracking? I don't know a thing about tracking" was my reaction when my friend Mhyra asked about tracking my first Dalmatian bitch. But Myhra was persistent, and next thing I knew, I was out in a field with one spotted dog complete with tracking harness (borrowed), leash, and glove.

"Now I'm going to put this stake in the ground right here where I am starting walking, and when I get out 30 feet I'll put out another one. You'll have that much of a hint as to where the track goes. It will give you 30 feet to be certain that Skye (the Dalmatian) has the scent. I'll drop the glove just a short way from the second stake. We don't want to try to rush Skye; just let her sniff her way along the short track with no turns until we're sure she's got the idea." Turns? Mhyra was really expecting miracles out of this, wasn't she?

Well, Mhyra took off, Skye watching with a lot of interest. I was sure that this was one of the silliest things I had ever tried with any of my dogs. Mhyra got to the second stake, walked a few more feet, dropped the glove, then turned around and walked back the same way she had come. "That's to set the scent into the ground even stronger. Now, you're going to take Skye to the first stake, put her nose to the ground, and tell her to find it." *Put* Skye's nose to the ground? Now I was sure this wasn't going to work, but if it would make Mhyra happy, why not? She likes to help with useful stuff like this.

So, I got Skye to the stake, pointed to the ground, and said, "Find it, Skye." Needless to say, she looked at me like I was the crazy one. So I pointed to the ground again, this time toying with the ground with my fingers until finally Skye put her nose down and took a whiff. Suddenly the six foot leash I was starting with was stretched taut as my spotted wonder took off down the track with her nose to the ground! She was tracking!

When Skye got to the glove, she came to a screeching halt, with me close behind her. But she was still sniffing and looking. Surely there must be more to this than a 35-foot run. Mhyra's reaction was, "Maybe she'd like to try a turn. You don't usually do turns

Ch. Roadrunner's Skye of Winemall, C.D., T.D. with owner-trainer Janis Butler, Kissimmee, Fla.

this quickly, but most people have to work for weeks to get their dogs to put their noses to the ground." Did that mean my Skye, the wonder dog, was exceptional?

So, in a different part of the field, Mhyra walked a track again, this time putting in a turn and marking it with a smaller stake so I would know where the turn was in case Skye missed it. Did she? No way! Skye got to the corner, made the turn, and took a few steps. Suddenly her head came up and she made a circle to the right, coming all the way around behind me. Mhyra hollered to me to stand still and see what Skye would do. She made a full circle, put her nose back on the track, and went on to the glove. Mhyra impressed upon me then that being able to "read" your dog was an important part of tracking. I must learn that when Skye makes a turn like that she is checking to be sure that she is still on the scent before going further.

Now I was on my own. I had to do my own tracks, learn about how wind and ground cover would disperse the scent, and start to let the scent age before letting Skye start to track. She had to be able to run approximately a quarter mile track that was at least an hour old, at the end of a 30-foot lead in order to earn her T.D. (Tracking Degree title). Suddenly a whole new world was open to me. I began walking fields at all hours of the day and night. Skye had her own tracking harness now, and she knew when I took the harness down what we were going to do. Those times with her became treasured. It was just the two of us learning to trust each other and work as a team to find the all-important glove.

The time came when I wanted to get Skye's T.D. First she had to be "certified," or run a shorter track for a tracking judge, who would sign a statement that he/she thought the dog ready to run a tracking test. Fortunately, our local obedience club was having a certification shortly, in which I entered Skye.

The day of the certification came. My nerves were on edge. Could Skye do it? Certainly, but *would* she? Would I do something to throw her off? Why did I have to be one of the last to run? Luck of the draw. But it wasn't helping my stomach any.

Skye's time finally came. I was so nervous that I forgot to hook her long leash to the tracking harness. Suddenly I realized she was ready to start her track and I hadn't taken off her collar. I backed up, removed the choke collar, and hooked the long lead to her harness. We were off. All the nerves were gone; it was just me and

Skye out there, she pulling me along like she had on all the other fields we had walked together. And there it was—the glove. Skye had passed her first step toward her T.D.

I quickly entered the first Tracking Test. Now all I had to do was run her one more time, right? *Wrong!* Mhyra said I had breezed through that one too easily. Now she was going to teach me to *really* trust my dog. Trust? That was the key word in tracking. The dog knows where the scent is. If you don't trust your dog, you will never have a true tracking dog. I had to come to Mhyra's house on Saturday evening and wait. She would meet me there shortly. I waited. Skye waited. Finally Mhyra showed up. No, we couldn't go now. But it was getting dark outside. That was the whole point. Finally the sky was pitch black, and Mhyra said that now it was time to go. We loaded Skye into her crate and drove to another part of town, where I had never been, fairly near the airport. We got Skye out and put her harness on. Then Mhyra led us to a stake in the ground. I could see the second stake 30 feet out. "This is the true test; go to it," said Mhyra. But I couldn't see anything at all. "This is the way you learn to trust your dog," Mhyra repeated.

I put Skye on the track and off we went. She pulled me across terrain so rough I could hardly keep my footing at the speed she was traveling. I remembered to stop and wait every time she circled. Then I felt my shoulders wrench as she took off on the scent again. We crossed ditches, both with and without water; we ploughed through piles of rubble; we crossed a dirt road; and we made a full circle before we found the glove. Mhyra was ecstatic. Skye had tracked across the roughest field Mhyra had been able to find. If she could track that, she could track anything. We found out the following week that particular field had been recently covered over and reclaimed. It used to be a dump.

Tracking Test day arrived. My nerves were worse than ever and I had a horrible cold. I couldn't breathe—how on earth was I going to get through a quarter mile track without breathing? Skye had drawn a later track again. We had to wait through a number of dogs, about half of whom did not pass their tests. Would Skye be one of them?

Skye's turn finally came. I put her harness on her and started to walk towards the track. Her track started in the cow pasture, so we had to climb over the fence to get in. As Skye came across the fence, she startled the calves penned next to the start of her track. They spooked and ran and Skye, being a city dog, jumped straight into the air and into my arms. That was it, I *knew*—she would never get off onto the track now. I put her down and hooked the long lead on to her harness, then removed the slip lead I had around her neck.

"Find it, Skye" and she was off. Finally she was past the 30 foot flag and I was at the end of the 30 foot lead. Skye was running as hard as she could go, and I was pulling trying to slow her up. The first turn, up came her head and she circled. Then my shoulders were wrenched as she took off again. By now I was running, too, trying to keep up with her and give my shoulders some relief. Here came the second turn, a quick breather while she turned and checked the scent. We were off again, pulling even harder. We must be near the end by now.

Then it happened. Suddenly the leash went slack and Skye, startled, stopped and looked back. Horrified I realized that she had pulled so hard the whole track that she had broken the front rivets on her harness. Skye was just a few feet from the end, and out of her harness. I was stunned! What do I do? Mhyra hadn't prepared me for this.

"Get a collar on her and see if she'll finish." That was the judge yelling from his position behind me. A collar! All I had was the slip-lead stuck into a jacket pocket somewhere. Finally I dug it out and got it around Skye. Had she been distracted for too long now? Would she remember what she was out here to be doing? Would she remember which scent she was following? All I could do was gasp for breath and try.

"Find it, Skye" and she was off again, remembering which scent she was on and going just as hard, this time only for 15 feet for the glove. I looked back, anxious to see the judges' reactions. They were grinning and waving their clipboards. Skye had done it! She was now Skye T.D. The gallery was cheering. In our enthusiasm, Skye was literally carried off the field, her little tail wagging.

Since that time I have had the opportunity to track Skye across different terrain. She has learned to cross water, fences, roads, and even to keep going in snow. Tracking is truly a lonely sport, but not if you enjoy the company of your dog in the great outdoors.

286

Chapter 16

Breeding Your Dalmatian

An earlier chapter discussed selection of a bitch you plan to use for breeding. In making this important purchase, you will be choosing a bitch who you hope will become the foundation of your kennel. Thus she must be of the finest producing bloodlines, excellent in temperament, of good type, and free of major faults or unsoundness. If you are offered a "bargain" brood bitch, be wary, as for this purchase you should not settle for less than the best and the price will be in accordance with the quality.

Conscientious breeders feel quite strongly that the only possible reason for producing puppies is the ambition to improve and uphold quality and temperament within the breed—definitely *not* because one hopes to make a quick cash profit on a mediocre litter, which never seems to work out that way in the long run and which accomplishes little beyond perhaps adding to the nation's heartbreaking number of unwanted canines. The only reason ever for breeding a litter is, with conscientious people, a desire to improve the quality of dogs in their own kennel or, as pet owners, to add to the number of dogs they themselves own with a puppy or two from their present favorites. In either case breeding should not take place unless one definitely has prospective owners for as many puppies as the litter may contain, lest you find yourself with several fast-growing young dogs and no homes in which to place them.

THE BROOD BITCH

Bitches should not be mated earlier than their second season, by which time they should be from fifteen to eighteen months old. Many breeders prefer to wait and first finish the championships of

Ch. Coachman's Paisley Candybar winning the Brood Bitch Class under judge Mrs. Alan Robson at The Dalmatian Club of Southern New England Specialty. *Left to right:* Candybar, Ch. Erin's Calculated Risk, and Ch. Coachman's Hot Coffee. "Hershey" is the dam of multi-Group and Specialty winners and was the No. 1 Dalmatian Brood Bitch and No. 2 Non-Sporting Brood Bitch in 1982. Owned by John and Sharon Lyons. Breeders, David and Sue McMillan.

their show bitches before breeding them, as pregnancy can be a disaster to a show coat and getting the bitch back in shape again takes time. When you have decided what will be the proper time, start watching at least several months ahead for what you feel would be the perfect mate to best complement your bitch's quality and bloodlines. Subscribe to the magazines which feature your breed exclusively and to some which cover all breeds in order to familiarize yourself with outstanding stud dogs in areas other than your own for there is no necessity nowadays to limit your choice to a local dog unless you truly like him and feel that he is the most suitable. It is quite usual to ship a bitch to a stud dog a distance away, and this generally works out with no ill effects. The important thing is that you need a stud dog strong in those features where your bitch is weak or lacking, a dog whose bloodlines are compatible with hers. Compare the background of both your bitch and the stud dog under consideration, paying particular attention to the quality of the puppies from bitches with backgrounds similar to your bitch's. If the puppies have been of the type and quality you admire, then this dog would seem a sensible choice for yours, too.

Stud fees may be a few hundred dollars, sometimes even more under special situations for a particularly successful sire. It is money well spent, however. *Do not* ever breed to a dog because he is less expensive than the others unless you honestly believe that he can sire the kind of puppies who will be a credit to your kennel and your breed.

Contacting the owners of the stud dogs you find interesting will bring you pedigrees and pictures which you can then study in relation to your bitch's pedigree and conformation. Discuss your plans with other breeders who are knowledgeable (including the one who bred your own bitch). You may not always receive an entirely unbiased opinion (particularly if the person giving it also has an available stud dog), but one learns by discussion so listen to what they say, consider their opinions, and then you may be better qualified to form your own opinion.

As soon as you have made a choice, phone the owner of the stud dog you wish to use to find out if this will be agreeable. You will be asked about the bitch's health, soundness, temperament, and freedom from serious faults. A copy of her pedigree may be requested, as might a picture of her. A discussion of her background over the telephone may be sufficient to assure the stud's owner that she is suitable for the stud dog and of type, breeding, and quality herself to produce puppies of the quality for which the dog is noted. The owner of a top-quality stud is often extremely selective in the bitches permitted to be bred to his dog, in an effort to keep the standard of his puppies high. The owner of a stud dog may require that the bitch be tested for brucellosis, which should be attended to not more than a month previous to the breeding.

Check out which airport will be most convenient for the person meeting and returning the bitch if she is to be shipped and also what airlines use that airport. You will find that the airlines are also apt to have special requirements concerning acceptance of animals for shipping. These include weather limitations and types of crates which are acceptable. The weather limits have to do with extreme heat and extreme cold at the point of destination, as some airlines will not fly dogs into temperatures above or below certain levels, fearing for their safety. The crate problem is a simple one, since, if your own crate is not suitable, most of the airlines have specially designed crates available for purchase at a fair and moderate price. It is a good plan to purchase one of these if you intend to be shipping dogs with any sort of frequency. They are made of fiberglass and are the safest type to use for shipping.

Normally you must notify the airline several days in advance to make a reservation, as they are able to accommodate only a certain number of dogs on each flight. Plan on shipping the bitch on about her eighth or ninth day of season, but be careful to avoid shipping her on a weekend when schedules often vary and freight offices are apt to be closed. Whenever you can, ship your bitch on a direct flight. Changing planes always carries a certain amount of risk of a dog being overlooked or wrongly routed at the middle stop, so avoid this danger if at all possible. The bitch must be accompanied by a health certificate which you must obtain from your veterinarian before taking her to the airport. Usually it will be necessary to have the bitch at the airport about two hours prior to flight time. Before finalizing arrangements, find out from the stud's owner at what time of day it will be most convenient to have the bitch picked up promptly upon arrival.

It is simpler if you can plan to bring the bitch to the stud dog yourself. Some people feel that the trauma of the flight may cause the bitch to not conceive; and, of course, undeniably there is a slight risk in shipping which can be avoided if you are able to drive the bitch to her destination. Be sure to leave yourself sufficient time to assure your arrival at the right time for her for breeding (normally the tenth to fourteenth day following the first signs of color); and remember that if you want the bitch bred twice, you should allow a day to elapse between the two matings. Do not expect the stud's owner to house you while you are there. Locate a nearby motel that takes dogs and make that your headquarters.

Just prior to the time your bitch is due in season, you should take her to visit your veterinarian. She should be checked for worms and should receive all the booster shots for which she is due plus one for parvovirus, unless she has had the latter shot fairly recently. The brucellosis test can also be done then, and the health certificate can be obtained for shipping if she is to travel by air. Should the bitch be at all overweight, now is the time to get the surplus off. She should be in good condition, neither underweight nor overweight, at the time of breeding.

The moment you notice the swelling of the vulva, for which you should be checking daily as the time for her season approaches, and the appearance of color, immediately contact the stud's owner and settle on the day for shipping or make the appointment for your arrival with the bitch for breeding. If you are shipping the bitch, the stud fee check should be mailed immediately, leaving ample time for it to have been received when the bitch arrives and the mating takes place. Be sure to call the airline, making her reservation at that time, too.

Do not feed the bitch within a few hours before shipping her. Be certain that she has had a drink of water and been well exercised before closing her in the crate. Several layers of newspapers, topped with some shredded newspaper, make a good bed and can be discarded when she arrives at her destination; these can be replaced with fresh newspapers for her return home. Remember that the bitch should be brought to the airport about two hours before flight time as sometimes the airlines refuse to accept late arrivals.

If you are taking your bitch by car, be certain that you will arrive at a reasonable time of day. Do not appear late in the evening. If your arrival in town is not until late, get a good night's sleep at your motel and contact the stud's owner first thing in the morning. If possible, leave children and relatives at home, as they will only be in the way and perhaps unwelcome by the stud's owner. Most stud dog owners prefer not to have any unnecessary people on hand during the actual mating.

After the breeding has taken place, if you wish to sit and visit for awhile and the stud's owner has the time, return the bitch to her crate in your car (first ascertaining, of course, that the temperature is comfortable for her and that there is proper ventilation). She should not be permitted to urinate for at least one hour following the breeding. This is the time when you get the business part of the transaction attended to. Pay the stud fee, upon which you should receive your breeding certificate and, if you do not al-

This lovely bitch with her owner Mary Barrett is Ch. Geraldine of Mainstay in May 1966. Winning under judge Frank Landgraf at the Dalmatian Club of Southern New England Specialty.

ready have it, a copy of the stud dog's pedigree. The owner of the stud dog does not sign or furnish a litter registration application until the puppies have been born.

Upon your return home, you can settle down and plan in happy anticipation a wonderful litter of puppies. A word of caution! Remember that although she has been bred, your bitch is still an interesting target for all male dogs, so guard her carefully for the next week or until you are absolutely certain that her season has entirely ended. This would be no time to have any unfortunate incident with another dog.

THE STUD DOG

Choosing the best stud dog to complement your bitch is often very difficult. The two principal factors to be considered should be the stud's conformation and his pedigree. Conformation is fairly obvious; you want a dog that is typical of the breed in the words of the Standard of perfection. Understanding pedigrees is a bit more subtle since the pedigree lists the ancestry of the dog and involves individuals and bloodlines with which you may not be entirely familiar.

To a novice in the breed, then, the correct interpretation of a pedigree may at first be difficult to grasp. Study the pictures and text of this book and you will find many names of important bloodlines and members of the breed. Also make an effort to discuss the various dogs behind the proposed stud with some of the more experienced breeders, starting with the breeder of your own bitch. Frequently these folks will be personally familiar with many of the dogs in question, can offer opinions of them, and may have access to additional pictures which you would benefit by seeing. It is very important that the stud's pedigree be harmonious with that of the bitch you plan on breeding to him. Do not rush out and breed to the latest winner with no thought of whether or not

Dalmatian Club of America National Specialty in 1975. *Left to right.* Ch. Coachman's Chuck-A-Luck, Ch. Lord Jim (D.C.A. Best of Breed in 1970), Ch. Coachman's Canicula (D.C.A. Best of Breed 1973), and Ch. Count Miguel of Tuckaway, D.C.A. Winners Dog, 1975. Canicula and Jimmy are sons of Chuck-A-Luck. Miguel is by Lord Jim ex a Canicula daughter. Photo courtesy of Dr. Sidney Remmele, Lexington, Kentucky.

293

he can produce true quality. By no means are all great show dogs great producers. It is the producing record of the dog in question and the dogs and bitches from which he has come that should be the basis on which you make your choice.

Breeding dogs is never a money-making operation. By the time you pay a stud fee, care for the bitch during pregnancy, whelp the litter, and rear the puppies through their early shots, worming, and so on, you will be fortunate to break even financially once the puppies have been sold. Your chances of doing this are greater if you are breeding for a show-quality litter which will bring you higher prices, as the pups are sold as show prospects. Therefore, your wisest investment is to use the best dog available for your bitch regardless of the cost; then you should wind up with more valuable puppies. Remember that it is equally costly to raise mediocre puppies as it is top ones, and your chances of financial return are better on the latter. To breed to the most excellent, most suitable stud dog you can find is the only sensible thing to do, and it is poor economy to quibble over the amount you are paying in a stud fee.

It will be your decision which course you decide to follow when you breed your bitch, as there are three options: linebreeding, inbreeding, and outcrossing. Each of these methods has its supporters and its detractors! Linebreeding is breeding a bitch to a dog belonging originally to the same canine family, being descended from the same ancestors, such as half-brother to half-sister, grandsire to granddaughter, niece to uncle (and vice-versa) or cousin to cousin. Inbreeding is breeding father to daughter, mother to son, or full brother to sister. Outcross breeding is breeding a dog and a bitch with no or only a few mutual ancestors.

Linebreeding is probably the safest course, and the one most likely to bring results, for the novice breeder. The more sophisticated inbreeding should be left to the experienced, longtime breeders who throughly know and understand the risks and the possibilities involved with a particular line. It is usually done in an effort to intensify some ideal feature in that strain. Outcrossing is the reverse of inbreeding, an effort to introduce improvement in a specific feature needing correction, such as a shorter back, better movement, more correct head or coat, and so on.

It is the serious breeder's ambition to develop a strain or bloodline of their own, one strong in qualities for which their dogs will

Mary Barrett with her widely admired bitch Ch. Roadcoach Spice taking Best of Breed at the 1962 Dalmatian Club of America Specialty Show under noted Dalmatian authority Mrs. Leonard W. (Flora) Bonney.

become distinguished. However, it must be realized that this will involve time, patience, and at least several generations before the achievement can be claimed. The safest way to embark on this plan, as we have mentioned, is by the selection and breeding of one or two bitches, the best you can buy and from top-producing kennels. In the beginning you do *not* really have to own a stud dog. In the long run it is less expensive and sounder judgement to pay a stud fee when you are ready to breed a bitch than to purchase a stud dog and feed him all year; a stud dog does not win any popularity contests with owners of bitches to be bred until he becomes a champion, has been successfully Specialed for a while,

Mrs. Alan Robson considers this lovely bitch, Ch. Albelarm Bittersweet, to be one of the best Dals she has ever bred or owned. Albelarm Dalmatians are at Glenmoore, Pa.

and has been at least moderately advertised, all of which adds up to quite a healthy expenditure.

The wisest course for the inexperienced breeder just starting out in dogs is as outlined above. Keep the best bitch puppy from the first several litters. After that you may wish to consider keeping your own stud dog if there has been a particularly handsome male in one of your litters that you feel has great potential or if you know where there is one available that you are interested in, with the feeling that he would work in nicely with the breeding program on which you have embarked. By this time, with several litters already born, your eye should have developed to a point enabling you to make a wise choice, either from one of your own litters or from among dogs you have seen that appear suitable.

The greatest care should be taken in the selection of your own stud dog. He must be of true type and highest quality as he may be responsible for siring many puppies each year, and he should come from a line of excellent dogs on both sides of his pedigree which themselves are, and which are descended from, successful producers. This dog should have no glaring faults in conformation; he should be of such a quality that he can hold his own in keenest competition within his breed. He should be in good health, be virile and be a keen stud dog, a proven sire able to transmit his correct qualities to his puppies. Need I say that such a dog will be enormously expensive unless you have the good fortune to produce him in one of your own litters? To buy and use a lesser stud dog, however, is downgrading your breeding program unnecessarily since there are so many dogs fitting the description of a fine stud whose services can be used on payment of a stud fee.

You should *never* breed to an unsound dog or one with any serious disqualifying faults according to the breed's standard. Not all champions by any means pass along their best features; and by the same token, occasionally you will find a great one who can pass along his best features but never gained his championship title due to some unusual circumstances. The information you need about a stud dog is what type of puppies he has produced and with what bloodlines and whether or not he possesses the bloodlines and attributes considered characteristic of the best in your breed.

If you go out to buy a stud dog, obviously he will not be a puppy but rather a fully mature and proven male with as many of the best attributes as possible. True, he will be an expensive investment, but if you choose and make his selection with care and forethought, he may well prove to be one of the best investments you have ever made.

Of course, the most exciting of all is when a young male you have decided to keep from one of your litters due to his tremendous show potential turns out to be a stud dog such as we have described. In this case he should be managed with care, for he is a valuable property that can contribute inestimably to this breed as a whole and to your own kennel specifically.

Do not permit your stud dog to be used until he is about a year old, and even then he should be bred to mature, proven matron accustomed to breeding who will make his first experience pleasant and easy. A young dog can be put off forever by a maiden bitch who fights and resists his advances. Never allow this to happen. Always start a stud dog out with a bitch who is mature, has been bred previously, and is of even temperament. The first

297

breeding should be performed in quiet surroundings with only you and one other person to hold the bitch. Do not make it a circus, as the experience will determine the dog's outlook about future stud work. If he does not enjoy the first experience or associates it with any unpleasantness, you may well have a problem in the future.

Your young stud must permit help with the breeding, as later there will be bitches who will not be cooperative. If right from the beginning you are there helping him and praising him, whether or not your assistance is actually needed, he will expect and accept this as a matter of course when a difficult bitch comes along.

Things to have handy before introducing your dog and the bitch are K-Y jelly (the only lubricant which should be used) and a length of gauze with which to muzzle the bitch should it be necessary to keep her from biting you or the dog. Some bitches put up a fight; others are calm. It is best to be prepared.

At the time of the breeding, the stud fee comes due, and it is expected that it will be paid promptly. Normally a return service is offered in case the bitch misses or fails to produce one live puppy. Conditions of the service are what the stud dog's owner makes them, and there are no standard rules covering this. The stud fee is paid for the act, not the result. If the bitch fails to conceive, it is customary for the owner to offer a free return service; but this is a courtesy and not to be considered a right, particularly in the case of a proven stud who is siring consistently and whose fault the failure obviously is *not*. Stud dog owners are always anxious to see their clients get good value and to have in the ring winning young stock by their dog; therefore, very few refuse to mate the second time. It is wise, however, for both parties to have the terms of the transaction clearly understood at the time of the breeding.

If the return service has been provided and the bitch has missed a second time, that is considered to be the end of the matter and the owner would be expected to pay a further fee if it is felt that the bitch should be given a third chance with the stud dog. The management of a stud dog and his visiting bitches is quite a task, and a stud fee has usually been well earned when one service has been achieved, let alone by repeated visits from the same bitch.

The accepted litter is one live puppy. It is wise to have printed a breeding certificate which the owner of the stud dog and the owner of the bitch both sign. This should list in detail the conditions of the breeding as well as the dates of the mating.

Upon occasion, arrangements other than a stud fee in cash are made for a breeding, such as the owner of the stud taking a pick-of-the-litter puppy in lieu of money. This should be clearly specified on the breeding certificate along with the terms of the age at which the stud's owner will select the puppy, whether it is to be a specific sex, or whether it is to be the pick of the entire litter.

The price of a stud fee varies according to circumstances. Usually, to prove a young stud dog, his owner will allow the first breeding to be quite inexpensive. Then, once a bitch has become pregnant by him, he becomes a "proven stud" and the fee rises accordingly for bitches that follow. The sire of championship quality puppies will bring a stud fee of at least the purchase price of one show puppy as the accepted "rule-of-thumb." Until at least one champion by your stud dog has finished, the fee will remain equal to the price of one pet puppy. When his list of champions starts to grow, so does the amount of the stud fee. For a top-producing sire of champions, the stud fee will rise accordingly.

Almost invariably it is the bitch who comes to the stud dog for the breeding. Immediately upon having selected the stud dog you wish to use, discuss the possibility with the owner of that dog. It is the stud dog owner's prerogative to refuse to breed any bitch deemed unsuitable for this dog. Stud fee and method of payment should be stated at this time and a decision reached on whether it is to be a full cash transaction at the time of the mating or a pick-of-the-litter puppy, usually at eight weeks of age.

If the owner of the stud dog must travel to an airport to meet the bitch and ship her for the flight home, an additional charge will be made for time, tolls, and gasoline based on the stud owner's proximity to the airport. The stud fee includes board for the day on the bitch's arrival through two days for breeding, with a day in between. If it is necessary that the bitch remain longer, it is very likely that additional board will be charged at the normal per-day rate for the breed.

Be sure to advise the stud's owner as soon as you know that your bitch is in season so that the stud dog will be available. This is especially important because if he is a dog being shown, he and his owner may be unavailable, owing to the dog's absence from home.

As the owner of a stud dog being offered to the public, it is essential that you have proper facilities for the care of visiting bitches. Nothing can be worse than a bitch being insecurely housed and slipping out to become lost or bred by the wrong dog. If you are taking people's valued bitches into your kennel or home, it is imperative that you provide them with comfortable, secure housing and good care while they are your responsibility.

There is no dog more valuable than the proven sire of champions, Group winners, and Best in Show dogs. Once you have such an animal, guard his reputation well and do *not* permit him to be bred to just any bitch that comes along. It takes two to make the puppies; even the most dominant stud cannot do it all himself, so never permit him to breed a bitch you consider unworthy. Remember that when the puppies arrive, it will be your stud dog who will be blamed for any lack of quality, while the bitch's shortcomings will be quickly and conveniently overlooked.

Going into the actual management of the mating is a bit superfluous here. If you have had previous experience in breeding a dog and bitch you will know how the mating is done. If you do not have such experience, you should not attempt to follow direction given in a book but should have a veterinarian, breeder friend, or handler there to help you with the first few times. You do not just turn the dog and bitch loose together and await developments, as too many things can go wrong and you may altogether miss getting the bitch bred. Someone should hold the dog and the bitch (one person each) until the "tie" is made and these two people should stay with them during the entire act.

If you get a complete tie, probably only the one mating is absolutely necessary. However, especially with a maiden bitch or one that has come a long distance for this breeding, we prefer following up with a second breeding, leaving one day in between the two matings. In this way there will be little or no chance of the bitch missing.

Once the tie has been completed and the dogs release, be certain that the male's penis goes completely back within its sheath. He should be allowed a drink of water and a short walk, and then he should be put into his crate or somewhere alone where he can settle down. Do not allow him to be with other dogs for a while as they will notice the odor of the bitch on him, and, particularly with other males present, he may become involved in a fight.

Dottidale puppy at eight days old. It is not unusual, and no cause for alarm, when Dalmatian puppies are born pure white. This is quite usual, and you will find that the spots will gradually develop as the puppy grows older. So please do not panic! Just wait and see what happens.

PREGNANCY, WHELPING, AND THE LITTER

Once the bitch has been bred and is back at home, remember to keep an ever watchful eye that no other males get to her until at least the twenty-second day of her season has passed. Until then, it will still be possible for an unwanted breeding to take place, which at this point would be catastrophic. Remember that she actually can have two separate litters by two different dogs, so take care.

In other ways, she should be treated normally. Controlled exercise is good, and necessary for the bitch throughout her pregnancy, tapering it off to just several short walks daily, preferably on lead, as she reaches about her seventh week. As her time grows close, be careful about her jumping or playing too roughly.

The theory that a bitch should be overstuffed with food when pregnant is a poor one. A fat bitch is never an easy whelper, so the overfeeding you consider good for her may well turn out to be a hindrance later on. During the first few weeks of pregnancy,

301

your bitch should be fed her normal diet. At four to five weeks along, calcium should be added to her food. At seven weeks her food may be increased if she seems to crave more than she is getting, and a meal of canned milk (mixed with an equal amount of water) should be introduced. If she is fed just once a day, add another meal rather than overload her with too much at one time. If twice a day is her schedule, then a bit more food can be added to each feeding.

A week before the pups are due, your bitch should be introduced to her whelping box so that she will be accustomed to it and feel at home there when the puppies arrive. She should be encouraged to sleep there but permitted to come and go as she wishes. The box should be roomy enough for her to lie down and stretch out in but not too large, lest the pups have more room than is needed in which to roam and possibly get chilled by going too far away from their mother. Be sure that the box has a "pig rail"; this will prevent the puppies from being crushed against the sides. The room in which the box is placed, either in your home or in the kennel, should be kept at about 70 degrees Fahrenheit. In winter it may be necessary to have an infrared lamp over the whelping box, in which case be careful not to place it too low or close to the puppies.

Newspapers will become a very important commodity, so start collecting them well in advance to have a big pile handy for the whelping box. With a litter of puppies, one never seems to have papers enough, so the higher pile to start with, the better off you will be. Other necessities for whelping time are clean, soft turkish towels, scissors, and a bottle of alcohol.

You will know that her time is very near when your bitch becomes restless, wandering in and out of her box and of the room. She may refuse food, and at that point her temperature will start to drop. She will dig at and tear up the newspapers in her box, shiver, and generally look uncomfortable. Only you should be with your bitch at this time. She does not need spectators; and several people, even though they may be family members whom she knows, hanging over her may upset her to the point where she may harm the puppies. You should remain nearby, quietly watching, not fussing or hovering; speak calmly and frequently to her to instill confidence. Eventually she will settle down in her box and begin panting; contractions will follow. Soon thereafter a

Coachmans Custom Maid, C.D., graduate of St. Louis Dog Breeders Obedience Club, has a final score of 198. Brains as well as beauty are to be found in Coachman Dalmatians. Mr. and Mrs. William Fetner, owners, St. Louis, Mo.

puppy will start to emerge, sliding out with the contractions. The mother immediately should open the sac, sever the cord with her teeth, and then clean up the puppy. She will also eat the placenta, which you should permit. Once the puppy is cleaned, it should be placed next to the bitch unless she is showing signs of having the next one immediately. Almost at once the puppy will start looking for a nipple on which to nurse, and you should ascertain that it is able to latch on successfully.

If the puppy is a breech (*i.e.*, born feet first), you must watch carefully for it to be completely delivered as quickly as possible and for the sac to be removed quickly so that the puppy does not drown. Sometimes even a normally positioned birth will seem extremely slow in coming. Should this occur, you might take a clean towel, and as the bitch contracts, pull the puppy out, doing so gently and with utmost care. If, once the puppy is delivered, it shows little signs of life, take a rough turkish towel and massage the puppy's chest by rubbing quite briskly back and forth. Con-

Ch. Starborn Summer Sunshine, liver and white, by Ch. Robbsdale's Baron Von Cross ex Ch. Cottondale's Candlelight, was Best of Winners at the 1983 DOH Specialty. The foundation bitch at Starburn Kennels, Sweeney, Texas.

Ch. Roadcoach Bandit, Best of Breed Dalmatian at Westminster in 1952. Owner-handled by Mrs. A.W. Barrett, Roadcoach Dalmatians, Dover, Mass.

Ch. Colonel Boots From Dalmatia was Winners Dog and Best of Breed from the Open Dog Class, Westchester K.C., 1954, which was the year of the Dalmatian Club of America National Specialty and judged by Mrs. Lloyd Reeves.

Dress Boots From Dalmatia, litter sister to the Winners Dog and Best of Breed (Ch. Colonel Boots From Dalmatia) was Winners Bitch at the 1954 National Specialty at Westchester under Mrs. Lloyd Reeves. Photos courtesy of Wendell J. Sammet.

tinue this for about fifteen minutes, and be sure that the mouth is free of liquid. It may be necessary to try mouth- to-mouth breathing, which is done by pressing the puppy's jaws open and, using a finger, depressing the tongue which may be stuck to the roof of the mouth. Then place your mouth against the puppy's and blow hard down the puppy's throat. Rub the puppy's chest with the towel again and try artificial respiration, pressing the sides of the chest together slowly and rhythmically—in and out, in and out. Keep trying one method or the other for at least twenty minutes before giving up. You may be rewarded with a live puppy who otherwise would not have made it.

If you are successful in bringing the puppy around, do not immediately put it back with the mother as it should be kept extra warm. Put it in a cardboard box on an electric heating pad or, if it is the time of year when your heat is running, near a radiator or near the fireplace or stove. As soon as the rest of the litter has been born, it then can join the others.

An hour or more may elapse between puppies, which is fine so long as the bitch seems comfortable and is neither straining nor contracting. She should not be permitted to remain unassisted for more than an hour if she does continue to contract. This is when you should get her to your veterinarian, whom you should already have alerted to the possibility of a problem existing. He should examine her and perhaps giver her a shot of Pituitrin. In some cases the veterinarian may find that a Caesarean section is necessary due to a puppy being lodged in a manner making normal delivery impossible. Sometimes this is caused by an abnormally large puppy, or it may just be that the puppy is simply turned in the wrong position. If the bitch does require a Caesarean section, the puppies already born must be kept warm in their cardboard box with a heating pad under the box.

Once the section is done, get the bitch and the puppies home. Do not attempt to put the puppies in with the bitch until she has regained consciousness as she may unknowingly hurt them. But do get them back to her as soon as possible for them to start nursing.

Should the mother lack milk at this time, the puppies must be fed by hand, kept very warm, and held onto the mother's teats several times a day in order to stimulate and encourage the secretion of milk, which should start shortly.

Assuming that there has been no problem and that the bitch has whelped naturally, you should insist that she go out to exercise, staying just long enough to make herself comfortable. She can be offered a bowl of milk and a biscuit, but then she should settle down with her family. Freshen the whelping box for her with fresh newspapers while she is taking this respite so that she and the puppies will have a clean bed.

Unless some problem arises, there is little you must do about the puppies until they become three to four weeks old. Keep the box clean and supplied with fresh newspapers the first few days, but then turkish towels should be tacked down to the bottom of the box so that the puppies will have traction as they move about.

If the bitch has difficulties with her milk supply, or if you should be so unfortunate as to lose her, then you must be prepared to either hand-feed or tube-feed the puppies if they are to survive. Tube-feeding is so much faster and easier. If the bitch is available, it is best that she continues to clean and care for the puppies in the normal manner excepting for the food supplements you will provide. If it is impossible for her to do this, then after every feeding you must gently rub each puppy's abdomen with wet cotton to make it urinate, and the rectum should be gently rubbed to open the bowels.

Newborn puppies must be fed every three to four hours around the clock. The puppies must be kept warm during this time. Have your veterinarian teach you how to tube-feed. You will find that it is really quite simple.

After a normal whelping, the bitch will require additional food to enable her to produce sufficient milk. In addition to being fed twice daily, she should be given some canned milk several times each day.

When the puppies are two weeks old, their nails should be clipped, as they are needle sharp at this age and can hurt or damage the mother's teats and stomach as the pups hold on to nurse.

Between three and four weeks of age, the puppies should begin to be weaned. Scraped beef (prepared by scraping it off slices of beef with a spoon so that none of the gristle is included) may be offered in very small quantities a couple of times daily for the first few days. Then by the third day you can mix puppy chow with warm water as directed on the package, offering it four times daily. By now the mother should be kept away from the puppies and out of the box for several hours at a time so that when they have reached five weeks of age she is left in with them only overnight. By the time the puppies are six weeks old, they should be entirely weaned and receiving only occasional visits from their mother.

Most veterinarians recommend a temporary DHL (distemper, hepatitis, leptospirosis) shot when the puppies are six weeks of age. This remains effective for about two weeks. Then at eight weeks of age, the puppies should receive the series of permanent shots for DHL protection. It is also a good idea to discuss with your vet the advisability of having your puppies inoculated against the dreaded parvovirus at the same time. Each time the pups go to the vet for shots, you should bring stool samples so that they can be examined for worms. Worms go through various stages of development and may be present in a stool sample even though the sample does not test positive in every checkup. So do not neglect to keep careful watch on this.

Dottidale puppies at four weeks old. Note that now the spots are appearing!

Phyllis Fetner with a current black spotted bitch, Coachman's Black Cat, taking first prize at the Dalmatian Club of Greater St. Louis Specialty in 1985.

The puppies should be fed four times daily until they are three months old. Then you can cut back to three feedings daily. By the time the puppies are six months of age, two meals daily are sufficient. Some people feed their dogs twice daily throughout their lifetime; others go to one meal daily when the puppy becomes one year of age.

The ideal age for puppies to go to their new homes is between eight and twelve weeks, although some puppies successfully adjust to a new home when they are six weeks old. Be sure that they go to their new owners accompanied by a description of the diet you've been feeding them and a schedule of the shots they have already received and those they still need. These should be included with the registration application and a copy of the pedigree.

Chapter 17

Traveling with Your Dalmatian

When you travel with your dog, to shows or on vacation or wherever, remember that everyone does not share your enthusiasm or love for dogs and that those who do not, strange creatures though they seem to us, have their rights, too. These rights, on which your should not encroach, include not being disturbed, annoyed, or made uncomfortable by the presence and behavior of other people's pets. Your dog should be kept on lead in public places and should recognize and promptly obey the commands "Down," "Come," "Sit," and "Stay."

Take along his crate if you are going any distance with your dog. And keep him in it when riding in the car. A crated dog has a far better chance of escaping injury than one riding loose in the car, should an accident occur or an emergency arise. If you do permit your dog to ride loose, never allow him to hang out a window, ears blowing in the breeze. An injury to his eyes could occur in this manner. He could also become overly excited by something he sees and jump out, or he could lose his balance and fall out.

Never, ever, under any circumstances, should a dog be permitted to ride loose in the back of a pick-up truck. Some people do transport dogs in this manner, which is cruel and shocking. How easily such a dog can be thrown out of the truck by sudden jolts or an impact! Doubtless many dogs have jumped out at the sight of something exciting along the way. Some unthinking individuals tie the dog, probably not realizing that were he to jump under those circumstances, his neck would be broken, he could be dragged alongside the vehicle, or he could be hit by another vehi-

The very famous Dalmatian Ch. Dottidale Jo Jo, was the Top Winning Liver Dal and the Top Winning Owner Handled Dal in the U.S. as well as No. 4 Dalmatian (Phillips System) for 1967. Bred, owned, and handled by Amy S. Lipschutz, Dottidale Kennels, Liberty, Kentucky.

cle. If you are for any reason taking your dog in an open-back truck, please have sufficient regard for that dog to at least provide a crate for him, and then remember that, in or out of a crate, a dog riding under the direct rays of the sun in hot weather can suffer and have his life endangered by the heat.

If you are staying at a hotel or motel with your dog, exercise him somewhere other than in the flower beds and parking lot of the property. People walking to and from their cars really are not thrilled at "stepping in something" left by your dog. Should an accident occur, pick it up with a tissue or paper towel and deposit it in a proper receptacle; do not just walk off leaving it to remain there. Usually there are grassy areas on the sides of and behind motels where dogs can be exercised. Use them rather than the

Ch. Homestead Forester of Anadel, owned by Tom Bechtle, Locust Valley, N.Y.

more conspicuous, usually carefully tended, front areas or those close to the rooms. If you are becoming a dog show enthusiast, you will eventually need an exercise pen to take with you to the show. Exercise pens are ideal to use when staying at motels, too, as they permit you to limit the dog's roaming space and to pick up after him more easily.

Never leave your dog unattended in the room of a motel unless you are absolutely, positively certain that he will stay there quietly and not damage or destroy anything. You do not want a long list of complaints from irate guests, caused by the annoying barking or whining of a lonesome dog in strange surroundings or an over-zealous watch dog barking furiously each time a footstep passes the door or he hears a sound from an adjoining room. And you certainly do not want to return to torn curtains or bedspreads, soiled rugs, or other embarrassing evidence of the fact that your dog is not really house-reliable after all.

If yours is a dog accustomed to traveling with you and you are positive that his behavior will be acceptable when left alone, that is fine. But if the slightest uncertainty exists, the wise course is to leave him in the car while you go to dinner or elsewhere; then bring him into the room when you are ready to retire for the night.

When you travel with a dog, it is often simpler to take along from home the food and water he will need rather than to buy food and look for water while you travel. In this way he will have the rations to which he is accustomed and which you know agree with him, and there will be no fear of problems due to different drinking water. Feeding on the road is quite easy now, at least for short trips, with all the splendid dry prepared foods and high-quality canned meats available. A variety of lightweight, refillable water containers can be bought at many types of stores.

Be careful always to leave sufficient openings to ventilate your car when the dog will be alone in it. Remember that during the summer, the rays of the sun can make an inferno of a closed car within only a few minutes, so leave enough window space open to provide air circulation. Again, if your dog is in a crate, this can be done quite safely. The fact that you have left the car in a shady spot is not always a guarantee that you will find conditions the same when you return. Don't forget that the position of the sun changes in a matter of minutes, and the car you left nicely shaded half an hour ago can be getting full sunlight far more quickly than you may realize. So, if you leave a dog in the car, make sure there is sufficient ventilation and check back frequently to ascertain that all is well.

If you are going to another country, you will need a health certificate from your veterinarian for each dog you are taking with you, certifying that each has had rabies shots within the required time preceding your visit.

Chapter 18

Responsibilities of Breeders and Owners

The first responsibility of any person breeding dogs is to do so with care, forethought, and deliberation. It is inexcusable to breed more litters than you need to carry on your show program or to perpetuate your bloodlines. A responsible breeder should not cause a litter to be born without definite plans for the safe and happy disposition of the puppies.

A responsible dog breeder makes absolutely certain, so far as is humanly possible, that the home to which one of his puppies will go is a good home, one that offers proper care and an enthusiastic owner. To be admired are those breeders who insist on visiting (although doing so is not always feasible) the prospective owners of their puppies to see if they have suitable facilities for keeping a dog and to find out if they understand the responsibility involved, and if all members of the household are in accord regarding the desirability of owning one. All breeders should carefully check out the credentials of prospective purchasers to be sure that the puppy is being placed in responsible hands.

No breeder ever wants a puppy or grown dog he has raised to wind up in an animal shelter, in an experimental laboratory, or as a victim of a speeding car. While complete control of such a situation may be impossible, it is at important to make every effort to turn over dogs to responsible people. When selling a puppy, it is a good idea to do so with the understanding that should it become necessary to place the dog in other hands, the purchaser will first contact you, the breeder. You may want to help in some way, possibly by buying back or taking back the dog or placing it else-

Ch. Tioga Sportscar was owned by Mrs. A.W. Barrett, Roadcoach Dalmatians, Dover, Mass. One of the Champions sired by Ch. Roadcoach Roadster.

where. It is not fair to just sell puppies and then never again give a thought to their welfare. Family problems arise, people may be forced to move where dogs are prohibited, or people just plain grow bored with a dog and its care. Thus the dog becomes a victim. You, as the dog's breeder, should concern yourself with the welfare of each of your dogs and see to it that the dog remains in good hands.

The final obligation every dog owner shares, be there just one dog or an entire kennel involved, is that of making detailed, explicit plans for the future of these dearly loved animals in the event of the owner's death. Far too many of people are apt to proscrastinate and leave this very important matter unattended to, feeling that everything will work out or that "someone will see to them." The latter is not too likely, at least not to the benefit of the dogs, unless you have done some advance planning which will assure their future well-being.

Life is filled with the unexpected, and even the youngest, healthiest, most robust of us may be the victim of a fatal accident or sudden illness. The fate of your dogs, so entirely in our hands, should never be left to chance. If you have not already done so, please get together with your lawyer and set up a clause in your will specifying what you want done with each of your dogs, to whom they will be entrusted (after first making absolutely certain that the person selected is willing and able to assume the responsibility), and telling the locations of all registration papers, pedigrees, and kennel records. Just think of the possibilities which might happen otherwise! If there is another family member who shares your love of the dogs, that is good and you have less to worry about. But if your heirs are not dog-oriented, they will hardly know how to proceed or how to cope with the dogs themselves, and they may wind up disposing of or caring for your dogs in a manner that would break your heart were you around to know about it.

It is advisable to have in your will specific instructions concerning each of your dogs. A friend, also a dog person who regards her own dogs with the same concern and esteem as we do, may agree to take over their care until they can be placed accordingly and will make certain that all will work out as you have planned. This person's name and phone number can be prominently displayed in your van or car and in your wallet. Your lawyer can be made aware of this fact. This can be spelled out in your will. The friend can have a signed check of yours to be used in case of an emergency or accident when you are traveling with the dogs; this check can be used to cover her expense to come and take over the care of your dogs should anything happen to make it impossible for us to do so. This is the least any dog owner should do in preparation for the time their dogs suddenly find themselves alone. There have been so many sad cases of dogs unprovided for by their loving owners, left to heirs who couldn't care less and who disposed of them in any way at all to get rid of them, or left to heirs who kept and neglected them under the misguided idea that they were providing them "a fine home with lots of freedom." These misfortunes must be prevented from befalling your own dogs who have meant so much you!

Index